# CORRECT *your* ITALIAN BLUNDERS

## Avoid **99**% of the Common Mistakes Made by Learners of Italian

### Marcel Danesi

New York  Chicago  San Francisco  Lisbon  London  Madrid  Mexico City
Milan  New Delhi  San Juan  Seoul  Singapore  Sydney  Toronto

**Library of Congress Cataloging-in-Publication Data**

Danesi, Marcel, 1946–
    Correct your Italian blunders : avoid 99% of the common mistakes made by
learners of Italian / Marcel Danesi.
        p.    cm.
    Includes index.
    ISBN 0-07-147215-0
    1. Italian language—Grammar.    2. Italian language—Errors of usage.    I. Title.

PC1112.D33    2006
455—dc22                                                                        2006048220

    2  3  4  5  6  7  8  9  10  11  12  13  14  15  16  17  18  19   VLP/VLP   0  9  8  7

ISBN-13: 978-0-07-147215-9
ISBN-10:      0-07-147215-0

McGraw-Hill books are available at special quantity discounts to use as premiums
and sales promotions, or for use in corporate training programs. For more information,
please write to the Director of Special Sales, Professional Publishing, McGraw-Hill,
Two Penn Plaza, New York, NY 10121-2298. Or contact your local bookstore.

This book is printed on acid-free paper.

# CONTENTS

# INTRODUCTION

The purpose of this book is to identify the most common errors for English-speaking students of Italian, to provide a basis for understanding why they typically arise, and to offer guidance for avoiding them in the future.

Most errors are caused by transferring the patterns and habits of English to Italian unconsciously. This happens in all areas of language, from pronunciation to word formation to sentence structure. Other errors can be traced to peculiarities within the Italian language itself. Following are examples of problems that English speakers experience when learning Italian.

- The sounds represented by *c* and *g* are problematic—the *c* is pronounced like the "ch" in "church" in words such as *cena* and *cinema,* but as "k" in words such as *cane* and *come.*
- Although articles and adjectives can indicate whether a noun ending in *-e* is masculine or feminine (for example, *il giornale* or *la televisione*), by and large a noun's gender must be memorized.
- Pluralizing nouns that end in *-co, -ca, -go,* and *-ga* is difficult, because in some cases the hard and soft sounds of the singular forms are retained, in others they are not.
- Knowing when to use the imperfect is tricky, because English often uses a perfect tense for the Italian imperfect.
- Learning how to use the equivalent of "some" (known as the partitive) is a knotty problem, given the variety of ways in which Italian renders this concept: *dei libri = alcuni libri = qualche libro =* "some books."
- Prepositions are particularly troublesome. In English, one says "I live in Rome"; in Italian, one says instead *Vivo a Roma* (literally, "at Rome"). Examples like this abound.
- False friends create difficulties. These are Italian and English words that have a common origin (and therefore look alike) but have different meanings. For example, *libreria* does not mean "library," as one might surmise, but "bookstore."

This book pinpoints all areas that constitute a source of blunders for most students. The ones that I have found to occur regularly in over three decades of teaching Italian are treated in this book. All blunders are printed in green type and marked by a stylized χ. You will be made aware of potential trouble spots and shown how to break bad habits and correct any mistakes you might be making. At the end of each unit (except the first unit on pronunciation) are exercises that test your knowledge. These will help you become even more conscious of potential blunder sources. At the back of the book is an Answer Key for the exercises, as well as an Index of Italian Words and Expressions and a Subject Index.

This is not a complete grammar of Italian. Its contents are structured around the most common blunders made by most students taking Italian classes in North America. This book will help you avoid these blunders and improve your proficiency in Italian. At the same time, you will get a synthetic overview of Italian grammar and its intricacies.

## Suggestions for Using This Book

This book is divided into two parts: (1) Pronunciation and Spelling and (2) Grammar. If you are unfamiliar with grammatical terminology, follow these suggestions:

- First look for the "Avoid the Blunder" boxes in each section. Read the examples, then the explanation.
- Do the exercises on a separate sheet of paper, then check your answers in the Answer Key at the back of the book. If you have made errors, reread the pertinent sections, then do the exercises again.
- Use the Subject Index, not the Contents, to find a particular topic that you are interested in.

The grammar and vocabulary explanations are based on current standard usage. However, be aware that Italian, like any language, is constantly changing, and that there are some aspects identified as blunders here that may be acceptable in colloquial or regional uses. Recognizing the differences you encounter in different places will enrich your knowledge of Italian and enable you to identify regional variations. The best way to learn a language is to listen to native speakers and practice by communicating with them.

# PRONUNCIATION AND SPELLING

# PRONUNCIATION

## Italian Letters and Sounds

There are two kinds of sounds in any language: vowels and consonants. Vowels are produced by expelling air through the mouth with no blockage. The letters that represent these sounds in Italian are as follows.

a   e   i   o   u

## Stressed Vowels

Italian stressed vowels—vowels bearing the main stress—are produced by expelling air from the mouth with no obstruction. Because Italian and English use many of the same alphabetic characters, it is important to keep in mind that sounds represented by certain letters in Italian are different from the sounds those letters represent in English.

a   pronounced like the *a* in "father" or in the exclamation "ah" but cut short: *cane* (KAH-neh) "dog"

e   pronounced like the *e* in "bet" but cut short: *bene* (BEH-neh) "well"

i   pronounced like the *i* in "machine" but cut short: *dico* (DEE-koh) "I say"

o   pronounced like the *o* in "go" or in the exclamation "oh" but cut short: *poco* (POH-koh) "little"

u   pronounced like the *oo* in "boot" or in the exclamation "ooh" but cut short: *tubo* (TOO-boh) "tube, pipe"

### AVOID THE Blunder

Stressed vowels are not pronounced with a glide, as in English (the /w/ sound in the middle of "going" or the /y/ sound in the middle of "baying").

✗ POHW-koh (poco)          ✗ BAY-nay (bene)

**3**

The vowels *e* and *o* are pronounced differently in different parts of Italy. In some areas, they are spoken with the mouth more open, in others more closed. In many areas, however, both pronunciations are used.

To give an English analogy: Consider how the *a* in "tomato" is pronounced in North America. In some areas, it is pronounced like the *a* in "father"; in others, it is pronounced like the *ay* in "pay." However it is pronounced, no one will have much difficulty understanding that the word is still "tomato." The same thing happens when Italian words with *e* and *o* are pronounced differently.

## Unstressed Single Vowels

Unstressed vowels—vowels that do not bear the main stress—are pronounced clearly and in the same way as stressed ones, unlike in English, where they are "reduced" to an indistinct sound.

| | | |
|---|---|---|
| amico | *friend* | ah-MEE-koh |
| italiano | *Italian* | ee-tah-LYAH-noh |

AVOID THE *Blunder*

Do not "glide" your pronunciation of unstressed vowels.

✗ ah-MEE-kohw (amico)
✗ ee-tah-LYAH-nohw (italiano)

## Vowel Combinations

Any combination of unstressed *i* or *u* plus stressed *a, e, o,* or *u* produces a one-syllable pronunciation; this combination is technically known as a diphthong.

| | |
|---|---|
| ia | yah |
| ie | yeh |
| io | yoh |
| iu | yoo |
| ua | wah |
| ue | weh |
| ui | wee |
| uo | woh |
| ai | ahee |
| ei | ay |
| oi | oy |
| au | ow |

In diphthongs, *i* sounds similar to the *y* in "yes" if it comes before a stressed vowel, and to the *y* in "say" if it comes after. Similarly, *u* sounds similar to the *w* in "way" if it comes before a stressed vowel, and to the *w* in "how" if it comes after.

| piano | *soft* | PYAH-noh |
| dieta | *diet* | DYEH-tah |
| pioggia | *rain* | PYOH-jjah |
| più | *more* | PYOO |
| quale | *which one* | KWAH-leh |
| questo | *this one* | KWEHS-toh |
| quinto | *fifth* | KWEEN-toh |
| buono | *good* | BWOH-noh |
| avrai | *you will have* | ah-VRAHEE |
| lei | *she* | LAY |
| noi | *we* | NOY |
| causa | *cause* | KOW-zah |

AVOID THE *Blunder*

✗ peeh-AH-noh (**piano**)
✗ KAH-leh (**quale**)
✗ KEHS-toh (**questo**)
✗ BOO-noh (**buono**)
✗ NWAH (**noi**)
✗ KOH-zah (**causa**)

When stressed *i* or *u* occurs before or after another stressed vowel, the vowels are pronounced as two separate syllables. In Italian, there is no accent mark to show this feature; you simply have to memorize the pronunciation of these words.

| via | *street* | VEE-ah |
| zio | *uncle* | TSEE-oh |
| bue | *ox* | BOO-eh |
| tuo | *yours* | TOO-oh |
| sei | *you are* | SEH-ee |
| baule | *trunk* | bah-OO-leh |

AVOID THE *Blunder*

✗ VYAH (**via**)
✗ BOW-leh (**baule**)

When a vowel is repeated within a word, like *ee* or *oo,* the two vowels are pronounced separately.

| linee aeree | *airlines* | LEE-neh-eh ah-EH-reh-eh |
| coordinare | *to coordinate* | koh-ohr-dee-NAH-reh |

**AVOID THE** *Blunder*

Do not add a /w/ or /y/ glide sound between double vowels, as you would in English.

✗ koh-wohr-dee-NAH-reh (coordinare)
✗ LEE-neh-yeh (linee)

## Stress

In most Italian words, the stress falls on the next-to-last syllable.

| amico | *friend* | ah-MEE-koh |
| sincero | *sincere* | seen-CHEH-roh |

But be careful! This is not always the case.

| lampada | *lamp* | LAHM-pah-dah |
| semplice | *simple* | SEHM-plee-cheh |

**AVOID THE** *Blunder*

✗ AH-mee-koh (amico)
✗ SEEN-cheh-roh (sincero)
✗ lahm-PAH-dah (lampada)
✗ sehm-PLEE-cheh (semplice)

Some Italian words are written with an accent mark on the final vowel. This means that you must put the main stress on that vowel.

| virtù | *virtue* | veer-TOO |
| perché | *because* | pehr-KEH |

**AVOID THE** *Blunder*

✗ VEER-too (virtù)
✗ PEHR-keh (perché)

## Single Consonants

Single consonants are produced by a blockage (partial or complete) of the air expelled through the mouth.

The Italian letters *b, f, m, n,* and *v* are sounded as in English.

The consonant represented by the letter *p* is not accompanied by a puff of air (aspiration), as it is at the beginning of some English words.

| | | |
|---|---|---|
| pane | *bread* | PAH-neh |
| poco | *little* | POH-koh |

The sounds represented by the letters *t* and *d* do not correspond exactly to the English sounds. In Italian, the tongue is placed on the upper teeth (not above them, as in English).

| | | |
|---|---|---|
| treno | *train* | TREH-noh |
| tutto | *everything* | TOO-ttoh |
| dare | *to give* | DAH-reh |
| dopo | *after* | DOH-poh |

**AVOID THE** *Blunder*

Do not pronounce words such as *pane, treno,* and *dopo* as you would in English. Make sure your tongue touches the upper teeth for the initial consonant and that no aspiration follows.

The letter *l* sounds identical to the /l/ sound in "love." However, in English, the back of the tongue is raised toward the back of the mouth when *l* occurs at the end of a syllable or word, as in "bill" or "filler." This feature, known as the dark /l/, is not found in Italian pronunciation.

| | | |
|---|---|---|
| latte | *milk* | LAH-tteh |
| alto | *tall* | AHL-toh |
| bello | *beautiful* | BEHL-loh |

**AVOID THE** *Blunder*

Do not pronounce words such as *alto* and *bello* with the dark /l/ sound of English.

The sound represented by *gli* is similar to the sound of *lli* in "million," but much more forceful.

| | | |
|---|---|---|
| figlio | *son* | FEE-llyoh |
| luglio | *July* | LOO-llyoh |

The sound represented by *gn* is similar to the sound of *ny* in "canyon," but—again—much more forceful.

| | | |
|---|---|---|
| giugno | *June* | JOO-nnyoh |
| sogno | *dream* | SOH-nnyoh |

AVOID THE *Blunder*

✗ LOOG-lee-oh (**luglio**)
✗ SOHG-noh (**sogno**)

The letter *s* represents either the /s/ sound in "sip" or the /z/ sound in "zip." The /z/ sound is used before *b, d, g, l, m, n, r,* and *v* and between vowels; otherwise, the /s/ sound is used.

| | | |
|---|---|---|
| sbaglio | *mistake* | ZBAH-llyoh |
| casa | *house* | KAH-zah |
| sapone | *soap* | sah-POH-neh |
| specchio | *mirror* | SPEH-kkyoh |

AVOID THE *Blunder*

✗ SBAH-llyoh (**sbaglio**)
✗ KAH-sah (**casa**)

The letter *z* represents either the /ts/ sound in "cats" or the /dz/ sound in "lads."

| | | |
|---|---|---|
| zio | *uncle* | TSEE-oh OR DZEE-oh |
| zero | *zero* | TSEH-roh OR DZEH-roh |

AVOID THE *Blunder*

✗ ZEE-oh (**zio**)
✗ ZEH-roh (**zero**)

The letter *h* does not represent any sound in Italian. It is silent, like the *h* in "hour."

| | | |
|---|---|---|
| ho | *I have* | oh |
| hai | *you have* | ahee |

AVOID THE *Blunder*

Do not pronounce the *h* in *ho* or *hai*.

The letter *r* represents a sound that is different from English *r*. To pronounce the Italian *r*, tap your tongue a few times on the ridge above your top front teeth.

| | | |
|---|---|---|
| caro | *dear* | KAH-roh |
| vero | *true* | VEH-roh |

AVOID THE *Blunder*

Do not pronounce words such as *caro* and *vero* with the English *r*.

## Double Consonants

Each single consonant may be doubled and have a corresponding double pronunciation, which lasts twice as long as and is slightly more forceful than its single counterpart.

| SINGLE CONSONANT | | | DOUBLE CONSONANT | | |
|---|---|---|---|---|---|
| fato | *fate* | FAH-toh | fatto | *fact* | FAH-ttoh |
| caro | *dear* | KAH-roh | carro | *cart* | KAH-rroh |
| pala | *shovel* | PAH-lah | palla | *ball* | PAH-llah |
| sono | *I am* | SOH-noh | sonno | *sleep* | SOH-nnoh |

AVOID THE *Blunder*

Do not use single consonants to pronounce double consonants in words like *fatto* and *palla*.

# SPELLING

Italian uses the same alphabetic characters as English does, except *j, k, w, x,* and *y*. These five are found, however, in words that Italian has borrowed from other languages, primarily English.

| | |
|---|---|
| il jazz | *jazz* |
| il karatè | *karate* |
| l'hardware | *hardware* |
| il software | *software* |
| il weekend | *weekend* |
| lo yacht | *yacht* |

## Single Consonants

The hard /k/ sound is spelled *c* before consonants and the vowels *a, o,* and *u*.

| | |
|---|---|
| clarino | *clarinet* |
| cravatta | *tie* |
| cane | *dog* |
| casa | *house* |
| collo | *neck* |
| come | *how* |
| cuore | *heart* |
| curioso | *curious, funny* |

It is spelled *ch* before the vowels *e* and *i*.

| | |
|---|---|
| anche | *also* |
| maniche | *sleeves* |
| chi | *who* |
| chimica | *chemistry* |

AVOID THE *Blunder*

✗ ance
✗ qui (chi)

The sound /kw/ is usually spelled *qu*.

| | |
|---|---|
| dunque | *therefore* |
| questo | *this* |
| quota | *quota* |

AVOID THE *Blunder*

✗ dunche
✗ chesto

The soft /ch/ sound (as in "church") is spelled *c* before the vowels *e* and *i*.

| | |
|---|---|
| cena | *dinner* |
| cento | *one hundred* |
| cinema | *movies* |
| cinque | *five* |

It is spelled *ci* before the vowels *a*, *o*, and *u*.

| | |
|---|---|
| ciao | *bye* |
| cominciare | *to begin, start* |
| bacio | *kiss* |
| comincio | *I begin, I start* |
| ciurma | *throng* |

AVOID THE *Blunder*

✗ chena
✗ chento

The hard /g/ sound is spelled *g* before consonants and before the vowels *a*, *o*, and *u*.

| | |
|---|---|
| globo | *globe* |
| grande | *big* |
| gara | *competition, match* |
| gatto | *cat* |
| gola | *throat* |
| gonna | *skirt* |
| gusto | *taste* |

It is spelled *gh* before the vowels *e* and *i*.

| | |
|---|---|
| ghetto | *ghetto* |
| luoghi | *places* |

The sound /gw/ is usually spelled *gu*.

| guanto | *glove* |
| guerra | *war* |

The soft /j/ sound (as in "jar") is spelled *g* before the vowels *e* and *i*.

| gelo | *frost* |
| gente | *people* |
| ginocchio | *knee* |
| giro | *turn; tour* |

It is spelled *gi* before the vowels *a, o,* and *u*.

| giacca | *jacket* |
| giapponese | *Japanese* |
| gioco | *game* |
| giovane | *young* |
| giugno | *June* |
| giusto | *just; correct* |

AVOID THE *Blunder*

✗ luogi
✗ jovane
✗ jugno

The sound /sk/ is spelled *sc* before consonants and before the vowels *a, o,* and *u*.

| scrivere | *to write* |
| scala | *stairs* |
| scopo | *scope* |
| scuola | *school* |

It is spelled *sch* before the vowels *e* and *i*.

| schermo | *screen* |
| schiena | *back* |

AVOID THE *Blunder*

✗ schuola
✗ sciena

The soft /sh/ sound (as in "shoe") is spelled *sc* before the vowels *e* and *i*.

| scena | *scene* |
| sciroppo | *syrup* |

It is spelled *sci* before the vowels *a, o,* and *u*.

| fascia | *dressing, bandage* |
| sciarpa | *scarf* |
| sciopero | *labor strike* |
| sciupare | *to waste* |

AVOID THE *Blunder*

✗ schiroppo
✗ schiopero

When grammar is responsible for a vowel change in the ending of a word, spelling adjustments are made to endings such as *-co* and *-cia*. These adjustments will be discussed in the unit on nouns.

## Double Consonants

Each single consonant may be doubled and have a corresponding double pronunciation. The double consonant is generally shown with double letters.

| fatto | *fact* |
| palla | *ball* |
| pizza | *pizza* |
| rosso | *red* |

AVOID THE *Blunder*

✗ fato (fatto)
✗ pala (palla)

The letter sequences *gl* and *gn* between vowels already represent double pronunciations.

| figlio | *son* |
| ragno | *spider* |

AVOID THE *Blunder*

✗ filio
✗ ranio

The double pronunciations of *ch, ci, gh,* and *gi* are indicated by doubling the first letter: *ch* becomes *cch, ci* becomes *cci, gh* becomes *ggh,* and *gi* becomes *ggi.*

| | |
|---|---|
| occhio | *eye* |
| faccia | *face* |
| agghiacciare | *to freeze* |
| aggiustare | *to fix* |

AVOID THE *Blunder*

✗ ochio
✗ facia

## Accent Marks

The accent mark in Italian is not used to indicate differences in pronunciation in most words. The grave accent is used in words that are stressed on the last vowel: *-à, -è, -ì, -ò,* and *-ù.*

| | |
|---|---|
| città | *city* |
| caffè | *coffee* |
| tassì | *taxi* |
| parlò | *he spoke* |
| virtù | *virtue* |

AVOID THE *Blunder*

✗ citta
✗ caffe

If the word ends in *-ché* or *-tré,* the acute accent is used instead.

| | |
|---|---|
| benché | *although* |
| perché | *because* |
| novantatré | *ninety-three* |
| trentatré | *thirty-three* |

The grave accent is used to avoid confusion in a few single-syllable words.

| | | | |
|---|---|---|---|
| è | *it is* | e | *and* |
| dà | *he gives* | da | *from* |

AVOID THE *Blunder*

✗ perche
✗ trentatre
✗ e (è)
✗ da (dà)

## Exercises

**A** *Fill in the blanks with the consonant(s) that produce the indicated sound.*

1. the hard /k/ sound

    a. ____a          d. ____e

    b. ____o          e. ____i

    c. ____u

2. the soft /ch/ sound

    a. ____a          d. ____e

    b. ____o          e. ____i

    c. ____u

3. the hard /g/ sound

    a. ____a          d. ____e

    b. ____o          e. ____i

    c. ____u

4. the soft /j/ sound

    a. ____a          d. ____e

    b. ____o          e. ____i

    c. ____u

5. the /sk/ sound

    a. ____a          d. ____e

    b. ____o          e. ____i

    c. ____u

6. the /sh/ sound

    a. ____a          d. ____e

    b. ____o          e. ____i

    c. ____u

**B** *The following words are misspelled. Write the correct form for each.*

1. ance          _____

2. cuesto          _____

3. chena          _____

4. luogi          _____

5. ganto     _____

6. govane     _____

7. gugno     _____

8. schuola     _____

9. sciena     _____

10. scharpa     _____

11. ochio     _____

12. facca     _____

13. buge     _____

14. amice     _____

15. perche     _____

# CAPITALIZATION

Many of the spelling conventions used in English with regard to capitalization apply to Italian as well. For example, like English, capital letters are used at the beginning of Italian sentences and to write proper nouns (for instance, *Alessandro, Sara, Italia,* and *Milano*). But there are exceptions.

The pronoun *io* "I" is not capitalized unless it is the first word of a sentence, but the pronouns *Lei* "you" (polite singular) and *Loro* "you" (polite plural) are generally capitalized, to distinguish them from *lei* "she" and *loro* "they," respectively.

Personal and professional titles are generally not capitalized, although this is optional, especially with professional titles used in direct speech.

| | |
|---|---|
| il signor Marchi | *Mr. Marchi* |
| la signora Dini | *Mrs./Ms. Dini* |
| la signorina Bruni | *Miss/Ms. Bruni* |
| il professor Rossini | *Professor Rossini* |
| la dottoressa Martini | *Dr. Martini* |

| | |
|---|---|
| Come sta, Professor Rossini? | *How are you, Professor Rossini?* |
| Come va, Dottoressa Martini? | *How are you, Dr. Martini?* |

## AVOID THE *Blunder*

✗ anch'Io
✗ lei (*you* (polite singular))

✗ la Signorina Bruni
✗ il Dottor Verdi

Names of the days of the week and the months of the year are not capitalized in Italian unless they are the first word in a sentence.

### DAYS

| | | | |
|---|---|---|---|
| lunedì | *Monday* | venerdì | *Friday* |
| martedì | *Tuesday* | sabato | *Saturday* |
| mercoledì | *Wednesday* | domenica | *Sunday* |
| giovedì | *Thursday* | | |

19

**MONTHS**

| | | | |
|---|---|---|---|
| gennaio | *January* | luglio | *July* |
| febbraio | *February* | agosto | *August* |
| marzo | *March* | settembre | *September* |
| aprile | *April* | ottobre | *October* |
| maggio | *May* | novembre | *November* |
| giugno | *June* | dicembre | *December* |

### AVOID THE Blunder

✗ Oggi è Lunedì.
✗ Oggi è Sabato.
✗ È il mese di Febbraio.
✗ È il mese di Gennaio.

Names of languages and nationalities are not capitalized in Italian.

| LANGUAGE | | NATIONALITY |
|---|---|---|
| il cinese | *Chinese* | cinese |
| il francese | *French* | francese |
| il giapponese | *Japanese* | giapponese |
| l'inglese | *English* | inglese |
| l'inglese | *English* | americano(-a) (*American*) |
| l'inglese | *English* | canadese (*Canadian*) |
| l'italiano | *Italian* | italiano(-a) |
| il portoghese | *Portuguese* | portoghese |
| il russo | *Russian* | russo(-a) |
| lo spagnolo | *Spanish* | spagnolo(-a) |
| il tedesco | *German* | tedesco(-a) |

### AVOID THE Blunder

✗ Tu studi il Giapponese.
✗ Io parlo Italiano.
✗ Lei ama il Portoghese.
✗ Lui studia lo Spagnolo.
✗ Tu sei Giapponese.
✗ Io sono Italiana.
✗ Lei è Portoghese.
✗ Lui è Spagnolo.

Names of religions and religious affiliations are usually not capitalized, although this is a convention and not a strict rule.

| RELIGION | | RELIGIOUS AFFILIATION | |
|---|---|---|---|
| il buddismo | *Buddhism* | buddista | *Buddhist* |
| il cattolicesimo | *Catholicism* | cattolico(-a) | *Catholic* |
| il cristianesimo | *Christianity* | cristiano(-a) | *Christian* |
| l'induismo | *Hinduism* | indù | *Hindu* |
| il protestantesimo | *Protestantism* | protestante | *Protestant* |

AVOID THE *Blunder*

✗ il Buddismo
✗ il Cattolicesimo
✗ Franco è Cristiano.
✗ Maria è Protestante.

In titles of books and articles, only the first word and proper names are capitalized.

«Grammatica della lingua italiana»          *Grammar of the Italian Language*

«Il significato della poesia di Dante»       *The Meaning of Dante's Poetry*

## Exercises

**A** *Circle the words that are capitalized incorrectly.*

1. la Signora Dini
2. la professoressa Franchi
3. Martedì
4. sabato
5. Bruno
6. Febbraio
7. marzo
8. tedesca
9. Russo
10. portoghese
11. Buddista
12. il protestantesimo

**B** *Each of the following sentences or titles has capitalization errors.*
*Rewrite each item, correcting the errors.*

1. giovanni è un Protestante.

   _____

2. "Il Significato della Matematica nella Vita Moderna"

   _____

3. oggi è Lunedì, il venti Marzo.

   _____

4. maria arriva a Gennaio.

   _____

# GRAMMAR

# NOUNS

A noun is a word that names a person, an animal, an object, a place, an event, a concept, or other abstract notion. In Italian, a noun can generally be recognized by its vowel ending, which often indicates its gender and number.

| | | | |
|---|---|---|---|
| ragazzo | *boy* | ragazzi | *boys* |
| ragazza | *girl* | ragazze | *girls* |
| madre | *mother* | madri | *mothers* |
| padre | *father* | padri | *fathers* |

A proper noun is the name given to a person or place.

| | |
|---|---|
| Alessandro | *Alexander* |
| Sara | *Sarah* |
| America | *America* |
| Italia | *Italy* |
| Stati Uniti | *United States* |
| Toscana | *Tuscany* |

All other nouns are called common.

## Gender

Every Italian noun has gender—that is to say, it is either masculine or feminine. With a few exceptions, nouns that refer to males (people or animals) are masculine, and those that refer to females are feminine.

Nouns ending in -*o* are generally masculine, and those ending in -*a* are generally feminine.

| MASCULINE (MALES) | | FEMININE (FEMALES) | |
|---|---|---|---|
| l'americano | *the male American* | l'americana | *the female American* |
| l'amico | *the male friend* | l'amica | *the female friend* |
| il figlio | *the son* | la figlia | *the daughter* |
| il gatto | *the male cat* | la gatta | *the female cat* |
| il ragazzo | *the boy* | la ragazza | *the girl* |
| lo zio | *the uncle* | la zia | *the aunt* |
| Carlo | *Charles* | Carla | *Carla* |
| Paolo | *Paul* | Paola | *Paula* |

But there are exceptions. For example, *il soprano* "soprano" is a masculine noun even though it refers to a female person, and *la spia* "spy" is a feminine noun even though it can refer to either a male or female person.

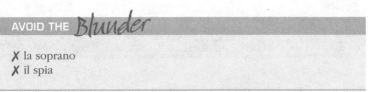

AVOID THE *Blunder*

✗ la soprano
✗ il spia

A noun that ends in *-e* may refer to either a male or female, and thus can be masculine or feminine. Since the gender of a noun is indicated by the form of the article that precedes it, you should learn a noun of this type along with its article (*il, lo,* and *l'* with masculine nouns and *la* and *l'* with feminine nouns). This will help you remember the noun's gender.

| MASCULINE (MALES) | | FEMININE (FEMALES) | |
|---|---|---|---|
| il cantante | *the male singer* | la cantante | *the female singer* |
| il francese | *the Frenchman* | la francese | *the Frenchwoman* |
| l'inglese | *the Englishman* | l'inglese | *the Englishwoman* |
| il nipote | *the nephew* | la nipote | *the niece* |
| il padre | *the father* | la madre | *the mother* |
| il parlante | *the male speaker* | la parlante | *the female speaker* |
| lo zio | *the uncle* | la zia | *the aunt* |

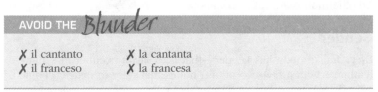

AVOID THE *Blunder*

✗ il cantanto     ✗ la cantanta
✗ il franceso     ✗ la francesa

In some cases, a masculine noun ending in *-e* has a corresponding feminine noun ending in *-a.*

| MASCULINE (MALES) | | FEMININE (FEMALES) | |
|---|---|---|---|
| il cameriere | *the waiter* | la cameriera | *the waitress* |
| l'infermiere | *the male nurse* | l'infermiera | *the female nurse* |

Note that a few nouns ending in *-a* refer to both males and females.

| | |
|---|---|
| la persona | *the person* (male or female) |
| la spia | *the spy* (male or female) |
| la stella | *the (movie) star* (male or female) |
| la vittima | *the victim* (male or female) |

AVOID THE *Blunder*

Do not confuse the ending of a noun with the gender of the person the noun refers to.

✗ il persona
✗ il vittimo

Nouns ending in *-ista* refer to both male and female persons. Many of these indicate a person's occupation.

| MASCULINE (MALES) | | FEMININE (FEMALES) | |
|---|---|---|---|
| il dentista | *the male dentist* | la dentista | *the female dentist* |
| il farmacista | *the male pharmacist* | la farmacista | *the female pharmacist* |
| il pianista | *the male pianist* | la pianista | *the female pianist* |
| lo specialista | *the male specialist* | la specialista | *the female specialist* |

AVOID THE *Blunder*

✗ il dentisto
✗ il pianisto

A masculine noun ending in *-tore* often has a corresponding feminine noun ending in *-trice*.

| MASCULINE (MALES) | | FEMININE (FEMALES) | |
|---|---|---|---|
| l'attore | *the male actor* | l'attrice | *the female actor* |
| l'autore | *the male author* | l'autrice | *the female author* |
| il pittore | *the male painter* | la pittrice | *the female painter* |

Some masculine nouns have corresponding feminine nouns ending in *-essa*.

| MASCULINE (MALES) | | FEMININE (FEMALES) | |
|---|---|---|---|
| il dottore | *the male doctor* | la dottoressa | *the female doctor* |
| l'elefante | *the male elephant* | l'elefantessa | *the female elephant* |
| il leone | *the lion* | la leonessa | *the lioness* |
| il professore | *the male professor* | la professoressa | *the female professor* |

Some feminine forms, however, have been eliminated in Italy, especially in nouns indicating professions.

| l'avvocato | the *lawyer* (male or female) |
|---|---|
| lo scultore | the *sculptor* (male or female) |

AVOID THE *Blunder*

When referring to females, be careful to use the correct ending.

✗ la pittora
✗ la professora
✗ l'avvocata

An Italian noun is either masculine or feminine, whether it refers to animate beings or to things. The general rules regarding gender remain the same. If a noun ends in -*o*, it is generally masculine; if it ends in -*a*, it is generally feminine.

**MASCULINE**

| il braccio | the *arm* (whether it is the arm of a male or a female) |
|---|---|
| il vestito | the *suit* (worn by either a male or a female) |
| l'anno | the *year* |
| l'occhio | the *eye* |

**FEMININE**

| la gamba | the *leg* (whether it is the leg of a male or a female) |
|---|---|
| la cravatta | the *necktie* (worn by either a male or a female) |
| la casa | the *house* |
| la cosa | the *thing* |

A noun ending in -*e* is either masculine or feminine. There is no choice; the noun's gender is fixed by the grammar of Italian. You will have to memorize the gender of such nouns. To be sure about the gender of a specific noun ending in -*e*, consult a dictionary if you cannot infer it from the article.

| **MASCULINE** | | **FEMININE** | |
|---|---|---|---|
| il cognome | the *surname* | la chiave | the *key* |
| il dente | the *tooth* | la gente | *people* |
| il giornale | the *newspaper* | la notte | the *night* |
| il nome | the *name* | la televisione | the *television* |

AVOID THE *Blunder*

✗ la braccia      ✗ il notte
✗ il gambo       ✗ il televisione
✗ il gente

In general, the name of a tree is masculine, whereas the name of the fruit it bears is feminine.

| MASCULINE | | FEMININE | |
|---|---|---|---|
| l'arancio | *the orange tree* | l'arancia | *the orange* |
| il ciliegio | *the cherry tree* | la ciliegia | *the cherry* |
| il melo | *the apple tree* | la mela | *the apple* |
| il pero | *the pear tree* | la pera | *the pear* |
| il pesco | *the peach tree* | la pesca | *the peach* |

Some exceptions are *il limone* "the lemon," *il fico* "the fig," and *il mandarino* "the mandarin"—each of these masculine nouns refers to both the tree and its fruit.

AVOID THE *Blunder*

✗ la limone
✗ la mandarina

Nouns of Greek origin ending in *-ema* and *-amma* correspond to English nouns ending in *-em* and *-am/-ama,* respectively. They are all masculine.

| il problema | *the problem* |
|---|---|
| il sistema | *the system* |
| il teorema | *the theorem* |
| il diagramma | *the diagram* |
| il dramma | *the drama* |
| il programma | *the program* |

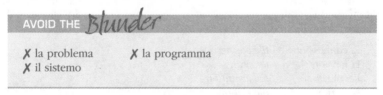

AVOID THE *Blunder*

✗ la problema ✗ la programma
✗ il sistemo

Nouns of Greek origin ending in *-si* correspond to English nouns ending in *-sis.* They are all feminine.

| l'analisi | *the analysis* |
|---|---|
| la crisi | *the crisis* |
| l'ipotesi | *the hypothesis* |
| la tesi | *the thesis* |

One exception is *il brindisi* "(the drinking) toast," which is masculine and of Germanic origin.

Some nouns ending in -*o* are feminine, and some ending in -*a* are masculine.

| | | | |
|---|---|---|---|
| la mano | *the hand* | il cometa | *the comet* |
| la radio | *the radio* | il pianeta | *the planet* |

A few nouns ending in -*o* are feminine because they are shortened forms of feminine nouns.

| FEMININE NOUN | | SHORTENED FORM | |
|---|---|---|---|
| la fotografia | *the photograph* | la foto | *the photo* |
| la motocicletta | *the motorcycle* | la moto | *the motorcycle* |

Similarly, a few nouns ending in -*a* are masculine because they are shortened forms of masculine nouns.

| MASCULINE NOUN | | SHORTENED FORM | |
|---|---|---|---|
| il cinematografo | *the movie theater* | il cinema | *the movies* |

Many nouns ending in -*ione,* especially those ending in -*sione* and -*zione,* are feminine.

| | |
|---|---|
| la connessione | *the connection* |
| la tensione | *tension, stress* |
| l'evoluzione | *the evolution* |
| la nazione | *the nation* |
| la regione | *the region* |
| la riunione | *the meeting* |

However, some nouns ending in *-ione* are masculine. Those ending in *-one* (but not *-ione*) are all masculine.

| | |
|---|---|
| il copione | *the script* |
| il padiglione | *the pavilion* |
| il cordone | *the rope* |
| il mattone | *the brick* |

Nouns ending in accented *-à* or *-ù* are generally feminine; those ending in other accented vowels are generally masculine.

| **MASCULINE** | | **FEMININE** | |
|---|---|---|---|
| il caffè | *the coffee* | la città | *the city* |
| il tè | *the tea* | l'università | *the university* |
| il lunedì | *Monday* | la gioventù | *youth* |
| il tassì | *the taxi* | la virtù | *virtue* |

There are several exceptions to this pattern, most notably *il papà* "dad."

AVOID THE *Blunder*

✗ la caffè
✗ il città

Nouns that have been borrowed from other languages (primarily English) are generally masculine. These typically end in a consonant.

| | |
|---|---|
| l'autobus | *the bus* |
| il clacson | *the car horn* |
| il computer | *the computer* |
| lo sport | *the sport* |
| il tennis | *tennis* |
| il tram | *the streetcar, trolley* |

BUT

| | |
|---|---|
| la chat | *chat room* |
| la mail (l'email) | *e-mail* |

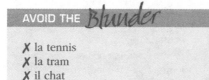

AVOID THE *Blunder*

✗ la tennis
✗ la tram
✗ il chat

# Plurals

Some nouns, known as collective nouns, have only a singular form.

| l'acqua | *water* |
|---------|---------|
| il pane | *bread* |
| la fame | *hunger* |
| la sete | *thirst* |
| il sale | *salt* |
| il pepe | *pepper* |
| il coraggio | *courage* |

A few nouns have only a plural form. These nouns refer to things made up of more than one part.

| i baffi | *mustache* |
|---------|-----------|
| le forbici | *scissors* |
| gli occhiali | *(eye)glasses* |
| le mutande | *underwear* |
| i pantaloni | *pants* |

AVOID THE *Blunder*

✗ i pani
✗ i pepi
✗ il baffo
✗ la forbice
✗ la mutanda
✗ il pantalone

Italian has several ways to make nouns plural.

- If a noun ends in *-o*, change the *-o* to *-i*.

| SINGULAR | | PLURAL | |
|----------|---|--------|---|
| il giorno | *the day* | i giorni | *the days* |
| la mano | *the hand* | le mani | *the hands* |
| il ragazzo | *the boy* | i ragazzi | *the boys* |

The main exception to this rule pertains to shortened nouns, which do not change in the plural.

| SINGULAR | | PLURAL | |
|----------|---|--------|---|
| la foto | *the photo* | le foto | *the photos* |
| la moto | *the motorcycle* | le moto | *the motorcycles* |
| la radio | *the radio* | le radio | *the radios* |

AVOID THE Blunder

✗ i foti
✗ i radi

■ If a noun ends in *-a*, change the *-a* to *-e*.

| SINGULAR | | PLURAL | |
|---|---|---|---|
| la gonna | *the skirt* | le gonne | *the skirts* |
| la mela | *the apple* | le mele | *the apples* |
| la ragazza | *the girl* | le ragazze | *the girls* |

Again, shortened nouns do not change in the plural.

| SINGULAR | | PLURAL | |
|---|---|---|---|
| il cinema | *the movie* | i cinema | *the movies* |

If a noun ends in *-ema* or *-amma*, the ending is changed to *-emi* or *-ammi*, respectively.

| SINGULAR | | PLURAL | |
|---|---|---|---|
| il problema | *the problem* | i problemi | *the problems* |
| il diagramma | *the diagram* | i diagrammi | *the diagrams* |
| il programma | *the program* | i programmi | *the programs* |

AVOID THE Blunder

✗ le probleme
✗ le programme

■ If a noun ends in *-e*, change the *-e* to *-i*.

| SINGULAR | | PLURAL | |
|---|---|---|---|
| il cameriere | *the waiter* | i camerieri | *the waiters* |
| la madre | *the mother* | le madri | *the mothers* |
| la notte | *the night* | le notti | *the nights* |
| il padre | *the father* | i padri | *the fathers* |

AVOID THE  Blunder

✗ le madre
✗ le notte

- If a noun ends in *-si* or in an accented vowel, it is not changed in the plural.

| SINGULAR | | PLURAL | |
|---|---|---|---|
| la crisi | *the crisis* | le crisi | *the crises* |
| la tesi | *the thesis* | le tesi | *the theses* |
| la città | *the city* | le città | *the cities* |
| l'università | *the university* | le università | *the universities* |
| il caffè | *the coffee* | i caffè | *the coffees* |
| il tè | *the tea* | i tè | *the teas* |
| il tassì | *the taxi* | i tassì | *the taxis* |

Be careful! The noun *la gente* "people" is singular in Italian; it has no plural form.

| La gente parla troppo. | *People speak too much.* |
|---|---|

Also, be careful with the plural of *l'uomo* "the man." It is *gli uomini* "the men."

AVOID THE *Blunder*

✗ i crisi          ✗ le genti
✗ le cittè         ✗ gli uomi

Italian has two ways to pluralize a noun ending in *-co* or *-go.*

- If the hard *c* and *g* sounds are to be retained, the plural endings are *-chi* and *-ghi,* which represent hard sounds.

| SINGULAR | | PLURAL | |
|---|---|---|---|
| il gioco | *the game* | i giochi | *the games* |
| il luogo | *the place* | i luoghi | *the places* |

- If soft sounds are required instead, the plural endings are *-ci* and *-gi,* which represent soft sounds.

| SINGULAR | | PLURAL | |
|---|---|---|---|
| l'amico | *the friend* | gli amici | *the friends* |
| il greco | *the Greek* | i greci | *the Greeks* |
| il biologo | *the biologist* | i biologi | *the biologists* |

In general, if the *-co* is preceded by *e* or *i* (as in *l'amico* and *il greco*), the tendency is to retain the soft sound in the plural (*gli amici, i greci*); otherwise, the hard sound is retained. In the case of *-go,* the tendency is the opposite—to retain the hard sound. But there are a number of exceptions to these guidelines, which are not strict grammatical rules even though they cover a large number of cases. If you have any doubt about these plurals, consult a dictionary.

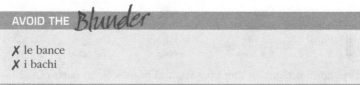

AVOID THE *Blunder*

✗ gli amichi
✗ i grechi
✗ i biologhi

Italian has only one way to pluralize a noun ending in -*ca* or -*ga*; these endings change to -*che* and -*ghe,* which represent hard sounds.

| SINGULAR | | PLURAL | |
|---|---|---|---|
| la banca | *the bank* | le banche | *the banks* |
| la riga | *the ruler* | le righe | *the rulers* |

There is also only one way to pluralize a noun ending in -*cio* or -*gio*; these endings change to -*ci* and -*gi,* which represent soft sounds.

| SINGULAR | | PLURAL | |
|---|---|---|---|
| il bacio | *the kiss* | i baci | *the kisses* |
| l'orologio | *the watch* | gli orologi | *the watches* |

AVOID THE *Blunder*

✗ le bance
✗ i bachi

Italian has two ways to pluralize a noun ending in -*cia* or -*gia.*

- If the *i* in the ending is stressed, it is pronounced in the plural and thus retained in the plural spelling.

| SINGULAR | PLURAL |
|---|---|
| bugia  *lie* | bugie  *lies* |
| (boo-JEE-ah) | (boo-JEE-eh) |
| farmacia  *pharmacy* | farmacie  *pharmacies* |
| (fahr-mah-CHEE-ah) | (fahr-mah-CHEE-eh) |

- If the *i* is not stressed, it is not pronounced and thus not retained in the plural spelling.

| SINGULAR | PLURAL |
|---|---|
| faccia  *face* | facce  *faces* |
| (FAH-chah) | (FAH-cheh) |
| valigia  *suitcase* | valige  *suitcases* |
| (vah-LEE-jah) | (vah-LEE-jeh) |

(The form *valigie* is also used.)

The only exception to these rules is *camicia*.

| SINGULAR | PLURAL |
|----------|--------|
| camicia *shirt* | camicie *shirts* |
| (kah-MEE-chah) | (kah-MEE-chee-eh) |

AVOID THE *Blunder*

✗ farmace      ✗ faccie
✗ buge         ✗ camice

Like the English nouns *memorandum* and *compendium,* which have the plural forms *memoranda* and *compendia,* Italian has a few nouns whose plural forms end in *-a.* These derive from Latin words that were pluralized in this way.

The following Italian nouns are masculine in the singular, but feminine in the plural.

| SINGULAR | | PLURAL | |
|----------|--|--------|--|
| il dito | *the finger* | le dita | *the fingers* |
| il ginocchio | *the knee* | le ginocchia | *the knees* |
| il labbro | *the lip* | le labbra | *the lips* |
| il paio | *the pair* | le paia | *the pairs* |

There are not many of these nouns, and most refer to parts of the human body.

AVOID THE *Blunder*

✗ i diti
✗ i labbri

## Titles

The final *-e* of a masculine title is dropped before a name. This rule does not apply to feminine titles. Keep in mind that this is a rule of style rather than of strict grammar; it is not technically wrong to keep the *-e,* but very few Italians do so.

| MASCULINE TITLE | | USED BEFORE A NAME | |
|-----------------|--|--------------------|--|
| il signore | *the gentleman* | il signor Marchi | *Mr. Marchi* |
| il professore | *the professor* | il professor Binni | *Professor Binni* |
| il dottore | *the doctor* | il dottor Franchi | *Dr. Franchi* |

| FEMININE TITLE | | USED BEFORE A NAME | |
|---|---|---|---|
| la signora | *the lady* | la signora Marchi | *Mrs. Marchi* |
| la professoressa | *the professor* | la professoressa Binni | *Professor Binni* |
| la dottoressa | *the doctor* | la dottoressa Franchi | *Dr. Franchi* |

AVOID THE *Blunder*

✗ il professore Binni
✗ il dottore Franchi

## Compound Nouns

Compound nouns are made up of two or more words. In English, the compound noun *handkerchief* is made up of two nouns, *hand* + *kerchief.*

To form the plural of such nouns in Italian, observe the following guidelines.

■ Most compound nouns are pluralized in the normal fashion, by changing the final vowel.

| SINGULAR | | PLURAL | |
|---|---|---|---|
| l'arcobaleno | *the rainbow* | gli arcobaleni | *the rainbows* |
| la ferrovia | *the railroad* | le ferrovie | *the railroads* |

■ There are exceptions. In some cases, both parts of the noun are changed.

| SINGULAR | | PLURAL | |
|---|---|---|---|
| la cassaforte | *the (money) safe* | le casseforti | *the safes* |

■ If the compound noun has a verb as one of its parts, it usually does not change.

| SINGULAR | | PLURAL | |
|---|---|---|---|
| il cacciavite | *the screwdriver* | i cacciavite | *the screwdrivers* |
| il salvagente | *the life jacket* | i salvagente | *the life jackets* |

Obviously, you need to consult a dictionary for the plural of many compound nouns.

# Exercises

**A** Complete the following chart by writing the male equivalent of the feminine nouns and the female equivalent of the masculine nouns.

| MASCULINE | FEMININE |
|---|---|
| 1. il ragazzo | _____ |
| 2. _____ | la madre |
| 3. l'americano | _____ |
| 4. _____ | la cantante |
| 5. il nipote | _____ |
| 6. _____ | la cameriera |
| 7. il pianista | _____ |
| 8. _____ | la persona |
| 9. l'autore | _____ |
| 10. _____ | la dottoressa |

**B** Complete the following chart by writing the plural form of the singular nouns and the singular form of the plural nouns.

| SINGULAR | PLURAL |
|---|---|
| 1. il problema | _____ |
| 2. _____ | i programmi |
| 3. la tesi | _____ |
| 4. _____ | i brindisi |
| 5. la mano | _____ |
| 6. _____ | le radio |
| 7. il caffè | _____ |
| 8. _____ | le città |
| 9. lo sport | _____ |

10. _____ i greci

11. il luogo _____

12. _____ gli amici

13. l'amica _____

14. _____ i baci

15. la farmacia _____

16. _____ gli orologi

17. la camicia _____

18. _____ le labbra

19. l'uomo _____

20. _____ le ferrovie

21. il cacciavite _____

**C** *Each of the following sentences contains an error. Rewrite the sentence, correcting the error.*

1. Le genti ama l'italiano. *(People love Italian.)*

_____

2. Io mangio sempre i meli. *(I always eat apples.)*

_____

3. Amo i pani. *(I love breads.)*

_____

4. Lui porta il baffo. *(He wears a mustache.)*

_____

5. Il professore Rossi è molto bravo. *(Professor Rossi is very good.)*

_____

# NUMBERS

## Cardinal Numbers

| | | | |
|---|---|---|---|
| 0 | zero | 11 | undici |
| 1 | uno | 12 | dodici |
| 2 | due | 13 | tredici |
| 3 | tre | 14 | quattordici |
| 4 | quattro | 15 | quindici |
| 5 | cinque | 16 | sedici |
| 6 | sei | 17 | diciassette |
| 7 | sette | 18 | diciotto |
| 8 | otto | 19 | diciannove |
| 9 | nove | 20 | venti |
| 10 | dieci | | |

**AVOID THE *Blunder***

✗ undieci          ✗ diecisette
✗ dodieci          ✗ dieciotto
✗ seidici

The number words above 20 are formed by adding the words for numbers one through nine to each larger number word, keeping the following adjustments in mind.

- In front of *uno* and *otto* (the two number words that start with a vowel), drop the final vowel of the higher-value word to which these are added.

| 21 | venti + uno | → | ventuno |
| 38 | trenta + otto | → | trentotto |

- When *tre* is added, it has an accented *é* (to show that the stress is on the final syllable).

| 23 | venti + tre | → | ventitré |
| 33 | trenta + tre | → | trentatré |

Here are examples of numbers from 20 to 100.

| | | | |
|---|---|---|---|
| 20 | venti | 52 | cinquantadue |
| 21 | ventuno | 53 | cinquantatré |
| 22 | ventidue | 60 | sessanta |
| 23 | ventitré | 61 | sessantuno |
| 24 | ventiquattro | 62 | sessantadue |
| 25 | venticinque | 63 | sessantatré |
| 26 | ventisei | 70 | settanta |
| 27 | ventisette | 71 | settantuno |
| 28 | ventotto | 72 | settantadue |
| 29 | ventinove | 73 | settantatré |
| 30 | trenta | 80 | ottanta |
| 31 | trentuno | 81 | ottantuno |
| 32 | trentadue | 82 | ottantadue |
| 33 | trentatré | 83 | ottantatré |
| 40 | quaranta | 90 | novanta |
| 41 | quarantuno | 91 | novantuno |
| 42 | quarantadue | 92 | novantadue |
| 43 | quarantatré | 93 | novantatré |
| 50 | cinquanta | 100 | cento |
| 51 | cinquantuno | | |

The same method of construction applies to numbers above 100.

| | |
|---|---|
| 101 | centuno |
| 102 | centodue |
| 103 | centotré |

To form the numbers 200, 300, and so on, simply add *cento* to the words for numbers two through nine.

| | |
|---|---|
| 200 | duecento |
| 300 | trecento |
| 900 | novecento |

Larger numbers are formed in the same way.

| | |
|---|---|
| 201 | duecentuno |
| 302 | trecentodue |
| 403 | quattrocentotré |
| 1000 | mille |
| 1001 | milleuno |
| 1002 | milledue |
| 2000 | duemila |
| 3000 | tremila |
| 100.000 | centomila |
| 200.000 | duecentomila |
| 1.000.000 | un milione |
| 2.000.000 | due milioni |
| 3.000.000 | tre milioni |

Notice that the plural of *mille* is *mila,* whereas *un milione* is pluralized in the normal way.

| | |
|---|---|
| duemila | *two thousand* |
| due milioni | *two million* |

**AVOID THE** *Blunder*

✗ due mille
✗ due milione

The cardinal numbers may be written as one word. But for large numbers, it is better to separate them into logical components, so that they can be read easily.

| | |
|---|---|
| 30.256 | trentamila duecento cinquantasei |
| | (RATHER THAN trentamiladuecentocinquantasei) |

**AVOID THE** *Blunder*

| | |
|---|---|
| ✗ 24.456 | ventiquattromilaquattrocento cinquantasei |
| ✗ 15.521 | quindicimilacinquecentoventuno |

Note that Italians use periods to separate thousands; Americans use commas.

| ITALIAN | AMERICAN |
|---------|----------|
| 30.256  | 30,256   |

AVOID THE *Blunder*

✗ 23,678
✗ 15,421

When the number *uno* (or any number constructed with it, such as *ventuno* or *trentuno*) is used with a noun, it is treated exactly like the indefinite article.

| uno zio | *one uncle* |
|---------|-------------|
| ventun anni | *21 years* |
| trentuna ragazze | *31 girls* |

AVOID THE *Blunder*

✗ ventuno anni
✗ trentuno ragazze

The word *nessuno* means "no" in the sense of "none." It is made up of *ness* plus *uno,* and thus it is treated like the indefinite article when used with a noun. In this case, however, the noun is always in the singular, even if its meaning is plural.

| nessuno zio | *no uncle(s)* |
|-------------|---------------|
| nessun amico | *no friend(s)* |
| nessuna zia | *no aunt(s)* |

AVOID THE *Blunder*

✗ nessuno amici
✗ nessuna amiche

The form *uno* also varies like the indefinite article in front of *altro* "other." Its two forms are *un altro* (masculine) and *un'altra* (feminine).

| un altro zio | *another uncle* |
|--------------|-----------------|
| un'altra ragazza | *another girl* |

*Milione* is always followed by *di* before a noun.

| | |
|---|---|
| un milione di dollari | *a million dollars* |
| due milioni di euro | *two million euros* |

AVOID THE *Blunder*

✗ uno altro zio
✗ un altra ragazza
✗ un milione persone

## Ordinal Numbers

| | |
|---|---|
| 1° | primo |
| 2° | secondo |
| 3° | terzo |
| 4° | quarto |
| 5° | quinto |
| 6° | sesto |
| 7° | settimo |
| 8° | ottavo |
| 9° | nono |
| 10° | decimo |

AVOID THE *Blunder*

✗ octavo
✗ diecimo

Ordinals above "tenth" are constructed in the following manner.

- Take the corresponding cardinal number, drop its vowel ending, and add *-esimo*.

| | | | |
|---|---|---|---|
| 11° | undici + -esimo | → | undicesimo |
| 42° | quaranta + -esimo | → | quarantesimo |

- In the case of numbers ending in *-tré*, remove the accent mark, but keep the *-e*.

| | | | |
|---|---|---|---|
| 23° | ventitré + -esimo | → | ventitreesimo |
| 33° | trentatré + -esimo | → | trentatreesimo |

- If the number ends in *-sei*, do not drop the vowel.

| | | | |
|---|---|---|---|
| 26° | ventisei + -esimo | → | ventiseiesimo |

Unlike the cardinal numbers, ordinals are adjectives. Therefore, they agree with the noun they modify in gender and number.

| | |
|---|---|
| il primo (1°) giorno | *the first day* |
| la ventesima (20ª) volta | *the twentieth time* |
| tutti gli ottavi (8ⁱ) capitoli | *all the eighth units* |

Like any adjective in Italian, the ordinals can be easily transformed into pronouns.

| | |
|---|---|
| È il terzo in fila. | *He is the third in line.* |
| Sono tra i primi della classe. | *They are among the first in their class.* |

The definite article is not used when the ordinals are used with a proper name.

| | |
|---|---|
| Papa Giovanni XXIII (= Ventitreesimo) | *Pope John XXIII (the Twenty-Third)* |
| Luigi XIV (= Quattordicesimo) | *Louis XIV (the Fourteenth)* |

## Fractions

As in English, cardinal numbers are used to express the numerator and ordinal numbers the denominator in fractions. If the numerator is greater than *1,* the denominator (being an ordinal adjective) must be plural.

| | |
|---|---|
| 1/17 | un diciassettesimo |
| 3/4 | tre quarti |
| 5/9 | cinque noni |

Be careful! The fraction 1/2 is different.

1/2    mezzo (*adjective*)
       metà (*noun*)

mezzo litro                     *a half liter*
la metà di tutto                *half of everything*

AVOID THE Blunder

✗ tre quarto (3/4)              ✗ mezzo caramella
✗ cinque dodicesimo (5/12)      ✗ mezzo della torta

## Numerical Expressions

+              più
23 + 36 = 59   Ventitré più trentasei fa cinquantanove.

−              meno
8 − 3 = 5      Otto meno tre fa cinque.

×              per
7 × 2 = 14     Sette per due fa quattordici.

÷              diviso per
16 ÷ 2 = 8     Sedici diviso per due fa otto.

AVOID THE Blunder

✗ Cinque più due è sette.
✗ Sette per due è quattordici.

The following expression is used to ask about age. It translates literally as "How many years do you have?"

Quanti anni hai (*familiar*)?     *How old are you?*
Quanti anni ha (*polite*)?        *How old are you?*
Ho ventidue anni.                 *I am 22 years old.*

The last sentence translates literally as "I have 22 years."

AVOID THE Blunder

✗ Quanti anni sei?
✗ Sono ventidue.

Here are a few other useful numerical expressions.

| | |
|---|---|
| il doppio | *double* |
| a due a due, a tre a tre, ... | *two by two, three by three, . . .* |
| una dozzina | *a dozen* |
| una ventina, una trentina, ... | *about twenty, about thirty, . . .* |
| un centinaio, due centinaia, ... | *about a hundred, about two hundred, . . .* |
| un migliaio, due migliaia, ... | *about a thousand, about two thousand, . . .* |

AVOID THE *Blunder*

✗ quattro per quattro
✗ una centina

## Telling Time

| | |
|---|---|
| Che ora è? | *What time is it?* (literally, *What hour is it?*) |

OR

| | |
|---|---|
| Che ore sono? | *What time is it?* (literally, *What hours are they?*) |

The word *ora* means "hour." The abstract concept of "time" is expressed by *il tempo*.

| | |
|---|---|
| Come passa il tempo! | *How time flies!* |

AVOID THE *Blunder*

✗ Che tempo è?
✗ Che ore è?

The hours are feminine and are, therefore, preceded by the feminine forms of the definite article.

| | |
|---|---|
| l'una | *one o'clock* (This is the only singular form.) |
| le due | *two o'clock* |
| le tre | *three o'clock* |
| le quattro | *four o'clock* |

✗ due
✗ quattro

In ordinary conversation, morning, afternoon, and evening hours are distinguished by the following expressions.

| | |
|---|---|
| di mattina / della mattina | *in the morning* |
| di pomeriggio | *in the afternoon* |
| di sera / della sera | *in the evening* |
| di notte / della notte | *in the night / at night* |
| Sono le otto di mattina. | *It's eight o'clock in the morning.* |
| Sono le nove di sera. | *It's nine o'clock in the evening.* |

✗ Sono le otto nella mattina.
✗ Sono le nove nella sera.

Official time in Italy is based on the 24-hour clock. Thus, after the noon hour, continue with the numbers as follows.

| | |
|---|---|
| le tredici | *1 P.M. (1300 hours)* |
| le quattordici | *2 P.M. (1400 hours)* |
| le quindici | *3 P.M. (1500 hours)* |
| le sedici | *4 P.M. (1600 hours)* |
| Sono le quindici. | *It's 3 P.M.* |
| Sono le venti. | *It's 8 P.M.* |
| Sono le ventiquattro. | *It's (12) midnight.* |

✗ È le venti.
✗ È le ventiquattro.

Minutes are simply added to the hour, after the conjunction *e* "and."

| | |
|---|---|
| Sono le tre e venti. | *It's 3:20.* |
| È l'una e quaranta. | *It's 1:40.* |
| Sono le sedici e cinquanta. | *It's 4:50 P.M.* |
| Sono le ventidue e cinque. | *It's 10:05 P.M.* |

AVOID THE *Blunder*

✗ Sono le tre venti.
✗ È l'una quaranta.

As the next hour approaches, an alternative way of expressing minutes is to give the next hour minus (*meno*) the number of minutes left to go.

| 8:58 | le otto e cinquantotto OR le nove meno due |
| 10:50 | le dieci e cinquanta OR le undici meno dieci |

AVOID THE *Blunder*

✗ È le due e cinquantasei.
✗ Sono l'una e cinquanta.

The expressions *un quarto* "a quarter" and *mezzo* or *mezza* "half" can be used to indicate the quarter and half hour.

| 3:15 | le tre e quindici OR le tre e un quarto |
| 4:30 | le quattro e trenta OR le quattro e mezzo/mezza |
| 5:45 | le cinque e quarantacinque OR le sei meno un quarto |
| | OR le cinque e tre quarti (*three quarters*) |

Noon and midnight can also be rendered by *mezzogiorno* and *mezzanotte*, respectively.

Sono le dodici. / È mezzogiorno.　　*It's noon.*
Sono le ventiquattro. / È mezzanotte.　　*It's midnight.*

Finally, note the following useful expressions.

preciso　*exactly*
È l'una precisa.　　　　　　　　*It's exactly one o'clock.*
Sono le otto precise.　　　　　　*It's exactly eight o'clock.*

in punto　*on the dot*
È l'una in punto.　　　　　　　　*It's one o'clock on the dot.*
Sono le otto in punto.　　　　　　*It's eight o'clock on the dot.*

AVOID THE *Blunder*

✗ Sono le tre e quarto.　　　　✗ Sono mezzogiorno.
✗ Sono le sette e tre quarto.　　✗ Sono mezzanotte.

## Dates

Dates are expressed by the following formula.

| | |
|---|---|
| il quindici settembre | *September 15* (literally, *the 15 September*) |
| il ventun settembre | *September 21* (literally, *the 21 September*) |

The exception to this formula is the first day of the month, for which the ordinal number *primo* is used.

| | |
|---|---|
| È il primo ottobre. | *It's October 1.* |
| È il primo giugno. | *It's June 1.* |

Years are preceded by the definite article.

| | |
|---|---|
| È il 2007. | *It's 2007.* |
| Sono nato(-a) nel 1994. | *I was born in 1994.* |

In complete dates, however, the article is omitted before the year.

| | |
|---|---|
| Oggi è il cinque febbraio, 2012. | *Today is February 5, 2012.* |

AVOID THE *Blunder*

✗ È l'uno ottobre.
✗ Oggi è cinque febbraio.

## Exercises

**A** Write the Italian words for the following numbers.

1. 7 _____

2. 12 _____

3. 17 _____

4. 18 _____

5. 19 _____

6. 24 _____

7. 31 _____

8. 43 _____

9. 58 _____

10. 398 _____

11. 2012 _____

12. 34.599 _____

**B** Write the following expressions in Italian.

1. four thousand euros _____

2. five million dollars _____

3. twenty-one girls _____

4. I am thirty-one years old. _____

5. no uncles _____

6. no aunts _____

7. another boy _____

8. another girl _____

9. a half liter _____

10. 16 divided by 4 equals 4 _____

**C** Write the words for the ordinal numbers in the chart.

1. first  il _____ ragazzo

  la _____ ragazza

2. second  il _____ figlio

  la _____ figlia

3. *third*  il _____ cugino

la _____ cugina

4. *fourth*  il _____ fratello

la _____ sorella

5. *fifth*  il _____ piano

la _____ casa

6. *fifteenth*  il _____ anno

la _____ volta

7. *twenty-first*  il _____ mese (*month*)

la _____ settimana (*week*)

8. *fifty-sixth*  il _____ giorno (*day*)

la _____ persona

9. *ninety-third*  il _____ ragazzo

la _____ ragazza

---

**◻** *Each of the following expressions contains an error. Rewrite the expression, correcting the error.*

1. un venti (*about twenty*)  _____

2. Che tempo è?  _____

3. i due e venti  _____

4. le ventitré di pomeriggio  _____

5. le nove e tre quarto  _____

6. Sono le dieci preciso.  _____

7. Oggi è quattro dicembre.  _____

8. Oggi è l'uno maggio.  _____

9. Sono nata 1998.  _____

# ARTICLES AND DEMONSTRATIVES

Articles are words used to identify nouns as specific or nonspecific.

| A SPECIFIC NOUN | | A NONSPECIFIC NOUN | |
| --- | --- | --- | --- |
| il libro | *the book* | un libro | *a book* |

Demonstratives also identify nouns; they indicate whether the person or thing a noun refers to is relatively near or far away.

| NEAR | | FAR AWAY | |
| --- | --- | --- | --- |
| questo libro | *this book* | quel libro | *that book* |

## The Indefinite Article

The indefinite article varies according to the gender, number, and initial sound of the noun or adjective it precedes. It may help to realize that the English indefinite article also varies, albeit only according to the initial sound of the following noun or adjective.

| BEFORE A CONSONANT | BEFORE A VOWEL |
| --- | --- |
| *a boy* | *an angel* |
| *a friend* | *an egg* |

The Italian indefinite article may take one of several forms.

■ *Uno* is used before a masculine noun or adjective beginning with *z, s* + consonant, *gn,* or *ps.*

| uno zio | *an uncle* |
| --- | --- |
| uno studente | *a student* |
| uno gnocco | *a dumpling* |
| uno psicologo | *a psychologist* |

■ *Un* is used before a masculine noun or adjective beginning with any other sound (consonant or vowel).

| un amico | *a friend* |
| --- | --- |
| un cane | *a dog* |
| un gatto | *a cat* |
| un ragazzo | *a boy* |

- *Una* is used before a feminine noun or adjective beginning with a consonant.

| | |
|---|---|
| una zia | *an aunt* |
| una studentessa | *a student* |
| una ragazza | *a girl* |
| una psicologa | *a psychologist* |

- *Un'* is used before a feminine noun or adjective beginning with a vowel.

| | |
|---|---|
| un'americana | *an American* |
| un'amica | *a friend* |
| un'isola | *an island* |
| un'ora | *an hour* |

---

### AVOID THE *Blunder*

✗ un zio      ✗ un'amico
✗ un psicologo      ✗ un amica

---

When an adjective precedes the noun, it is necessary to adjust the indefinite article according to the initial sound of the adjective.

| | | | |
|---|---|---|---|
| uno zio | *an uncle* | un caro zio | *a dear uncle* |
| un'amica | *a friend* | una cara amica | *a dear friend* |

It may help to remember that a similar pattern applies in English.

| | |
|---|---|
| *a boy* | *an intelligent boy* |
| *an apple* | *a good apple* |

---

### AVOID THE *Blunder*

✗ uno caro zio
✗ una amica canadese

---

The uses of the indefinite article in Italian are generally the same as those in English. However, there are two differences that are a constant cause of blunders.

- The Italian indefinite article is omitted in exclamations of the following type.

| | |
|---|---|
| Che buon caffè! | *What a good coffee!* |
| Che lingua bella! | *What a beautiful language!* |

■ The Italian indefinite article is omitted in expressions that refer to an ailment with *mal di....*

| | |
|---|---|
| mal di testa | *a headache* |
| mal di gola | *a sore throat* |

The indefinite article must be repeated before every noun.

| | |
|---|---|
| un ragazzo e una ragazza | *a boy and girl* |
| un amico e uno zio | *a friend and uncle* |

## The Definite Article

The singular forms of the Italian definite article are as follows.

■ *Lo* is used before a masculine singular noun or adjective beginning with *z, s* + consonant, *gn,* or *ps.*

| | |
|---|---|
| lo zio | *the uncle* |
| lo studente | *the student* |
| lo gnocco | *the dumpling* |
| lo psicologo | *the psychologist* |

■ *Il* is used before a masculine singular noun or adjective beginning with any other consonant.

| | |
|---|---|
| il cane | *the dog* |
| il gatto | *the cat* |
| il ragazzo | *the boy* |

■ *La* is used before a feminine singular noun or adjective beginning with a consonant.

| | |
|---|---|
| la zia | *the aunt* |
| la studentessa | *the student* |
| la ragazza | *the girl* |
| la psicologa | *the psychologist* |

- *L'* is used before a masculine or feminine singular noun or adjective beginning with a vowel.

| | |
|---|---|
| l'amico | *the (male) friend* |
| l'orologio | *the watch* |
| l'isola | *the island* |
| l'ora | *the hour* |

AVOID THE *Blunder*

✗ il zio          ✗ il amico
✗ lo ragazzo      ✗ la amica

There are also corresponding plural forms of the definite article, as follows.

- *Gli* is used before a masculine plural noun or adjective beginning with *z, s* + consonant, *gn, ps,* or a vowel.

| | |
|---|---|
| gli zii | *the uncles* |
| gli studenti | *the students* |
| gli gnocchi | *the dumplings* |
| gli psicologi | *the psychologists* |
| gli amici | *the friends* |
| gli orologi | *the watches* |

- *I* is used before a masculine plural noun or adjective beginning with any other consonant.

| | |
|---|---|
| i cani | *the dogs* |
| i gatti | *the cats* |
| i ragazzi | *the boys* |

- *Le* is used before a feminine plural noun or adjective beginning with any sound.

| | |
|---|---|
| le zie | *the aunts* |
| le ragazze | *the girls* |
| le isole | *the islands* |
| le ore | *the hours* |

AVOID THE *Blunder*

✗ i zii            ✗ l'amici
✗ gli ragazzi      ✗ l'amiche

As with the indefinite article, when an adjective precedes the noun, it is necessary to adjust the definite article according to the initial sound of the adjective.

| lo zio | *the uncle* | il caro zio | *the dear uncle* |
|--------|-------------|-------------|------------------|
| l'amica | *the friend* | la cara amica | *the dear friend* |

The definite article must also be repeated before every noun.

| il ragazzo e la ragazza | *the boy and girl* |
|-------------------------|---------------------|
| l'amico e lo zio | *the friend and uncle* |

AVOID THE *Blunder*

✗ lo caro zio
✗ la amica canadese
✗ il ragazzo e ragazza

The definite article is used before collective nouns used as subjects (normally at the beginning of a sentence).

| L'acqua è un liquido. | *Water is a liquid.* |
|-----------------------|----------------------|
| Il cibo è necessario per vivere. | *Food is necessary to live.* |
| La pazienza è una virtù. | *Patience is a virtue.* |

AVOID THE *Blunder*

✗ Acqua è un liquido.
✗ Pazienza è una virtù.

The definite article is also used with nouns in the plural that express generalizations.

| Gli italiani sono simpatici. | *Italians are nice.* |
|------------------------------|----------------------|
| Le macchine stanno rovinando l'ambiente. | *Cars are wrecking the environment.* |

As a general guideline, remember that you cannot start an Italian sentence with a noun without its article.

AVOID THE *Blunder*

✗ Americani sono simpatici.
✗ Macchine rovinano l'ambiente.

The definite article is used before geographical names (continents, countries, states, rivers, islands, mountains, and so forth)—except cities.

| | |
|---|---|
| l'Italia | *Italy* |
| la Sicilia | *Sicily* |
| gli Stati Uniti | *the United States* |
| la California | *California* |
| il Belgio | *Belgium* |
| il Piemonte | *Piedmont* |
| il Tevere | *the Tiber* |
| il Mediterraneo | *the Mediterranean* |
| le Alpi | *the Alps* |

BUT

| | |
|---|---|
| Roma | *Rome* |
| Firenze | *Florence* |
| Venezia | *Venice* |

**AVOID THE** *Blunder*

✗ Italia è bella.
✗ California è magnifica.

The definite article is usually dropped after the preposition *in* before an unmodified geographical noun.

| | |
|---|---|
| Vado in Italia. | *I'm going to Italy.* |
| Vivo in Francia. | *I live in France.* |

But when the noun is modified, the definite article must be used. Note: *nell'* = *in* + *l'* and *nella* = *in* + *la*.

| | |
|---|---|
| Vado nell'Italia centrale. | *I'm going to central Italy.* |
| Vivo nella Francia meridionale. | *I live in southern France.* |

**AVOID THE** *Blunder*

✗ Domani vado all'Italia.
✗ Vivo in Francia meridionale.

The definite article is commonly used instead of a possessive adjective when referring to family members in the singular, parts of the body, or clothing.

| | |
|---|---|
| Oggi vado in centro con la zia. | *Today I'm going downtown with my aunt.* |
| Mi fa male la testa. | *My head hurts.* |
| Franco non si mette mai la giacca. | *Franco never puts his jacket on.* |

AVOID THE *Blunder*

✗ Oggi vado in centro con zio.
✗ Mi fa male gola.

The definite article is used with the days of the week to indicate a habitual action.

| | |
|---|---|
| Il lunedì gioco sempre a tennis. | *On Mondays I always play tennis.* |
| La domenica vado regolarmente in chiesa. | *On Sundays I regularly go to church.* |

AVOID THE *Blunder*

✗ Martedì vado sempre a scuola.
✗ Sabato gioco regolarmente a tennis.

The definite article is used with titles, unless the person is being spoken to.

| | |
|---|---|
| Il dottor Rossi è italiano. | *Dr. Rossi is Italian.* |
| La professoressa Bianchi è molto brava. | *Professor Bianchi is very good.* |

BUT

| | |
|---|---|
| Dottor Rossi, come va? | *Dr. Rossi, how is it going?* |
| Professoressa Bianchi, come sta? | *Professor Bianchi, how are you?* |

AVOID THE *Blunder*

✗ Dottor Smith è americano.
✗ Signorina Corelli è italiana.

The definite article is used before the names of languages and nouns referring to school subjects.

| | |
|---|---|
| Amo lo spagnolo. | *I love Spanish.* |
| Sto studiando la matematica. | *I am studying mathematics.* |

It is dropped after the prepositions *di* and *in*.

| | |
|---|---|
| Ecco il mio libro di spagnolo. | *Here is my Spanish book.* |
| Lui è molto bravo in matematica. | *He is very good at math.* |

AVOID THE *Blunder*

✗ Amo italiano.
✗ Ecco il mio libro della matematica.

The definite article is used with *scorso* "last" and *prossimo* "next" in time expressions.

| | |
|---|---|
| la settimana scorsa | *last week* |
| il mese prossimo | *next month* |

The definite article is not used in some common expressions.

| | |
|---|---|
| a destra | *on/to the right* |
| a sinistra | *on/to the left* |
| a casa | *at home* |

AVOID THE *Blunder*

✗ Sono andata al cinema settimana scorsa.
✗ Il tuo libro è alla destra.

## The Demonstratives

The demonstrative indicating "nearness" is *questo*. Its form varies as follows.

- *Questo* (plural: *questi*) is used before a masculine noun or adjective.

| SINGULAR | | PLURAL | |
|---|---|---|---|
| questo zio | *this uncle* | questi zii | *these uncles* |
| questo studente | *this student* | questi studenti | *these students* |
| questo amico | *this friend* | questi amici | *these friends* |
| questo cane | *this dog* | questi cani | *these dogs* |
| questo ragazzo | *this boy* | questi ragazzi | *these boys* |

- *Questa* (plural: *queste*) is used before a feminine noun or adjective.

| SINGULAR | | PLURAL | |
|---|---|---|---|
| questa zia | *this aunt* | queste zie | *these aunts* |
| questa studentessa | *this student* | queste studentesse | *these students* |
| questa amica | *this friend* | queste amiche | *these friends* |
| questa camicia | *this shirt* | queste camicie | *these shirts* |
| questa ragazza | *this girl* | queste ragazze | *these girls* |

The form *quest'* can be used (optionally) before a singular noun or adjective beginning with a vowel.

questo amico OR quest'amico
questa amica OR quest'amica

AVOID THE *Blunder*

✗ quest zio
✗ quest'amici
✗ quest'amiche

The demonstrative indicating "farness" is *quello*. Its form varies as follows.

- *Quello* (plural: *quegli*) is used before a masculine noun or adjective beginning with *z, s* + consonant, *gn*, or *ps*.

| SINGULAR | | PLURAL | |
|---|---|---|---|
| quello zio | *that uncle* | quegli zii | *those uncles* |
| quello studente | *that student* | quegli studenti | *those students* |
| quello gnocco | *that dumpling* | quegli gnocchi | *those dumplings* |
| quello psicologo | *that psychologist* | quegli psicologi | *those psychologists* |

- *Quel* (plural: *quei*) is used before a masculine noun or adjective beginning with any other consonant.

| SINGULAR | | PLURAL | |
|---|---|---|---|
| quel cane | *that dog* | quei cani | *those dogs* |
| quel ragazzo | *that boy* | quei ragazzi | *those boys* |

- *Quell'* (plural: *quegli*) is used before a masculine noun or adjective beginning with a vowel.

| SINGULAR | | PLURAL | |
|---|---|---|---|
| quell'amico | *that friend* | quegli amici | *those friends* |
| quell'orologio | *that watch* | quegli orologi | *those watches* |

- *Quella* (plural: *quelle*) is used before a feminine noun or adjective beginning with a consonant.

| SINGULAR | | PLURAL | |
|---|---|---|---|
| quella zia | *that aunt* | quelle zie | *those aunts* |
| quella studentessa | *that student* | quelle studentesse | *those students* |
| quella ragazza | *that girl* | quelle ragazze | *those girls* |

- *Quell'* (plural: *quelle*) is used before a feminine noun or adjective beginning with a vowel.

| SINGULAR | | PLURAL | |
|---|---|---|---|
| quell'amica | *that friend* | quelle amiche | *those friends* |
| quell'ora | *that hour* | quelle ore | *those hours* |

AVOID THE *Blunder*

✗ quel zio       ✗ quei amici
✗ quello ragazzo  ✗ quell'amiche
✗ quegli ragazzi

Be careful! As with the articles, when an adjective precedes the noun, it is necessary to adjust the demonstrative according to the initial sound of the adjective.

| quello zio | *that uncle* | quel simpatico zio | *that nice uncle* |
|---|---|---|---|
| quegli amici | *those friends* | quei simpatici amici | *those nice friends* |

The demonstrative must be repeated before every noun.

| questo ragazzo e questa ragazza | *this boy and girl* |
|---|---|
| quel ragazzo e quella ragazza | *that boy and girl* |

AVOID THE *Blunder*

✗ quello simpatico zio
✗ quel ragazzo e ragazza

Demonstrative pronouns can replace noun phrases constructed with demonstratives.

| Quel ragazzo è italiano. | *That boy is Italian.* |
|---|---|
| Quello è italiano. | *That one is Italian.* |
| | |
| Questa ragazza è americana. | *This girl is American.* |
| Questa è americana. | *This one is American.* |

The pronouns retain the gender and number of—and are mainly the same in form as—the demonstratives they replace, with a few exceptions. Following are all the possibilities.

### MASCULINE DEMONSTRATIVES

| SINGULAR FORM | | CORRESPONDING PRONOUN FORM | |
|---|---|---|---|
| questo ragazzo | *this boy* | questo | *this one* (*referring to* ragazzo) |
| quest'amico | *this friend* | questo | *this one* (*referring to* amico) |
| quel ragazzo | *that boy* | quello | *that one* (*referring to* ragazzo) |
| quello zio | *that uncle* | quello | *that one* (*referring to* zio) |
| quell'amico | *that friend* | quello | *that one* (*referring to* amico) |

| SINGULAR FORM | | CORRESPONDING PRONOUN FORM | |
|---|---|---|---|
| questi ragazzi | *these boys* | questi | *these ones* (*referring to* ragazzi) |
| questi amici | *these friends* | questi | *these ones* (*referring to* amici) |
| quei ragazzi | *those boys* | quelli | *those ones* (*referring to* ragazzi) |
| quegli zii | *those uncles* | quelli | *those ones* (*referring to* zii) |
| quegli amici | *those friends* | quelli | *those ones* (*referring to* amici) |

### FEMININE DEMONSTRATIVES

| SINGULAR FORM | | CORRESPONDING PRONOUN FORM | |
|---|---|---|---|
| questa ragazza | *this girl* | questa | *this one* (*referring to* ragazza) |
| quest'amica | *this friend* | questa | *this one* (*referring to* amica) |
| quella ragazza | *that girl* | quella | *that one* (*referring to* ragazza) |
| quell'amica | *that friend* | quella | *that one* (*referring to* amica) |

| PLURAL FORM | | CORRESPONDING PRONOUN FORM | |
|---|---|---|---|
| queste ragazze | *these girls* | queste | *these ones* (*referring to* ragazze) |
| queste amiche | *these friends* | queste | *these ones* (*referring to* amiche) |
| quelle ragazze | *those girls* | quelle | *those ones* (*referring to* ragazze) |
| quelle amiche | *those friends* | quelle | *those ones* (*referring to* amiche) |

AVOID THE *Blunder*

✗ Quel è Marco.
✗ Quei sono studenti.
✗ Quegli sono i miei zii.

# Exercises

**A** *Write the corresponding definite article expression for each indefinite article expression.*

| INDEFINITE ARTICLE | DEFINITE ARTICLE |
|---|---|
| 1. un ragazzo | _____ |
| 2. una ragazza | _____ |
| 3. un americano | _____ |
| 4. un'italiana | _____ |
| 5. uno studente | _____ |
| 6. uno psicologo | _____ |
| 7. un orologio | _____ |
| 8. un'amica | _____ |
| 9. una zia | _____ |

**B** *Complete the following chart by writing the plural equivalent of the singular nouns and the singular equivalent of the plural nouns.*

| SINGULAR | PLURAL |
|---|---|
| 1. il ragazzo | _____ |
| 2. _____ | le madri |
| 3. l'americano | _____ |
| 4. _____ | le cantanti |
| 5. lo studente | _____ |
| 6. _____ | gli italiani |
| 7. il cane | _____ |
| 8. _____ | gli orologi |
| 9. lo gnocco | _____ |
| 10. _____ | le ore |
| 11. questo gatto | _____ |
| 12. _____ | queste zie |
| 13. quest'amico | _____ |
| 14. _____ | quegli psicologi |
| 15. quel ragazzo | _____ |
| 16. _____ | quegli amici |

17. quell'amica                     _____

18. _____     quelle ragazze

**C**  Fill in the blank with the article or other word necessary to complete each sentence. If no word is necessary, write an X in the blank.

1. Che _____ bel film! (What a nice movie!)

2. Ho _____ mal di stomaco. (I have a stomachache.)

3. Loro hanno un cane e _____ gatto. (They have a dog and cat.)

4. Sono la zia e _____ zio dall'Italia.
   (They're the aunt and uncle from Italy.)

5. Io amo _____ carne. (I love meat.)

6. _____ italiani sanno vivere. (Italians know how to live.)

7. Loro vanno spesso _____ Italia. (They go often to Italy.)

8. _____ Francia è un bel paese. (France is a beautiful country.)

9. Spesso vado in centro con _____ zio.
   (Often I go downtown with my uncle.)

10. _____ venerdì vanno spesso al cinema.
    (On Fridays they often go to the movies.)

11. Conosci _____ professor Martini?
    (Do you know Professor Martini?)

12. Mio fratello ama _____ matematica. (My brother loves math.)

13. Lei è andata al cinema _____ settimana scorsa.
    (She went to the movies last week.)

14. Loro vivono _____ destra. (They live on the right.)

**D**  Match the words and expressions in the left column with those in the right column to make complete, logical sentences.

_____  1. Lui è ...              a. dottoressa Rossi, come va?

_____  2. Lui va spesso ...      b. il mio libro.

_____  3. Buongiorno, ...        c. i miei libri.

_____  4. Mio fratello è bravo ...  d. le mie amiche.

_____  5. Questo è ...           e. nell'Italia meridionale.

_____  6. Quelli sono ...        f. un caro zio.

_____  7. Quelle sono ...        g. in matematica.

# DESCRIPTIVE ADJECTIVES

Descriptive adjectives are words that modify or describe nouns. With some exceptions, they are placed after the noun they modify.

| | |
|---|---|
| È una casa nuova. | *It's a new house.* |
| Sono due macchine italiane. | *They are two Italian cars.* |

Adjectives are easily recognized, generally by predictable changes in their ending.

| | |
|---|---|
| il libro nuovo | *the new book* |
| i libri nuovi | *the new books* |
| la rivista nuova | *the new magazine* |
| le riviste nuove | *the new magazines* |

## Forms

An adjective agrees with the noun it modifies. This means, in concrete terms, that the adjective's final vowel is changed to match the gender and number of the noun. There are two types of adjectives: (1) adjectives that end in *-o* (such as *alto* "tall") and (2) those that end in *-e* (such as *intelligente* "intelligent").

■ With masculine nouns, an adjective such as *alto* ends in *-o* if the noun it modifies is singular and in *-i* if it is plural; an adjective such as *intelligente* ends in *-e* if the noun is singular and in *-i* if it is plural.

| SINGULAR | PLURAL |
|---|---|
| il padre alto | i padri alti |
| *the tall father* | *the tall fathers* |
| il padre intelligente | i padri intelligenti |
| *the intelligent father* | *the intelligent fathers* |
| l'uomo alto | gli uomini alti |
| *the tall man* | *the tall men* |
| l'uomo intelligente | gli uomini intelligenti |
| *the intelligent man* | *the intelligent men* |

- With feminine nouns, an adjective such as *alto* ends in -*a* if the noun it modifies is singular and in -*e* if it is plural; an adjective such as *intelligente* ends in -*e* if the noun is singular and in -*i* if it is plural.

| SINGULAR | PLURAL |
|---|---|
| la donna alta | le donne alte |
| *the tall woman* | *the tall women* |
| la donna intelligente | le donne intelligenti |
| *the intelligent woman* | *the intelligent women* |
| la madre alta | le madri alte |
| *the tall mother* | *the tall mothers* |
| la madre intelligente | le madri intelligenti |
| *the intelligent mother* | *the intelligent mothers* |

### AVOID THE *Blunder*

✗ gli uomini intelligente
✗ le ragazze intelligente
✗ le donne intelligente
✗ le madri alti

A few adjectives are invariable, that is, their ending does not change. The most common are the color adjectives *marrone* "brown," *arancione* "orange," *viola* "violet, purple," *rosa* "pink," and *blu* "dark blue."

| SINGULAR | PLURAL |
|---|---|
| la giacca marrone | le giacche marrone |
| *the brown jacket* | *the brown jackets* |
| la matita arancione | le matite arancione |
| *the orange crayon* | *the orange crayons* |
| lo zaino viola | gli zaini viola |
| *the purple backpack* | *the purple backpacks* |
| il vestito rosa | i vestiti rosa |
| *the pink dress* | *the pink dresses* |
| la sciarpa blu | le sciarpe blu |
| *the dark blue scarf* | *the dark blue scarves* |

### AVOID THE *Blunder*

✗ i vestiti marroni
✗ gli zaini arancioni
✗ le sciarpe viole
✗ le sciarpe rose

Adjectives ending in *-co, -go, -cio,* or *-gio* undergo the same spelling changes when pluralized as the nouns that end in these sounds do (see pages 34–35 in the unit on nouns).

| SINGULAR | PLURAL |
|---|---|
| un uomo simpatico | due uomini simpatici |
| *a nice man* | *two nice men* |
| una strada lunga | due strade lunghe |
| *a long street* | *two long streets* |
| un vestito grigio | due vestiti grigi |
| *a gray suit* | *two gray suits* |

### AVOID THE *Blunder*

✗ Ho due amici simpatichi.
✗ Ha anche due amiche simpatice.

When two nouns are modified by an adjective, the adjective must be in the plural. If the two nouns are feminine, the appropriate feminine plural form of the adjective is used; if the two nouns are both masculine, or of mixed gender, then the appropriate masculine plural form is used.

**BOTH FEMININE**
La maglia e la borsa sono rosse.    *The sweater and the purse are red.*

**BOTH MASCULINE**
Il cappotto e l'impermeabile       *The coat and the raincoat are red.*
sono rossi.

**MIXED GENDER**
La maglia e il cappotto sono rossi.  *The sweater and the coat are red.*

### AVOID THE *Blunder*

✗ La camicia e la sciarpa sono rossi.
✗ Il vestito e la sciarpa sono nuove.

## Position

A descriptive adjective generally comes after the noun or nouns it modifies.

una camicia bianca    *a white shirt*
un libro interessante  *an interesting book*

Some adjectives, however, can occur before or after the noun(s).

È una bella camicia.
È una camicia bella. } *It's a beautiful shirt.*

Maria è una ragazza simpatica. }
Maria è una simpatica ragazza. } *Mary is a nice girl.*

You learn which descriptive adjectives can precede a noun through practice and use. As you read Italian, take note of the position of adjectives.

AVOID THE *Blunder*

✗ È una bianca camicia.
✗ È un'arancione matita.

Following is a list of the most common descriptive adjectives that can come before or after a noun.

| | | | |
|---|---|---|---|
| bello | *beautiful* | grande | *big, large* |
| brutto | *ugly* | nuovo | *new* |
| buono | *good* | povero | *poor* |
| caro | *dear* | simpatico | *nice, charming* |
| cattivo | *bad* | vecchio | *old* |
| giovane | *young* | | |

A few of these adjectives change in meaning according to their position before or after the noun.

È un ragazzo povero.     *He is a poor boy.* (not wealthy)
È un povero ragazzo.     *He is a poor boy.* (deserving of pity)

È un amico vecchio.     *He is an old friend.* (elderly)
È un vecchio amico.     *He is an old friend.* (for many years)

AVOID THE *Blunder*

✗ È un povero ragazzo. (when "He is not wealthy" is meant)
✗ È una vecchia persona. (when "He is elderly" is meant)

A descriptive adjective can be separated from the noun it modifies by what is called a linking verb. The most common linking verbs are the following three.

| essere | *to be* |
|--------|---------|
| sembrare | *to seem* |
| diventare | *to become* |

| Quella macchina è nuova. | *That car is new.* |
|--------------------------|--------------------|
| Quell'uomo sembra giovane. | *That man seems young.* |
| Questa macchina sta diventando vecchia. | *This car is getting old.* |

An adjective used in this way is called a predicate adjective, because it occurs in the predicate slot, after the verb that links it to the noun it modifies.

AVOID THE *Blunder*

✗ Quella macchina nuova è.
✗ Quell'uomo giovane sembra.

One final word about the position of descriptive adjectives: When such an adjective is accompanied by an adverb, another adjective, or some other part of speech, the adjective must follow the noun.

| È un simpatico ragazzo. | *He is a pleasant boy.* |
|-------------------------|-------------------------|

BUT

| È un ragazzo molto simpatico. | *He is a very pleasant boy.* |
|-------------------------------|------------------------------|
| È un ragazzo simpatico e bravo. | *He is a pleasant and good boy.* |

AVOID THE *Blunder*

✗ È una molto simpatica ragazza.
✗ Questo è un bello e elegante vestito.

## Form-Changing Adjectives

Of the adjectives that can come before the noun, the following change form when they are placed before.

### buono *good*

Before masculine nouns beginning with *z, s* + consonant, *gn,* or *ps,* the forms of *buono* are as follows (*dei* means "some").

| SINGULAR | PLURAL |
|----------|--------|
| un buono studente | dei buoni studenti |
| un buono zio | dei buoni zii |

Before masculine nouns beginning with any other consonant or a vowel, the forms are as follows.

| SINGULAR | PLURAL |
|---|---|
| un buon medico | dei buoni medici |
| un buon amico | dei buoni amici |

Before feminine nouns beginning with a consonant, the forms are as follows (*delle* means "some").

| SINGULAR | PLURAL |
|---|---|
| una buona caramella | delle buone caramelle |
| una buona studentessa | delle buone studentesse |

Before feminine nouns beginning with a vowel, the forms are as follows.

| SINGULAR | PLURAL |
|---|---|
| una buon'amica | delle buone amiche |
| una buon'ora | delle buone ore |

**AVOID THE Blunder**

✗ un buon zio
✗ un buon'amico
✗ un buono caffè

When *buono* is placed after the noun, it is treated as a normal descriptive adjective ending in -*o*.

| BEFORE | AFTER |
|---|---|
| un buon amico | un amico buono |
| una buon'amica | un'amica buona |

When referring to people, *buono* means "good" in the sense "good in nature." If "good at doing something" is intended, the appropriate adjective is *bravo*.

| È un buon ragazzo. | *He is a good(-natured) boy.* |
| È un bravo studente. | *He is a good student.* |

## bello *beautiful, handsome*

Before masculine nouns beginning with *z, s* + consonant, *gn,* or *ps,* the forms of *bello* are as follows.

| SINGULAR | PLURAL |
|---|---|
| un bello sport | dei begli sport |
| un bello zaino | dei begli zaini |

Before masculine nouns beginning with any other consonant, the forms are as follows.

| SINGULAR | PLURAL |
|---|---|
| un bel cane | dei bei cani |
| un bel gatto | dei bei gatti |

Before masculine nouns beginning with a vowel, the forms are as follows.

| SINGULAR | PLURAL |
|---|---|
| un bell'amico | dei begli amici |
| un bell'orologio | dei begli orologi |

Before feminine nouns beginning with a consonant, the forms are as follows.

| SINGULAR | PLURAL |
|---|---|
| una bella borsa | delle belle borse |
| una bella camicia | delle belle camicie |

Before feminine nouns beginning with a vowel, the forms are as follows.

| SINGULAR | PLURAL |
|---|---|
| una bell'amica | delle belle amiche |
| una bell'isola | delle belle isole |

AVOID THE *Blunder*

✗ un bel zaino
✗ dei belli amici
✗ un bel amico
✗ delle bell'amiche

When *bello* is placed after the noun, it is treated like a normal descriptive adjective ending in -*o*.

| BEFORE | AFTER |
|---|---|
| una bell'amica | un'amica bella |
| un bel vestito | un vestito bello |
| dei begli zaini | degli zaini belli |

## santo *saint*

There is only one plural form of *santo* in the masculine (*santi*) and only one plural form in the feminine (*sante*). Form changes apply to the singular uses of this adjective.

Before masculine singular nouns beginning with *z, s* + consonant, *gn,* or *ps,* the form is *santo.*

| | |
|---|---|
| Santo Stefano | *St. Stephen* |

Before masculine singular nouns beginning with any other consonant, the form is *san.*

| | |
|---|---|
| San Giovanni | *St. John* |
| San Paolo | *St. Paul* |

Before masculine and feminine singular nouns beginning with a vowel, the form is *sant'.*

| | |
|---|---|
| Sant'Antonio | *St. Anthony* |
| Sant'Anna | *St. Anne* |

Before feminine nouns beginning with a consonant, the form is *santa.*

| | |
|---|---|
| Santa Caterina | *St. Catherine* |
| Santa Maria | *St. Mary* |

AVOID THE *Blunder*

✗ San Stefano
✗ Santo Pietro
✗ San Antonio

## grande *big, great*

*Grande* has the optional forms *gran* (before a masculine singular noun beginning with any consonant except *z, s* + consonant, *ps,* or *gn*), and *grand'* (before any singular noun beginning with a vowel). Otherwise, it is treated as a normal adjective ending in -*e.* There is only one plural form: *grandi.*

| | |
|---|---|
| un gran film OR un grande film | *a great film* |
| un grand'amico OR un grande amico | *a great friend* |

AVOID THE *Blunder*

✗ un gran amica
✗ un gran studente

## Other Types of Adjectives

In addition to possessive, partitive, and interrogative adjectives, which are treated in the next three units, there are certain words that have various adjectival functions. Some grammars classify them as adjectives, others as different types of elements. Here are the most common.

| | |
|---|---|
| abbastanza | *enough* |
| altro | *other* |
| assai | *quite, enough* |
| certo | *certain* |
| molto | *much, many, a lot* |
| ogni | *each, every* |
| parecchio | *several, quite a few* |
| poco | *little, few* |
| qualsiasi | *whichever, any* |
| qualunque | *whichever, any* |
| stesso | *same* |
| tanto | *much, many, a lot* |
| troppo | *too much* |
| tutto | *all* |
| ultimo | *last* |

Of these, the following are invariable in form.

| | |
|---|---|
| Non ho abbastanza soldi. | *I do not have enough money.* |
| Lui mangia assai carne. | *He eats quite a lot of meat.* |
| Ogni mattina leggiamo il giornale. | *Every morning we read the newspaper.* |
| Mi piace qualsiasi/qualunque cibo. | *I like any food.* |

And the following are variable (like most descriptive adjectives).

| | |
|---|---|
| Chi è l'altra ragazza? | *Who is the other girl?* |
| Conosci un certo signore che si chiama Marco? | *Do you know a certain gentleman named Mark?* |
| Ieri ho mangiato molti/tanti dolci. | *Yesterday I ate a lot of sweets.* |
| Parecchi turisti visitano Venezia. | *Quite a few tourists visit Venice.* |

| | |
|---|---|
| Ci sono poche studentesse in questa classe. | *There are few female students in this class.* |
| Loro sono gli stessi studenti. | *They are the same students.* |
| Abbiamo mangiato troppo gelato. | *We ate too much ice cream.* |
| Ho mangiato tutta la pizza. | *I ate all the pizza.* |
| Questa è l'ultima volta che ti telefonerò. | *This is the last time I'm going to call you.* |

AVOID THE *Blunder*

| | |
|---|---|
| ✗ Non ho abbastanzi soldi. | ✗ Ho mangiato poco caramelle. |
| ✗ Ho mangiato molto dolci. | ✗ Ho mangiato troppo pizza. |

*Molto, poco, tanto,* and *troppo* are also used as adverbs, in which case there is no agreement. This topic will be taken up in the unit on adverbs.

## Comparison of Adjectives

Adjectives can be used to indicate that someone or something has a relatively equal, greater, or lesser degree of some quality. The three degrees of comparison are called positive, comparative, and superlative.

For the positive degree, either *così ... come* or *tanto ... quanto* is used.

| | |
|---|---|
| Alessandro è così felice come sua sorella. | *Alexander is as happy as his sister.* |
| Loro sono tanto noiosi quanto gli altri. | *They are as boring as the others.* |

The first word of these expressions (*così* or *tanto*) is optional.

Alessandro è felice come sua sorella.
Loro sono noiosi quanto gli altri.

For the comparative degree, *più* "more" or *meno* "less" is used, as appropriate.

| | |
|---|---|
| Marco è studioso. Maria è più studiosa. | *Mark is studious. Mary is more studious.* |
| Sara è alta. Alessandro è più alto. | *Sarah is tall. Alexander is taller.* |
| Lui è simpatico. Lei è meno simpatica. | *He is nice. She is less nice.* |

AVOID THE *Blunder*

✗ Maria è più studioso.
✗ Lui è meno simpatica.

For the superlative degree, the definite article followed by *più* or *meno* is used, as appropriate.

| | |
|---|---|
| Maria è la più studiosa della sua classe. | *Mary is the most studious in her class.* |
| Quel ragazzo è il più simpatico della famiglia. | *That boy is the nicest in the family.* |
| Le patate sono le meno costose. | *Potatoes are the least expensive.* |

In superlative constructions, the definite article is not repeated if it is already in front of a noun.

| | |
|---|---|
| Maria è la ragazza più studiosa della classe. | *Mary is the most studious girl in the class.* |
| Lui è il ragazzo meno intelligente della classe. | *He is the least intelligent boy in the class.* |

AVOID THE *Blunder*

✗ Marco è il ragazzo il più simpatico della classe.
✗ Lei è la persona la meno intelligente della famiglia.

In comparative constructions, the word "than" is rendered in two ways in Italian.

▪ If two elements (nouns, substantives, or noun phrases) are compared using one adjective, the preposition *di* is used.

| | |
|---|---|
| Giovanni è più alto di Pietro. | *John is taller than Peter.* |
| Maria è meno elegante di sua sorella. | *Mary is less elegant than her sister.* |

▪ If two adjectives are used to compare one element (a noun, a substantive, or a noun phrase), the word *che* is used instead.

| | |
|---|---|
| Giovanni è più simpatico che furbo. | *John is nicer than he is clever.* |
| Maria è meno elegante che simpatica. | *Mary is less elegant than she is nice.* |

The construction *di quello che* (also *di quel che* or *di ciò che*) translates "than" before a subordinate clause.

| | |
|---|---|
| Giovanni è più intelligente di quel che crede. | *John is more intelligent than he thinks* (literally, *than what he believes*). |
| Maria è meno elegante di quello che pensa. | *Mary is less elegant than she thinks* (literally, *than what she thinks*). |

AVOID THE *Blunder*

✗ Mio fratello è più alto che il suo amico.
✗ Maria è meno elegante di simpatica.
✗ Giovanni è più intelligente che crede.

Some adjectives have both regular and irregular comparative and superlative forms.

| | | | |
|---|---|---|---|
| buono | *good* | più buono OR migliore | *better* |
| cattivo | *bad* | più cattivo OR peggiore | *worse* |
| grande | *big* | più grande OR maggiore | *bigger, older* |
| piccolo | *small* | più piccolo OR minore | *smaller, younger* |

| | |
|---|---|
| Questo vino è buono, ma quello è migliore. | *This wine is good, but that one is better.* |
| Questo caffè è cattivo, ma quello è peggiore. | *This coffee is bad, but that one is worse.* |
| Lui è il fratello maggiore. | *He is the oldest brother.* |
| Lei è la sorella minore. | *She is the youngest sister.* |

AVOID THE *Blunder*

✗ Questo vino è buono, ma quello è più migliore.
✗ Questo caffè è cattivo, ma quello è più peggiore.

To express *very* as part of the adjective, the final vowel is dropped and *-issimo* is added.

| | | | | | | |
|---|---|---|---|---|---|---|
| buono | CHANGE TO | buon- | ADD -issimo | buonissimo | *very good* |
| alto | CHANGE TO | alt- | ADD -issimo | altissimo | *very tall* |
| grande | CHANGE TO | grand- | ADD -issimo | grandissimo | *very big* |
| facile | CHANGE TO | facil- | ADD -issimo | facilissimo | *very easy* |

| | |
|---|---|
| Giovanni è intelligentissimo. | *John is very intelligent.* |
| Anche Maria è intelligentissima. | *Mary is also very intelligent.* |
| Quelle ragazze sono bravissime. | *Those girls are very good.* |
| Quelle lezioni sono facilissime. | *Those classes are very easy.* |

AVOID THE *Blunder*

✗ Giovanni è molto intelligentissimo.
✗ Quelle ragazze sono molto bravissime.

## Exercises

**A** Complete the following chart by writing the male equivalent of the feminine noun phrases and the female equivalent of the masculine noun phrases.

| MASCULINE | FEMININE |
|---|---|
| 1. il ragazzo intelligente | _____ |
| 2. _____ | l'amica elegante |
| 3. lo zio alto | _____ |
| 4. _____ | la donna alta |
| 5. il fratello simpatico | _____ |
| 6. _____ | l'amica italiana |
| 7. il ragazzo francese | _____ |
| 8. _____ | una buon'amica |
| 9. un buono zio | _____ |
| 10. _____ | una bella ragazza |
| 11. un bell'amico | _____ |
| 12. _____ | Santa Maria |

**B** Complete the following chart by writing the plural equivalent of the singular noun phrases and the singular equivalent of the plural noun phrases.

| SINGULAR | PLURAL |
|---|---|
| 1. il vestito rosa | _____ |
| 2. _____ | le sciarpe rosse |
| 3. l'uomo alto | _____ |
| 4. _____ | gli zaini marrone |
| 5. il fratello simpatico | _____ |
| 6. _____ | le camicie blu |
| 7. la ragazza francese | _____ |
| 8. _____ | i bei ragazzi |
| 9. la bell'amica | _____ |
| 10. _____ | i begli amici |
| 11. il gran ragazzo | _____ |
| 12. _____ | i begli orologi |

**C** *Each of the following sentences contains an error. Rewrite each sentence, correcting the error.*

1. La maglia e la borsa sono nuovi.

_____

2. Il vestito e la camicia sono nuove.

_____

3. È una bianca sciarpa.

_____

4. Lui è un molto intelligente studente.

_____

5. Ho mangiato molto carne.

_____

6. Maria è la ragazza la più intelligente della classe.

_____

7. Marco è molto intelligentissimo.

_____

**D** *Choose the correct response for each item.*

1. *To refer to a man who is not wealthy, you would say . . .*
   a. un povero uomo
   b. un uomo povero

2. *To refer to a friend who is elderly, you would say . . .*
   a. un vecchio amico
   b. un amico vecchio

3. Ci sono _____ turisti a Venezia.
   a. molti
   b. molte

4. Sono _____ amici.
   a. le stesse
   b. gli stessi

5. Marco è così bravo _____ suo fratello.
   a. tanto
   b. come

6. Marco è più simpatico _____ Maria.

   a. di

   b. che

7. Marco è più simpatico _____ furbo.

   a. di

   b. che

8. Marco è più intelligente _____ quel che crede.

   a. di

   b. che

9. Questo vino è buono, ma quello è _____.

   a. migliore

   b. ciò che

# POSSESSIVES

Possessives are adjectives that indicate ownership of, or relationship to, someone or something.

il mio libro          *my book* (ownership)
le nostre amiche      *our friends* (relationship)

## Forms

Like descriptive adjectives, a possessive adjective agrees in gender and number with the noun or nouns it modifies. Unlike most descriptive adjectives, however, a possessive adjective comes before the noun.

The definite article is part of the possessive adjective; it is not optional. Following are the forms of the possessive.

### mio *my*

| | SINGULAR | PLURAL |
|---|---|---|
| MASCULINE | il mio amico<br>*my (male) friend* | i miei amici<br>*my (male) friends* |
| FEMININE | la mia amica<br>*my (female) friend* | le mie amiche<br>*my (female) friends* |

### tuo *your* (familiar singular)

| | SINGULAR | PLURAL |
|---|---|---|
| MASCULINE | il tuo orologio<br>*your watch* | i tuoi orologi<br>*your watches* |
| FEMININE | la tua camicia<br>*your shirt* | le tue camicie<br>*your shirts* |

### suo *his, her, its*

| | SINGULAR | PLURAL |
|---|---|---|
| MASCULINE | il suo orologio<br>*his/her watch* | i suoi orologi<br>*his/her watches* |
| FEMININE | la sua camicia<br>*his/her shirt* | le sue camicie<br>*his/her shirts* |

## Suo *your* (polite singular)

|  | SINGULAR | PLURAL |
|---|---|---|
| MASCULINE | il Suo orologio<br>*your watch* | i Suoi orologi<br>*your watches* |
| FEMININE | la Sua camicia<br>*your shirt* | le Sue camicie<br>*your shirts* |

## nostro *our*

|  | SINGULAR | PLURAL |
|---|---|---|
| MASCULINE | il nostro amico<br>*our friend* | i nostri amici<br>*our friends* |
| FEMININE | la nostra amica<br>*our friend* | le nostre amiche<br>*our friends* |

## vostro *your* (familiar plural)

|  | SINGULAR | PLURAL |
|---|---|---|
| MASCULINE | il vostro orologio<br>*your watch* | i vostri orologi<br>*your watches* |
| FEMININE | la vostra camicia<br>*your shirt* | le vostre camicie<br>*your shirts* |

## loro *their* (invariable)

|  | SINGULAR | PLURAL |
|---|---|---|
| MASCULINE | il loro amico<br>*their friend* | i loro amici<br>*their friends* |
| FEMININE | la loro amica<br>*their friend* | le loro amiche<br>*their friends* |

## Loro *your* (polite plural, invariable)

|  | SINGULAR | PLURAL |
|---|---|---|
| MASCULINE | il Loro amico<br>*your friend* | i Loro amici<br>*your friends* |
| FEMININE | la Loro amica<br>*your friend* | le Loro amiche<br>*your friends* |

The only invariable possessive is *loro/Loro*.

AVOID THE *Blunder*

✗ È mia camicia.
✗ Sono nostre amiche.
✗ Ecco la lora amica.

When the noun is a singular, unmodified kinship noun (like *padre* or *madre*), the definite article is dropped from all forms except *loro*.

| SINGULAR KINSHIP NOUN | PLURAL KINSHIP NOUN |
|---|---|
| tuo cugino | i tuoi cugini |
| *your cousin* | *your cousins* |
| mia sorella | le mie sorelle |
| *my sister* | *my sisters* |
| nostro fratello | i nostri fratelli |
| *our brother* | *our brothers* |

| SINGULAR KINSHIP NOUN | MODIFIED OR ALTERED KINSHIP NOUN |
|---|---|
| tuo cugino | il tuo cugino americano |
| *your cousin* | *your American cousin* |
| mia sorella | la mia sorellina |
| *my sister* | *my little sister* |
| nostra cugina | la nostra cugina italiana |
| *our cousin* | *our Italian cousin* |

The article is always retained with *loro*.

| il loro figlio | *their son* |
|---|---|
| la loro figlia | *their daughter* |
| il loro fratello | *their brother* |

AVOID THE *Blunder*

✗ Ecco il mio fratello.
✗ Ecco nostri cugini.
✗ Lei è mia sorella minore.
✗ Lui è loro figlio.

The above rule is optional with the following kinship nouns (when singular and unmodified).

| mamma | *mom* |
|---|---|
| papà OR babbo | *dad* |
| nonno | *grandfather* |
| nonna | *grandmother* |
| mia mamma OR la mia mamma | *my mom* |
| tuo papà/babbo OR il tuo papà/babbo | *your dad* |
| mio nonno OR il mio nonno | *my grandfather* |
| mia nonna OR la mia nonna | *my grandmother* |

AVOID THE *Blunder*

✗ Ecco mio simpatico nonno.
✗ Ecco nostra buona mamma.

Both "his" and "her" are expressed by the same possessive, *suo*, which takes the appropriate form before the noun. This is a constant source of blunders.

| "HIS" | | "HER" | |
|---|---|---|---|
| il suo libro | *his book* | il suo libro | *her book* |
| i suoi libri | *his books* | i suoi libri | *her books* |
| la sua penna | *his pen* | la sua penna | *her pen* |
| le sue penne | *his pens* | le sue penne | *her pens* |

**AVOID THE** *Blunder*

✗ Sono le sue libri.
✗ È il suo penna.

To avoid making such blunders, keep this simple rule in mind: Make the possessive adjective agree with the noun in gender and number, without worrying about what it means in English. Otherwise, you will confuse its form with its meaning.

## Uses

Note that there are familiar and polite possessives that correspond to the English possessive "your." As these terms imply, familiar forms are used with the people you know well and with whom you are on familiar terms; otherwise, the polite forms are used.

The polite forms are identical to the *suo* forms in the singular and to the *loro* forms in the plural. To distinguish the two types in writing, the polite forms are often capitalized, as shown here.

| il suo amico | *his/her friend* | il Suo amico | *your* (singular) *friend* |
|---|---|---|---|
| le sue cose | *his/her things* | le Sue cose | *your* (singular) *things* |
| il loro amico | *their friend* | il Loro amico | *your* (plural) *friend* |
| le loro cose | *their things* | le Loro cose | *your* (plural) *things* |

When you see or hear these forms, you must figure out from the context which form is meant—*his/her/their* or *your.*

In current Italian, it is not unusual to find only the *vostro* forms used as the plural of both the familiar and polite singular forms. The use of *Loro* as the polite plural possessive is restricted to very formal situations.

AVOID THE *Blunder*

✗ Signor Verdi, come si chiama il tuo amico?
✗ Signora Rossini, dov'è tuo cugino?

The possessive adjective can be placed after the noun for emphasis.

| | |
|---|---|
| È il mio cane. | *It's my dog.* |
| È il cane mio! | *It's my dog!* |
| Chiama tuo cugino. | *Call your cousin.* |
| Chiama il cugino tuo! | *Call your cousin!* |

When preceded by the indefinite, rather than the definite, article, the possessive adjective expresses the notion "of mine," "of yours," etc.

| | |
|---|---|
| un mio zio | *an uncle of mine* |
| una sua amica | *a friend of his/hers* |

To express "own," the adjective *proprio* is used.

| | |
|---|---|
| il mio proprio cane | *my own dog* |
| la (sua) propria chiave | *his/her own key* |

AVOID THE *Blunder*

✗ Lui è un zio di mio.
✗ Lei è un'amica di loro.

## Possessive Pronouns

A possessive pronoun replaces a noun phrase containing a possessive adjective. The pronoun corresponds to English "mine," "yours," "his," "hers," "ours," or "theirs."

| | |
|---|---|
| La mia amica è simpatica, e la tua? | *My friend is nice, and yours?* |
| Ecco la nostra macchina. Dov'è la vostra? | *Here is our car. Where is yours?* |

There is an exact match between the adjective and pronoun forms of the possessive (see the chart on pages 85–86).

The definite article is always used with the pronoun forms, even when the noun phrase replacement contains a singular, unmodified kinship noun.

| | |
|---|---|
| Sua sorella è simpatica. | *His/Her sister is pleasant.* |
| La sua è simpatica. | *His/Hers is pleasant.* |
| Nostro zio è amichevole. | *Our uncle is friendly.* |
| Il nostro è amichevole. | *Ours is friendly.* |

The article can be dropped if the pronoun is in the predicate, that is, if it occurs after the verb *essere* "to be" or some other linking verb.

| | |
|---|---|
| Questo denaro è mio. | *This money is mine.* |
| È tua questa borsa? | *Is this purse yours?* |
| Quei biglietti sono suoi. | *Those tickets are his/hers.* |

AVOID THE *Blunder*

✗ Dov'è tua?
✗ Nostro è italiano.
✗ È la tua questa borsa?

# Exercises

**A** *Complete the following chart by writing the plural form of the singular noun phrases and the singular form of the plural noun phrases.*

| SINGULAR | PLURAL |
|---|---|
| 1. il mio orologio | _____ |
| 2. _____ | le nostre amiche |
| 3. la mia camicia | _____ |
| 4. _____ | i nostri libri |
| 5. il tuo cane | _____ |
| 6. _____ | le vostre amiche |
| 7. la tua macchina | _____ |
| 8. _____ | i vostri amici |
| 9. il suo gatto | _____ |
| 10. _____ | le sue amiche |
| 11. il loro amico | _____ |
| 12. _____ | le loro case |

**B** *Fill in the blank with the appropriate form of the indefinite or definite article. If no article is necessary, write an X in the blank.*

1. Lui è _____ mio fratello. *(He is my brother.)*

2. Lei è _____ nostra sorella maggiore. *(She is our bigger sister.)*

3. Quel ragazzo è _____ loro figlio. *(That boy is their son.)*

4. Lei è _____ sua figlia più grande. *(She is his oldest daughter.)*

5. Signora Marchi, come si chiama _____ Sua figlia?
   *(Mrs. Marchi, what's your daughter's name?)*

6. Signora e signor Marchi, come si chiama _____ Loro figlio?
   *(Mrs. and Mr. Marchi, what's your son's name?)*

7. Lui è _____ mio amico, tra molti amici.
   *(He is one of my friends, among many friends.)*

8. Anche lei è _____ mia amica, tra molte amiche.
   *(She too is one of my friends, among many friends.)*

9. Questo libro è mio. Dov'è _____ tuo?
   *(This book is mine. Where is yours?)*

**C** *Fill in the blank with the appropriate form of* **suo, Suo, loro,** *or* **Loro.**

1. Questo è il libro di mia sorella. *(This is my sister's book.)*

   È _____ libro. *(This is her book.)*

2. Questo è il libro di mio fratello. *(This is my brother's book.)*

   È _____ libro. *(This is his book.)*

3. Queste sono le riviste di mia madre. *(These are my mother's magazines.)*

   Sono _____ riviste. *(These are her magazines.)*

4. Queste sono le riviste di mio padre. *(These are my father's magazines.)*

   Sono _____ riviste. *(These are his magazines.)*

5. Signora Verdi, come si chiama _____ figlia?
   *(Mrs. Verdi, what's your daughter's name?)*

6. Signor Verdi, come si chiama _____ figlia?
   *(Mr. Verdi, what's your daughter's name?)*

7. Signora e signor Verdi, come si chiama _____ figlia?
   *(Mrs. and Mr. Verdi, what's your daughter's name?)*

# PARTITIVES

A partitive is a construction used as a noun phrase to indicate a part of something that is distinct from the whole.

| | |
|---|---|
| dell'acqua | *some water* |
| degli esami | *some exams* |

## With Count Nouns

Before a count noun (a noun that has a plural form), the partitive can be considered to function grammatically as the plural of the indefinite article. The most commonly used type of partitive in this case consists of the preposition *di* + the appropriate plural form of the definite article.

**MASCULINE CONTRACTIONS**

| | | |
|---|---|---|
| di + i → dei | di + i libri → dei libri | *some books* |
| di + gli → degli | di + gli studenti → degli studenti | *some students* |

**FEMININE CONTRACTION**

| | | |
|---|---|---|
| di + le → delle | di + le penne → delle penne | *some pens* |

| SINGULAR | | PLURAL | |
|---|---|---|---|
| un bicchiere | *a glass* | dei bicchieri | *some glasses* |
| un coltello | *a knife* | dei coltelli | *some knives* |
| un albero | *a tree* | degli alberi | *some trees* |
| uno sbaglio | *a mistake* | degli sbagli | *some mistakes* |
| un'automobile | *an automobile* | delle automobili | *some automobiles* |
| una forchetta | *a fork* | delle forchette | *some forks* |
| una sedia | *a chair* | delle sedie | *some chairs* |

AVOID THE *Blunder*

✗ Voglio di le forchette.
✗ Ho comprato sedie ieri.

93

In place of these forms, the pronouns *alcuni* (masculine plural) and *alcune* (feminine plural) can be used to render more precisely the idea of "several."

| dei bicchieri | *some glasses* | alcuni bicchieri | *several / a few glasses* |
|---|---|---|---|
| degli zii | *some uncles* | alcuni zii | *several / a few uncles* |
| delle amiche | *some friends* | alcune amiche | *several / a few friends* |
| delle forchette | *some forks* | alcune forchette | *several / a few forks* |

AVOID THE *Blunder*

✗ alcun zii
✗ alcun'amiche

The invariable pronoun *qualche* can also be used to express the partitive with count nouns. But be careful with this one! It must be followed by a singular noun, even though the meaning is plural.

| dei bicchieri | *some glasses* | qualche bicchiere | *some glasses* |
|---|---|---|---|
| degli zii | *some uncles* | qualche zio | *some uncles* |
| delle amiche | *some friends* | qualche amica | *some friends* |
| delle forchette | *some forks* | qualche forchetta | *some forks* |

Think of *qualche* as translating "whichever"; it will then be easy to see why the noun is singular. Note that the verb is also singular.

| qualche amico | *whichever friend* |
|---|---|
| qualche libro | *whichever book* |

AVOID THE *Blunder*

✗ Voglio qualche forchette.
✗ Qualche amico nostro studiano l'italiano.
✗ Qualche persona mangiano gli spaghetti.

A pronoun form (*qualche* or *alcuni/alcune*) is often used at the beginning of a sentence, rather than a *dei/degli/delle* form.

| Alcuni studenti studiano il francese. | *Some students study French.* |
|---|---|
| Qualche studente studia il francese. | *Some students study French.* |

In colloquial Italian, it is not unusual to find that the partitive is omitted (when the noun is not the first word of the sentence).

Voglio della carne. ⎤
Voglio carne. ⎦      *I want (some) meat.*

Mangio degli spaghetti. ⎤
Mangio spaghetti. ⎦      *I'm eating (some) spaghetti.*

In negative sentences, the partitive must be omitted.

| AFFIRMATIVE SENTENCE | NEGATIVE SENTENCE |
|---|---|
| Ho dei biglietti. | Non ho biglietti. |
| *I have some tickets.* | *I don't have any tickets.* |
| Ho alcune riviste. | Non ho riviste. |
| *I have some magazines.* | *I don't have any magazines.* |

The negative partitive can also be rendered by *non ... nessuno*. *Nessuno* is made up of *ness* + the indefinite article; it renders the idea "not . . . any." This means that the noun is always singular, even though the meaning is plural.

Non ho nessun biglietto.      *I don't have any tickets.*
Non ho nessuna rivista.      *I don't have any magazines.*

AVOID THE *Blunder*

✗ Non ho dei biglietti.
✗ Non ho nessuna riviste.

## With Collective Nouns

With collective nouns (nouns that normally do not have a plural form), the partitive is rendered by either *di* + a singular form of the definite article or by the expression *un po' di* "a bit of."

**MASCULINE CONTRACTIONS**

| di + il → del | di + il vino → del vino | *some wine* |
|---|---|---|
| di + lo → dello | di + lo zucchero → dello zucchero | *some sugar* |
| di + l' → dell' | di + l'orzo → dell'orzo | *some barley* |

**FEMININE CONTRACTIONS**

| di + la → della | di + la pasta → della pasta | *some pasta* |
|---|---|---|
| di + l' → dell' | di + l'acqua → dell'acqua | *some water* |

del vino      un po' di vino
  *some wine*      *some wine, a little wine*
dello zucchero      un po' di zucchero
  *some sugar*      *some sugar, a little sugar*

| dell'orzo | un po' di orzo |
|---|---|
| *some barley* | *some barley, a little barley* |
| della pasta | un po' di pasta |
| *some pasta* | *some pasta, a little pasta* |
| dell'acqua | un po' di acqua |
| *some water* | *some water, a little water* |

**AVOID THE Blunder**

✗ Voglio qualche vino.
✗ Voglio qualche acqua.

There is no negative form of the partitive in this case.

| Prendo dello zucchero. | *I will take some sugar.* |
|---|---|
| Non voglio zucchero. | *I do not want any sugar.* |

| Ho mangiato un po' di pasta. | *I ate some pasta.* |
|---|---|
| Non ho mangiato pasta. | *I did not eat any pasta.* |

**AVOID THE Blunder**

✗ Non prendo nessuno zucchero.
✗ Non voglio dello zucchero.

Remember, as in the case of articles and demonstratives, you may have to change the partitive form when an adjective precedes the noun.

| degli zii | *some uncles* | dei simpatici zii | *some nice uncles* |
|---|---|---|---|
| dell'acqua | *some water* | della buon'acqua | *some good water* |

**AVOID THE Blunder**

✗ degli simpatici zii
✗ degli bravi studenti

# Exercises

**A** Complete the following chart by writing in the missing noun phrases.

ESEMPIO    dei ragazzi    <u>alcuni ragazzi</u>    <u>qualche ragazzo</u>

1. delle penne    _____    _____

2. _____    _____    qualche zio

3. _____    alcune mele    _____

4. degli amici    _____    _____

5. _____    _____    qualche ragazza

**B** Choose the correct response for each item.

1. Non ho _____.

   a. dei cugini.

   b. cugini.

2. Non ho mangiato _____.

   a. delle mele.

   b. nessuna mela.

3. Prendo _____ zucchero.

   a. qualche

   b. un po' di

4. Non prendo _____.

   a. nessun vino.

   b. vino.

5. Voglio _____ acqua.

   a. dell'

   b. qualche

6. Ecco _____ buono zucchero.

   a. del

   b. dello

# QUESTIONS

Interrogative sentences are used to ask questions. In writing, they always have a question mark at the end.

| | |
|---|---|
| Anna è italiana? | *Is Ann Italian?* |
| Di che nazionalità è Anna? | *(Of) what nationality is Ann?* |
| Anna è italiana, non è vero? | *Ann is Italian, isn't she?* |

There are three main types of interrogative sentences: those that are designed to elicit a yes-or-no response, those that seek information of some kind, and those that simply seek consent or agreement.

## Interrogative Sentences Eliciting a Yes-or-No Response

The most common method of forming an interrogative sentence designed to get a yes-or-no response is to add a question mark at the end of the corresponding affirmative sentence. In spoken Italian, a yes-or-no question is distinguished from a statement by rising intonation at the end of the sentence.

| | |
|---|---|
| Anna è italiana? | *Is Ann Italian?* |
| Sì, è italiana. | *Yes, she's Italian.* |
| | |
| Lui parla francese? | *Does he speak French?* |
| Sì, parla francese. | *Yes, he speaks French.* |
| | |
| Tua sorella va in Italia quest'anno? | *Is your sister going to Italy this year?* |
| No, lei non ci va. | *No, she's not going.* |
| | |
| I tuoi amici giocano a tennis? | *Do your friends play tennis?* |
| No, non giocano a tennis, giocano a calcio. | *No, they don't play tennis, they play soccer.* |

Another way to form this type of interrogative sentence is to put the entire subject at the end.

| | |
|---|---|
| È italiana Anna? | *Is Ann Italian?* |
| Parla francese lui? | *Does he speak French?* |

**99**

| | |
|---|---|
| Va in Italia quest'anno tua sorella? | *Is your sister going to Italy this year?* |
| Giocano a tennis i tuoi amici? | *Do your friends play tennis?* |

AVOID THE *Blunder*

✗ È Anna italiana?
✗ Giocano i tuoi amici a tennis?

## Interrogative Sentences Eliciting Information

Interrogative sentences can also be formed with words such as "what?", "when?", and "where?" that request information from someone.

| | |
|---|---|
| Quale macchina preferisci? | *Which car do you prefer?* |
| Come va? | *How's it going?* |

Such sentences are formed with question words. The main ones in Italian are as follows.

### che *what* (ALSO che cosa OR cosa)

| | |
|---|---|
| Che libro leggi? | *What book are you reading?* |
| Che leggi? | *What are you reading?* |
| Che cosa fai? | *What are you doing?* |
| Cosa sono quelle cose? | *What are those things?* |

### chi *who*

| | |
|---|---|
| Chi è quella persona? | *Who is that person?* |
| Chi viene alla festa? | *Who is coming to the party?* |

| | |
|---|---|
| di chi | *whose* |
| a chi | *to whom* |
| da chi | *from whom* |

| | |
|---|---|
| Di chi è questa rivista? | *Whose magazine is this?* |
| A chi hai dato la rivista? | *To whom did you give the magazine?* |

### come *how*

| | |
|---|---|
| Maria, come stai? | *Mary, how are you?* |
| Come si chiama il tuo amico? | *What is the name of your friend?* |

### dove *where*

| | |
|---|---|
| Dove vivono i tuoi amici? | *Where do your friends live?* |
| Dove vai a scuola? | *Where do you go to school?* |

## perché *why*

Perché dici questo?
Perché non vai alla festa?

*Why are you saying this?*
*Why are you not going to the party?*

✗ Chi è questa rivista?
✗ Perche dici questo?

## quale *which*

The ending changes according to the number of the noun that *quale* modifies.

Quale persona parla italiano?
Quali sono gli studenti italiani?

*Which person speaks Italian?*
*Which ones are the Italian students?*

## quando *when*

Quando vai in Italia?
Quando arrivano?

*When are you going to Italy?*
*When are they arriving?*

## quanto *how much, how many*

The ending changes according to the gender and number of the noun that *quanto* modifies.

Quanto zucchero prendi?
Quanta carne mangi?
Quanti studenti sono italiani?
Quante studentesse conosci?

*How much sugar do you take?*
*How much meat do you eat?*
*How many students are Italian?*
*How many (female) students do you know?*

Used as a pronoun, however, the only form possible is *quanto*.

Quanto sai?

*How much do you know?*

AVOID THE *Blunder*

✗ Quale riviste leggi?
✗ Quanto studenti sono italiani?
✗ Quanta sai?

In writing, it is normal to drop the *-e* from *come, dove,* and *quale* before the verb form *è* "is." In the case of both *come* and *dove,* an apostrophe is added. But this is not the case for *quale.*

| | |
|---|---|
| Com'è? | *How is it?* |
| Dov'è? | *Where is it?* |
| Qual è? | *Which is it?* |

AVOID THE *Blunder*

✗ Dovè?
✗ Qual'è?

## Tag Sentences

Tag sentences are interrogative sentences designed to elicit consent or agreement of some kind. They are called "tag" because they end with an expression "tagged on." In Italian, that expression is one of the following.

| | |
|---|---|
| vero? | *right?* |
| non è vero? | *isn't that correct?* |
| no? | *no?* |
| non pensi? | *don't you think (so)?* |
| non credi? | *don't you believe (it)?* |
| non dici? | *don't you say (so)?* |

| | |
|---|---|
| Viene anche lei, vero? | *She's coming too, isn't she?* |
| Lui è americano, non è vero? | *He's American, isn't he?* |
| Prendi molto zucchero, no? | *You take a lot of sugar, don't you?* |
| L'italiano e una lingua bella, non pensi? | *Italian is a beautiful language, don't you think?* |

AVOID THE *Blunder*

✗ Lui è americano, non lui è?
✗ Prendi molto zucchero, non tu?

# Exercises

**A** *Each of the following sentences is a response to a yes-or-no question. Write the question for each.*

1. Sì, Maria è italiana.

2. No, loro non prendono zucchero.

3. Sì, Marco parla italiano molto bene.

4. No, lui non è andato al cinema ieri. *(No, he didn't go to the movies yesterday.)*

**B** *Each of the following sentences is a response to an information-seeking question. Write the question for each.*

1. Leggo una rivista.

2. È un amico.

3. È la mia penna.

4. Il mio amico si chiama Alessandro.

5. I miei amici vivono negli Stati Uniti.

6. Non vado alla festa perché sono stanco. *(I'm not going to the party, because I'm tired.)*

7. Mi piace questa rivista, non quella.

8. Vado a Roma domani.

9. Prendo tanto zucchero.

**C** *Each of the following sentences is a response to a tag question. Write the question for each.*

1. Sì, prendo molto zucchero nel caffè. *(Yes, I take a lot of sugar with my coffee.)*

_____

2. Non, non mi piace quel programma. *(No, I don't like that program.)*

_____

3. Sì, penso che l'italiano sia una bella lingua. *(Yes, I think that Italian is a beautiful language.)*

_____

4. No, mio fratello non è francese. *(No, my brother is not French.)*

_____

# VERBS
## infinitives and gerunds

A verb is a word that conveys the action performed by the subject of its clause. For this reason, it agrees with the subject's person (first, second, or third) and number (singular or plural). Verbs are also marked for tense (for instance, present, past, or future).

| io canto | *I sing* | tu canti | *you sing* |
| io ho cantato | *I sang* | tu hai cantato | *you sang* |
| io canterò | *I will sing* | tu canterai | *you will sing* |

A verb tense indicates the time the action occurred: now (present tense), earlier (past tense), or later (future tense).

La mangio adesso.
(PRESENT TENSE)

*I am eating it now.*

L'ho mangiata ieri.
(PAST TENSE)

*I ate it yesterday.*

La mangerò domani.
(FUTURE TENSE)

*I will eat it tomorrow.*

Not only do verbs express a time relationship, they also convey a way of thinking or point of view. This characteristic of a verb is known as its mood.

Maria mangia gli spaghetti.
(INDICATIVE MOOD)

*Mary is eating the spaghetti.*

Maria, mangia gli spaghetti!
(IMPERATIVE MOOD)

*Mary, eat the spaghetti!*

Penso che Maria mangi gli spaghetti. (SUBJUNCTIVE MOOD)

*I think that Mary is eating the spaghetti.*

## Infinitives

The infinitive, on the other hand, is a verb form with no reference to a particular tense, person, or other marker of this kind. It is the form you find in a dictionary. Italian verbs are divided into three main conjugations according to their infinitive endings. Verbs of the first conjugation end in *-are,* those of the second in *-ere,* and those of the third in *-ire.*

| FIRST CONJUGATION | | SECOND CONJUGATION | | THIRD CONJUGATION | |
|---|---|---|---|---|---|
| parlare | *to speak* | vendere | *to sell* | dormire | *to sleep* |
| arrivare | *to arrive* | cadere | *to fall* | partire | *to leave* |

There is also a past infinitive, which is a compound form consisting of an auxiliary verb, *avere* "to have" or *essere* "to be" (itself in the infinitive), and the past participle of the verb. The past participle of regular verbs is formed by changing the *-are* ending to *-ato,* the *-ere* ending to *-uto,* and the *-ire* ending to *-ito.* For now, it is enough to realize that a verb in a compound tense is conjugated with either *avere* or *essere.* This topic will be taken up in the unit on the present perfect tense.

| CONJUGATED WITH avere | | CONJUGATED WITH essere | |
|---|---|---|---|
| aver(e) parlato | *having spoken* | esser(e) arrivato(-a) | *having arrived* |
| aver(e) venduto | *having sold* | esser(e) caduto(-a) | *having fallen* |
| aver(e) dormito | *having slept* | esser(e) partito(-a) | *having left* |

Note that the final *-e* of the auxiliary may be dropped. Note too that the past participle of a verb conjugated with *essere* is treated exactly like an adjective ending in *-o.*

| | |
|---|---|
| Dopo essere arrivato, Marco mi ha chiamato. | *After having arrived, Mark called me.* |
| Dopo essere arrivata, Maria mi ha chiamato. | *After having arrived, Mary called me.* |
| Dopo essere arrivati, i miei amici mi hanno chiamato. | *After having arrived, my (male) friends called me.* |
| Dopo essere arrivate, le mie amiche mi hanno chiamato. | *After having arrived, my (female) friends called me.* |

AVOID THE *Blunder*

✗ avere arrivato(-a)
✗ Dopo essere arrivato, mia sorella mi ha chiamata.

Infinitives and past infinitives express actions that make no specific reference to time. They are translated by English forms like "to eat," "eating," and "having eaten."

| | |
|---|---|
| Stasera spero di studiare. | *Tonight, I am hoping to study.* |
| Invece di studiare, uscirò. | *Instead of studying, I am going to go out.* |
| Dopo avere studiato, uscirò. | *After having studied, I will go out.* |

This pattern of translation is a major source of blunders. The tendency of students is to use the gerund in Italian (see below) instead of the infinitive (present or past).

AVOID THE *Blunder*

✗ Invece di studiando, uscirò.
✗ Dopo avendo studiato, uscirò.

The infinitive can function as a substantive (a form replacing a noun), in which case it is assigned the masculine gender.

| | |
|---|---|
| Mangiare bene è una cosa importante. | *Eating well is an important thing.* |
| Studiare è importante. | *Studying is important.* |

When the subjects of two clauses are the same, the infinitive is used.

**DIFFERENT SUBJECTS**

| | |
|---|---|
| Lui crede che io scriva bene. | *He believes that I write well.* |
| Maria pensa che loro parlino italiano bene. | *Mary thinks that they speak Italian well.* |

**SAME SUBJECTS**

| | |
|---|---|
| Lui crede di scrivere bene. | *He believes that he writes well.* |
| Maria pensa di parlare italiano bene. | *Mary thinks that she speaks Italian well.* |

AVOID THE *Blunder*

✗ Mangiando bene è una cosa importante.
✗ Lui crede che lui scriva bene.

Some verbs are followed by *a* before an infinitive, as in the following sentences.

| | |
|---|---|
| Cominciano a capire. | *They are starting to understand.* |
| Devo imparare a usare Internet. | *I must learn how to use the Internet.* |

Some are followed instead by *di.*

| | |
|---|---|
| Finiranno di lavorare alle sei. | *They will finish working at six o'clock.* |
| Cercheremo di rientrare presto. | *We will try to get back home early.* |

Others are not followed by a preposition.

| | |
|---|---|
| Voglio capire meglio. | *I want to understand better.* |
| Desiderano andare in Italia. | *They want to go to Italy.* |
| Preferisco rimanere a casa stasera. | *I prefer staying home tonight.* |

The only sure way to learn which preposition (if any) is used in a certain construction or idiomatic expression is to consult a dictionary.

AVOID THE *Blunder*

✗ Cominciano di capire.
✗ Finiranno lavorare alle sei.
✗ Desiderano di andare in Italia.

## Gerunds

A gerund is formed by dropping the infinitive ending and adding *-ando* to the stem of a first-conjugation verb and *-endo* to the stem of a second- or third-conjugation verb.

| FIRST CONJUGATION | | SECOND CONJUGATION | | THIRD CONJUGATION | |
|---|---|---|---|---|---|
| parlando | *speaking* | vendendo | *selling* | dormendo | *sleeping* |
| arrivando | *arriving* | cadendo | *falling* | partendo | *leaving* |

AVOID THE *Blunder*

✗ dormiendo
✗ partiendo

The most important use of the gerund is in progressive tenses, which are made up of the verb *stare* plus the gerund. This will be treated in the unit on progressive tenses.

The gerund is also used, as in English, to express indefinite actions, replacing *mentre* "while" + the imperfect tense when the subjects of the two clauses are the same.

Mentre camminavo, ho visto Marco.  *While I was walking, I saw Mark.*

OR

Camminando, ho visto Marco.  *While walking, I saw Mark.*

There is also a past gerund, consisting of an auxiliary verb in the gerund (*avendo* or *essendo*) and a past participle.

| | | | |
|---|---|---|---|
| avendo parlato | *having spoken* | essendo arrivato(-a) | *having arrived* |
| avendo venduto | *having sold* | essendo caduto(-a) | *having fallen* |
| avendo dormito | *having slept* | essendo partito(-a) | *having left* |

---

AVOID THE *Blunder*

✗ avendo arrivata
✗ avendo partito

---

Once again, the past participle of a verb conjugated with *essere* is treated like an adjective. More will be said about this in the unit on the present perfect tense.

| | |
|---|---|
| Avendo mangiato tutto, siamo usciti. | *Having eaten everything, we went out.* |
| Essendo andati in Italia, visitarono tanti bei posti. | *Having gone to Italy, they visited many nice places.* |

---

AVOID THE *Blunder*

✗ Mentre camminando, ho visto Marco.
✗ Essendo andato in Italia, visitarono tanti bei posti.

---

## A Fourth Type of Verb

A fourth type of infinitive ends in *-rre*. Verbs of this type are, however, uncommon.

| | |
|---|---|
| porre | *to put* |
| produrre | *to produce* |
| tradurre | *to translate* |
| trarre | *to pull* |

All verbs of this type have irregular conjugations. Their past participle and gerund forms are shown below. Note that these particular verbs are conjugated with *avere* in compound tenses.

| INFINITIVE | PAST PARTICIPLE | GERUND |
|---|---|---|
| porre | posto | ponendo |
| produrre | prodotto | producendo |
| tradurre | tradotto | traducendo |
| trarre | tratto | traendo |

---

AVOID THE *Blunder*

✗ produtto
✗ porrendo

---

## Exercises

**A**  *Complete the following chart by writing in the missing infinitive, past infinitive, gerund, and past gerund.*

ESEMPIO    parlare
        _avere parlato_    _parlando_    _avendo parlato_

1. _____

  essere arrivato(-a)    _____    _____

2. _____

  _____    cadendo    _____

3. _____

  _____    _____    avendo venduto

4. dormire

  _____    _____    _____

5. _____

  _____    _____    essendo partito(-a)

6. produrre

  _____    _____    _____

7. _____

  _____    _____    avendo tratto

8. _____

  _____    traducendo    _____

9. porre

  _____    _____    _____

**B**  *Choose the correct response for each item.*

1. Dopo essere _____, loro mi hanno chiamato.

  a. arrivati

  b. arrivato

2. Stasera lui spera _____ studiare molto.

  a. a

  b. di

3. Dopo —————————— studiato, noi usciremo.

    a. avere

    b. essere

4. —————————— molto è importante.

    a. Dormire

    b. Dormendo

5. Alessandro crede —————————— molto intelligente.

    a. che sia

    b. di essere

6. Devo imparare —————————— parlare italiano bene.

    a. a

    b. di

7. Loro finiranno —————————— studiare alle sei.

    a. a

    b. di

# VERBS
## the present indicative

The indicative mood is used to express or indicate facts. It is the most commonly used mood in everyday conversation. As its name implies, the present indicative is used to express statements and questions in the present or related to the present in some way.

## Conjugation of Regular Verbs

To conjugate regular verbs in the present indicative, the infinitive ending is dropped and the following endings according to conjugation are added.

**FIRST CONJUGATION**

parlare *to speak*

**ENDINGS** -o, -i, -a, -iamo, -ate, -ano

| | |
|---|---|
| (io) parlo | *I speak, I am speaking, I do speak* |
| (tu) parli | *you* (familiar singular) *speak, you are speaking, you do speak* |
| (lui/lei/Lei) parla | *he/she speaks / you* (polite singular) *speak, he/she is / you are speaking, he/she does / you do speak* |
| (noi) parliamo | *we speak, we are speaking, we do speak* |
| (voi) parlate | *you* (familiar plural) *speak, you are speaking, you do speak* |
| (loro/Loro) parlano | *they/you* (polite plural) *speak, they/you are speaking, they/you do speak* |

AVOID THE *Blunder*

X noi parlamo
X loro parliano

**113**

**SECOND CONJUGATION**
vendere *to sell*

**ENDINGS** -o, -i, -e, -iamo, -ete, -ono

| | |
|---|---|
| (io) vendo | *I sell, I am selling, I do sell* |
| (tu) vendi | *you* (familiar singular) *sell, you are selling, you do sell* |
| (lui/lei/Lei) vende | *he/she sells / you* (polite singular) *sell, he/she is / you are selling, he/she does / you do sell* |
| (noi) vendiamo | *we sell, we are selling, we do sell* |
| (voi) vendete | *you* (familiar plural) *sell, you are selling, you do sell* |
| (loro/Loro) vendono | *they/you* (polite plural) *sell, they/you are selling, they/you do sell* |

AVOID THE *Blunder*

✗ noi vendamo
✗ loro vendano

**THIRD CONJUGATION (TYPE I)**
dormire *to sleep*

**ENDINGS** -o, -i, -e, -iamo, -ite, -ono

| | |
|---|---|
| (io) dormo | *I sleep, I am sleeping, I do sleep* |
| (tu) dormi | *you* (familiar singular) *sleep, you are sleeping, you do sleep* |
| (lui/lei/Lei) dorme | *he/she sleeps / you* (polite singular) *sleep, he/she is / you are sleeping, he/she does / you do sleep* |
| (noi) dormiamo | *we sleep, we are sleeping, we do sleep* |
| (voi) dormite | *you* (familiar plural) *sleep, you are sleeping, you do sleep* |
| (loro/Loro) dormono | *they/you* (polite plural) *sleep, they/you are sleeping, they/you do sleep* |

AVOID THE *Blunder*

✗ noi dormimo
✗ loro dormano

### THIRD CONJUGATION (TYPE II)
finire *to finish*

**ENDINGS** -isco, -isci, -isce, -iamo, -ite, -iscono

| | |
|---|---|
| (io) finisco | *I finish, I am finishing, I do finish* |
| (tu) finisci | *you* (familiar singular) *finish, you are finishing, you do finish* |
| (lui/lei/Lei) finisce | *he/she finishes / you* (polite singular) *finish, he/she is / you are finishing, he/she does / you do finish* |
| (noi) finiamo | *we finish, we are finishing, we do finish* |
| (voi) finite | *you* (familiar plural) *finish, you are finishing, you do finish* |
| (loro/Loro) finiscono | *they/you* (polite plural) *finish, they/you are finishing, they/you do finish* |

Note that there are two sets of endings for third-conjugation verbs; this fact is a constant source of blunders. Essentially, you must learn to which category (Type I or II) a third-conjugation verb belongs; this information is contained in a dictionary.

Two other verbs conjugated like *dormire* (Type I) are the following.

| | |
|---|---|
| aprire | *to open* |
| partire | *to leave* |

Two other verbs conjugated like *finire* (Type II) are the following.

| | |
|---|---|
| capire | *to understand* |
| preferire | *to prefer* |

AVOID THE *Blunder*

| | |
|---|---|
| ✗ noi finisciamo | ✗ noi capisciamo |
| ✗ loro apriscono | ✗ io prefiero |

The subject pronouns are optional with the present indicative. The reason for this is obvious: The ending makes it clear which person is being referred to.

Second-person forms are used for familiar (informal) address; third-person forms are used for polite (formal) address.

#### FAMILIAR

| | |
|---|---|
| Maria, (tu) cosa preferisci? | *Mary, what do you prefer?* |
| Marco e Maria, capite (voi)? | *Mark and Mary, do you (both) understand?* |

**POLITE**

| | |
|---|---|
| Professore, (Lei) cosa preferisce? | *Professor, what do you prefer?* |
| Signor Marchi e Signora Verdi, | *Mr. Marchi and Mrs. Verdi,* |
| capiscono (Loro)? | *do you (both) understand?* |

The English subject pronoun "it" (plural: "they") is not normally expressed in Italian.

| | |
|---|---|
| Apre a mezzogiorno. | *It opens at noon.* |
| Chiudono alle sei. | *They close at six.* |

AVOID THE *Blunder*

✗ Professore, cosa preferisci?
✗ Signora, parli italiano?

## Verbs That Undergo Spelling Changes

If a verb ends in -*care* or -*gare,* the preservation of the hard sound is indicated by the insertion of *h* before the endings -*i* and -*iamo.*

### cercare *to search for*

| | |
|---|---|
| (io) cerco | *I search* |
| (tu) cerchi | *you (familiar singular) search* |
| (lui/lei/Lei) cerca | *he/she searches / you (polite singular) search* |
| (noi) cerchiamo | *we search* |
| (voi) cercate | *you (familiar plural) search* |
| (loro/Loro) cercano | *they/you (polite plural) search* |

### pagare *to pay*

| | |
|---|---|
| (io) pago | *I pay* |
| (tu) paghi | *you (familiar singular) pay* |
| (lui/lei/Lei) paga | *he/she pays / you (polite singular) pay* |
| (noi) paghiamo | *we pay* |
| (voi) pagate | *you (familiar plural) pay* |
| (loro/Loro) pagano | *they/you (polite plural) pay* |

AVOID THE *Blunder*

✗ tu cerci
✗ noi cerciamo
✗ tu pagi
✗ noi pagiamo

If a verb ends in *-ciare* or *-giare*, the *-i* of these endings is dropped before *-i* and *-iamo*.

### cominciare *to start, begin*

| | |
|---|---|
| (io) comincio | *I start* |
| (tu) cominci | *you* (familiar singular) *start* |
| (lui/lei/Lei) comincia | *he/she starts / you* (polite singular) *start* |
| (noi) cominciamo | *we start* |
| (voi) cominciate | *you* (familiar plural) *start* |
| (loro/Loro) cominciano | *they/you* (polite plural) *start* |

### mangiare *to eat*

| | |
|---|---|
| (io) mangio | *I eat* |
| (tu) mangi | *you* (familiar singular) *eat* |
| (lui/lei/Lei) mangia | *he/she eats / you* (polite singular) *eat* |
| (noi) mangiamo | *we eat* |
| (voi) mangiate | *you* (familiar plural) *eat* |
| (loro/Loro) mangiano | *they/you* (polite plural) *eat* |

AVOID THE *Blunder*

✗ tu comincii
✗ noi mangiiamo

## Irregular Verbs

Irregular verbs—that is, verbs that are not conjugated according to one of the regular patterns above—are a major source of blunders. It is not possible to cover all the irregular verbs here; however, those that are particularly troublesome in the present indicative follow.

### andare *to go*

(io) vado, (tu) vai, (lui/lei/Lei) va,
(noi) andiamo, (voi) andate, (loro/Loro) vanno

### avere *to have*

(io) ho, (tu) hai, (lui/lei/Lei) ha,
(noi) abbiamo, (voi) avete, (loro/Loro) hanno

### bere *to drink*

(io) bevo, (tu) bevi, (lui/lei/Lei) beve,
(noi) beviamo, (voi) bevete, (loro/Loro) bevono

## dare *to give*

(io) do, (tu) dai, (lui/lei/Lei) dà,
(noi) diamo, (voi) date, (loro/Loro) danno

## dire *to say, tell*

(io) dico, (tu) dici, (lui/lei/Lei) dice,
(noi) diciamo, (voi) dite, (loro/Loro) dicono

## dovere *to have to, must*

(io) devo, (tu) devi, (lui/lei/Lei) deve,
(noi) dobbiamo, (voi) dovete, (loro/Loro) devono

## essere *to be*

(io) sono, (tu) sei, (lui/lei/Lei) è,
(noi) siamo, (voi) siete, (loro/Loro) sono

## fare *to do, make*

(io) faccio, (tu) fai, (lui/lei/Lei) fa,
(noi) facciamo, (voi) fate, (loro/Loro) fanno

## potere *to be able to, can*

(io) posso, (tu) puoi, (lui/lei/Lei) può,
(noi) possiamo, (voi) potete, (loro/Loro) possono

## sapere *to know*

(io) so, (tu) sai, (lui/lei/Lei) sa,
(noi) sappiamo, (voi) sapete, (loro/Loro) sanno

## stare *to stay*

(io) sto, (tu) stai, (lui/lei/Lei) sta,
(noi) stiamo, (voi) state, (loro/Loro) stanno

## tenere *to hold, keep*

(io) tengo, (tu) tieni, (lui/lei/Lei) tiene,
(noi) teniamo, (voi) tenete, (loro/Loro) tengono

## uscire *to go out*

(io) esco, (tu) esci, (lui/lei/Lei) esce,
(noi) usciamo, (voi) uscite, (loro/Loro) escono

## venire *to come*

(io) vengo, (tu) vieni, (lui/lei/Lei) viene,
(noi) veniamo, (voi) venite, (loro/Loro) vengono

## volere *to want*

(io) voglio, (tu) vuoi, (lui/lei/Lei) vuole,
(noi) vogliamo, (voi) volete, (loro/Loro) vogliono

AVOID THE *Blunder*

| | |
|---|---|
| ✗ ando | ✗ sapono |
| ✗ aviamo | ✗ stano |
| ✗ da (as verb) | ✗ teno |
| ✗ dicio | ✗ usco |
| ✗ doviamo | ✗ esciamo |
| ✗ facciano | ✗ veno |
| ✗ posse | ✗ volo |
| ✗ sape | |

# Uses

The present indicative is mainly used to state facts in the present, to indicate an ongoing action, to indicate a continuous or habitual action, or to indicate an immediate future action.

**FACTS IN THE PRESENT**

Studio l'italiano.                    *I study Italian.*
Finisco di lavorare alle sei.         *I finish working at six.*

**ONGOING ACTIONS**

In questo momento mangio una          *At this moment, I am eating*
  pizza.                                *a pizza.*
Loro guardano la TV.                  *They are watching TV.*

**CONTINUOUS OR HABITUAL ACTIONS**

Il lunedì mangio sempre la pizza.     *On Mondays I always eat pizza.*
Ogni giorno studio l'italiano.        *Every day I study Italian.*

**IMMEDIATE FUTURE ACTIONS**

Domani mangio gli spaghetti.          *Tomorrow I am going to eat*
                                        *spaghetti.*
Loro arrivano la settimana            *They are arriving next week.*
  prossima.

AVOID THE *Blunder*

✗ Domani vado a mangiare la pizza.
✗ In questo momento io sono mangiando la pizza.

The present indicative is also used with the preposition *da* (which can mean "since" or "for") to render the English present perfect progressive tense.

| | |
|---|---|
| Aspetto da lunedì. | *I have been waiting since Monday.* |
| Aspetto da due giorni. | *I have been waiting for two days.* |
| Lui dorme da ieri. | *He has been sleeping since yesterday.* |
| Lui dorme da 48 ore. | *He has been sleeping for 48 hours.* |

**AVOID THE** *Blunder*

✗ Noi aspettiamo per due giorni.
✗ Lui dorme per 48 ore.

# Exercises

**A** *Circle the correct verb form according to subject.*

1. io **parlo** | **parliamo**
2. tu **apre** | **apri**
3. Lei **apre** | **apri**
4. loro **capiscono** | **capiamo**
5. voi **mangiate** | **mangiano**
6. noi **preferiamo** | **preferiscono**
7. io **vendo** | **vende**
8. io **dormo** | **dorme**
9. tu **capisci** | **capisce**
10. tu **comincia** | **cominci**
11. tu **vendi** | **vende**
12. Lei **parla** | **parli**
13. Lei **preferisce** | **preferisci**
14. voi **pagate** | **pagano**
15. loro **parlano** | **parlate**
16. loro **vendono** | **vendete**
17. loro **dormono** | **dormite**
18. loro **finiscono** | **finiamo**

**B** *Each of the following sentences contains an error. Rewrite the sentence, correcting the error.*

1. Io fino alle sei.

_____

2. Noi non capisciamo l'italiano.

_____

3. Loro partiscono per l'Italia domani.

_____

4. Dottor Marchi, capisci l'inglese?

_____

5. Maria, parla italiano anche tu?

_____

6. Maria, che cosa cerci?

_____

7. Noi non pagiamo mai (*never*).

_____

8. A che ora comincate a lavorare?

_____

9. Noi vanno al cinema domani.

_____

10. Noi deviamo studiare l'italiano oggi.

_____

**C** *Express the following English sentences in Italian.*

1. *Mary, are you studying Italian?*

_____

2. *He finishes working at six.*

_____

3. *At this moment, my sister is eating a pizza.*

_____

4. *On Mondays I always study Italian.*

_____

5. *Tomorrow I am going to eat pasta.*

_____

6. *I have been sleeping since yesterday.*

_____

7. *He also has been sleeping for eight hours.*

_____

# VERBS
## the present perfect

The present perfect tense is used to express simple actions that have been completed at the present time (at the time of speaking). It is a compound tense, formed with the present indicative form of the auxiliary verb plus the past participle of the verb, in that order.

| | |
|---|---|
| Ieri ho mangiato tutto. | *Yesterday I ate everything.* |
| Marco è andato al cinema ieri. | *Mark went to the movies yesterday.* |

The present indicative conjugations of the auxiliary verbs *avere* and *essere* are found in the previous unit (pages 117 and 118), and the formation of the past participle has already been discussed in the unit on infinitives and gerunds.

### Verbs Conjugated with *avere*

Following are complete conjugations of three verbs conjugated with *avere* in the present perfect tense.

**parlare** *to speak*

| | |
|---|---|
| (io) ho parlato | *I have spoken, I spoke, I did speak* |
| (tu) hai parlato | *you (familiar singular) have spoken, you spoke, you did speak* |
| (lui/lei/Lei) ha parlato | *he/she has / you (polite singular) have spoken, he/she/you spoke, he/she/you did speak* |
| (noi) abbiamo parlato | *we have spoken, we spoke, we did speak* |
| (voi) avete parlato | *you (familiar plural) have spoken, you spoke, you did speak* |
| (loro/Loro) hanno parlato | *they/you (polite plural) have spoken, they/you spoke, they/you did speak* |

## vendere *to sell*

| | |
|---|---|
| (io) ho venduto | *I have sold, I sold, I did sell* |
| (tu) hai venduto | *you (familiar singular) have sold, you sold, you did sell* |
| (lui/lei/Lei) ha venduto | *he/she has / you (polite singular) have sold, he/she/you sold, he/she/you did sell* |
| (noi) abbiamo venduto | *we have sold, we sold, we did sell* |
| (voi) avete venduto | *you (familiar plural) have sold, you sold, you did sell* |
| (loro/Loro) hanno venduto | *they/you (polite plural) have sold, they/you sold, they/you did sell* |

## finire *to finish*

| | |
|---|---|
| (io) ho finito | *I have finished, I finished, I did finish* |
| (tu) hai finito | *you (familiar singular) have finished, you finished, you did finish* |
| (lui/lei/Lei) ha finito | *he/she has / you (polite singular) have finished, he/she/you finished, he/she/you did finish* |
| (noi) abbiamo finito | *we have finished, we finished, we did finish* |
| (voi) avete finito | *you (familiar plural) have finished, you finished, you did finish* |
| (loro/Loro) hanno finito | *they/you (polite plural) have finished, they/you finished, they/you did finish* |

AVOID THE *Blunder*

✗ tu ai finito
✗ noi aviamo parlato

The past participles of these verbs agree with the object pronouns *lo, la, li, le,* and *ne,* which will be discussed in the unit on pronouns.

### AGREEMENT WITH lo

Hai visto il nuovo film?          *Did you see the new movie?*
Sì, lo ho / l'ho visto.           *Yes, I saw it.*

### AGREEMENT WITH la

Hai comprato la pasta?            *Did you buy the pasta?*
Sì, la ho / l'ho comprata ieri.   *Yes, I bought it yesterday.*

**AGREEMENT WITH li**

Hai finito gli spaghetti?
Sì, li ho finiti.

*Did you finish the spaghetti?*
*Yes, I finished it.*

**AGREEMENT WITH le**

Hai mangiato le pesche?
Sì, le ho mangiate.

*Did you eat the peaches?*
*Yes, I ate them.*

**AGREEMENT WITH ne**

Quante pesche hai mangiato?
Ne ho mangiate tre.

*How many peaches did you eat?*
*I ate three of them.*

Quanti gnocchi hai mangiato?

*How many dumplings did you eat?*

Ne ho mangiati tanti.

*I ate a lot.*

AVOID THE *Blunder*

✗ la abbiamo mangiato
✗ le ho comprato
✗ li hanno finito

## Verbs Conjugated with *essere*

The past participle of a verb conjugated with *essere* agrees in gender and number with the subject of the sentence. Following are complete conjugations of three verbs conjugated with *essere* in the present perfect.

**arrivare *to arrive***

| | |
|---|---|
| (io) sono arrivato(-a) | *I have arrived, I arrived, I did arrive* |
| (tu) sei arrivato(-a) | *you (familiar singular) have arrived, you arrived, you did arrive* |
| (lui/lei/Lei) è arrivato(-a) | *he/she has / you (polite singular) have arrived, he/she/you arrived, he/she/you did arrive* |
| (noi) siamo arrivati(-e) | *we have arrived, we arrived, we did arrive* |
| (voi) siete arrivati(-e) | *you (familiar plural) have arrived, you arrived, you did arrive* |
| (loro/Loro) sono arrivati(-e) | *they/you (polite plural) have arrived, they/you arrived, they/you did arrive* |

## cadere *to fall*

| | |
|---|---|
| (io) sono caduto(-a) | *I have fallen, I fell, I did fall* |
| (tu) sei caduto(-a) | *you* (familiar singular) *have fallen, you fell, you did fall* |
| (lui/lei/Lei) è caduto(-a) | *he/she has / you* (polite singular) *have fallen, he/she/you fell, he/she/you did fall* |
| (noi) siamo caduti(-e) | *we have fallen, we fell, we did fall* |
| (voi) siete caduti(-e) | *you* (familiar plural) *have fallen, you fell, you did fall* |
| (loro/Loro) sono caduti(-e) | *they/you* (polite plural) *have fallen, they/you fell, they/you did fall* |

## partire *to leave*

| | |
|---|---|
| (io) sono partito(-a) | *I have left, I left, I did leave* |
| (tu) sei partito(-a) | *you* (familiar singular) *have left, you left, you did leave* |
| (lui/lei/Lei) è partito(-a) | *he/she has / you* (polite singular) *have left, he/she/you left, he/she/you did leave* |
| (noi) siamo partiti(-e) | *we have left, we left, we did leave* |
| (voi) siete partiti(-e) | *you* (familiar plural) *have left, you left, you did leave* |
| (loro/Loro) sono partiti(-e) | *they/you* (polite plural) *have left, they/you left, they/you did leave* |

**AVOID THE Blunder**

✗ ho arrivato
✗ siamo caduto
✗ abbiamo partito

## Selecting the Auxiliary Verb

When do you use *avere,* when do you use *essere?* The best learning strategy is to assume that most verbs are conjugated with *avere* (which is true), and then memorize the verbs conjugated with *essere.* All of the latter verbs are intransitive, that is, they do not take a direct object. Moreover, many of them express motion of some type (going, arriving, staying, entering, etc.).

**COMMON VERBS CONJUGATED WITH essere IN COMPOUND TENSES**

| | |
|---|---|
| andare | *to go* |
| arrivare | *to arrive* |
| cadere | *to fall* |
| diventare | *to become* |
| entrare | *to enter* |
| essere | *to be* |
| morire | *to die* |
| nascere | *to be born* |
| partire | *to leave* |
| sembrare | *to seem* |
| stare | *to stay* |
| tornare | *to return* |
| uscire | *to go out* |
| venire | *to come* |

All impersonal verbs are conjugated with *essere*. These are verbs that have only third-person forms.

**costare** *to cost*

Quanto sono costate le arance? *How much did the oranges cost?*

**durare** *to last*

Lo spettacolo è durato tre ore. *The show lasted three hours.*

AVOID THE *Blunder*

✗ ho andato        ✗ hanno tornato
✗ abbiamo diventato   ✗ ho uscito
✗ hai entrato       ✗ ha venuto
✗ avete stato

## Irregular Past Participles

The following irregular past participles constitute a major source of blunders. Verbs conjugated with *essere* are marked with an asterisk.

| | | | |
|---|---|---|---|
| aprire | *to open* | aperto | *opened* |
| bere | *to drink* | bevuto | *drunk* |
| chiedere | *to ask for* | chiesto | *asked* |
| chiudere | *to close* | chiuso | *closed* |

| dare | to give | dato | given |
|------|---------|------|-------|
| decidere | to decide | deciso | decided |
| dire | to say, tell | detto | said |
| essere* | to be | stato | been |
| fare | to do, make | fatto | done, made |
| leggere | to read | letto | read |
| mettere | to put | messo | put |
| morire* | to die | morto | died |
| nascere* | to be born | nato | born |
| perdere | to lose | perso | lost |
| prendere | to take | preso | taken |
| scegliere | to choose, select | scelto | chosen, selected |
| scendere* | to descend, go down | sceso | descended, gone down |
| scrivere | to write | scritto | written |
| stare* | to stay | stato | stayed |
| vedere | to see | visto | seen |
| venire* | to come | venuto | come |
| vincere | to win | vinto | won |

AVOID THE *Blunder*

✗ ha aprito
✗ abbiamo chieduto
✗ hai chiuduto
✗ ho datto
✗ hanno deciduto
✗ avete ditto
✗ hai leggiuto
✗ abbiamo mettuto
✗ sei morito
✗ è nasciuto
✗ ha prenduto
✗ avete scegliuto
✗ sono scenduto
✗ ho scrivuto
✗ siamo veniti
✗ ho vinciuto

## Uses

Basically, the present perfect corresponds to three English past tenses (exemplified by *I have spoken, I spoke, I did speak*).

| Maria ha venduto la sua macchina. | *Mary sold her car.* |

| | |
|---|---|
| Ieri ho parlato al signor Verdi. | *Yesterday I spoke to Mr. Verdi.* |
| Loro hanno dormito troppo ieri. | *They slept too much yesterday.* |
| Ho già mangiato. | *I have already eaten.* |
| Il nostro amico è arrivato ieri. | *Our friend arrived yesterday.* |
| Tua cugina è arrivata la settimana scorsa. | *Your cousin arrived last week.* |
| Quando siete venuti? | *When did you come?* |
| Quando è partita, signora Verdi? | *When did you leave, Mrs. Verdi?* |

AVOID THE *Blunder*

✗ Loro dormito troppo ieri.
✗ Lui venuto ieri.

Remember that third-person forms are used in polite address. The past participle of a verb conjugated with *essere* agrees in gender and number with the person(s) you are addressing.

| | |
|---|---|
| Signor Verdi, è uscito ieri? | *Mr. Verdi, did you go out yesterday?* |
| Signora Verdi, è uscita ieri? | *Mrs. Verdi, did you go out yesterday?* |

AVOID THE *Blunder*

✗ Signorina, è andato al cinema ieri?
✗ Signora Verdi e signorina Marchi, sono usciti ieri?

## Exercises

**A** Write the present perfect form of the verb according to the pronoun in parentheses.

ESEMPIO (tu) cantare   <u>hai cantato</u>

1. (io) mangiare   _____
2. (lui) pagare   _____
3. (noi) vendere   _____
4. (voi) leggere   _____
5. (loro) scrivere   _____
6. (lei) nascere   _____
7. (io) capire   _____
8. (tu) finire   _____
9. (lui) venire   _____
10. (loro) dire   _____
11. (voi) dare   _____
12. (noi) fare   _____
13. (io) chiedere   _____
14. (lui) aprire   _____

**B** Write the appropriate form of the auxiliary verb in the longer blank and the final vowel of the past participle in the shorter blank.

1. Marco _____ vendut____ la sua macchina ieri.
2. Marco la _____ vendut____ ieri.
3. Maria _____ andat____ al cinema ieri.
4. Maria _____ comprat____ le scarpe nuove ieri.
5. Maria le _____ comprat____ ieri.
6. I miei amici _____ andat____ in Italia la settimana scorsa.
7. Anche le sue amiche _____ andat____ in Italia qualche giorno fa (ago).
8. Loro _____ vist____ quel film già.
9. Voi _____ già mangiat____, non è vero?
10. Noi tutti _____ andat____ al cinema ieri.
11. Signor Franchi, quando _____ uscit____ ieri Lei?
12. Signora Franchi, quando _____ uscit____ ieri Lei?

**C** *Express the following English sentences in Italian.*

1. *The show lasted three hours.*

_____

2. *How much did the meat cost?*

_____

3. *My sister sold her car.*

_____

4. *Yesterday we spoke to Mr. Verdi.*

_____

5. *He slept too much yesterday.*

_____

6. *I have already eaten.*

_____

7. *Our grandfather arrived yesterday.*

_____

8. *Their grandmother arrived last week.*

_____

# VERBS
## the imperfect

The present perfect tense (discussed in the previous unit) expresses a finished past action—an action that can be visualized as having started and ended.

| | |
|---|---|
| Ieri ho dormito due ore. | *Yesterday I slept two hours.* |

If, however, it is necessary to express an action that continued for an indefinite period of time, the imperfect tense is used.

| | |
|---|---|
| Ieri, mentre io dormivo, lui guardava la TV. | *Yesterday, while I was sleeping, he was watching TV.* |

The imperfect is also used to indicate habitual or repeated actions in the past, as well as to describe the characteristics of people and things as they used to be.

| | |
|---|---|
| Quando ero giovane, suonavo il pianoforte. | *When I was young, I used to play the piano.* |
| Da giovane, lei aveva i capelli biondi. | *As a youth, she had / used to have blonde hair.* |

## Conjugation

The imperfect tense is formed by dropping the infinitive ending and adding the following endings according to conjugation.

**FIRST-CONJUGATION ENDINGS**  -avo, -avi, -ava, -avamo, -avate, -avano

parlare *to speak*

| | |
|---|---|
| (io) parlavo | *I was speaking, I used to speak* |
| (tu) parlavi | *you* (familiar singular) *were speaking, you used to speak* |
| (lui/lei/Lei) parlava | *he/she was / you* (polite singular) *were speaking, he/she/you used to speak* |
| (noi) parlavamo | *we were speaking, we used to speak* |
| (voi) parlavate | *you* (familiar plural) *were speaking, you used to speak* |
| (loro/Loro) parlavano | *they/you* (polite plural) *were speaking, they/you used to speak* |

**SECOND-CONJUGATION ENDINGS**  -evo, -evi, -eva, -evamo, -evate, -evano
scrivere *to write*

| | |
|---|---|
| (io) scrivevo | *I was writing, I used to write* |
| (tu) scrivevi | *you (familiar singular) were writing, you used to write* |
| (lui/lei/Lei) scriveva | *he/she was / you (polite singular) were writing, he/she/you used to write* |
| (noi) scrivevamo | *we were writing, we used to write* |
| (voi) scrivevate | *you (familiar plural) were writing, you used to write* |
| (loro/Loro) scrivevano | *they/you (polite plural) were writing, they/you used to write* |

**THIRD-CONJUGATION ENDINGS**  -ivo, -ivi, -iva, -ivamo, -ivate, -ivano
finire *to finish*

| | |
|---|---|
| (io) finivo | *I was finishing, I used to finish* |
| (tu) finivi | *you (familiar singular) were finishing, you used to finish* |
| (lui/lei/Lei) finiva | *he/she was / you (polite singular) were finishing, he/she/you used to finish* |
| (noi) finivamo | *we were finishing, we used to finish* |
| (voi) finivate | *you (familiar plural) were finishing, you used to finish* |
| (loro/Loro) finivano | *they/you (polite plural) were finishing, they/you used to finish* |

## Irregular Forms

Irregular verb forms constitute a major source of blunders. Following are the most common verbs with irregular imperfect forms.

**bere** *to drink*

(io) bevevo, (tu) bevevi, (lui/lei/Lei) beveva,
(noi) bevevamo, (voi) bevevate, (loro/Loro) bevevano

**dare** *to give*

(io) davo, (tu) davi, (lui/lei/Lei) dava,
(noi) davamo, (voi) davate, (loro/Loro) davano

**dire** *to say, tell*

(io) dicevo, (tu) dicevi, (lui/lei/Lei) diceva,
(noi) dicevamo, (voi) dicevate, (loro/Loro) dicevano

**essere** *to be*

(io) ero, (tu) eri, (lui/lei/Lei) era,
(noi) eravamo, (voi) eravate, (loro/Loro) erano

**fare** *to do, make*

(io) facevo, (tu) facevi, (lui/lei/Lei) faceva,
(noi) facevamo, (voi) facevate, (loro/Loro) facevano

**stare** *to stay*

(io) stavo, (tu) stavi, (lui/lei/Lei) stava,
(noi) stavamo, (voi) stavate, (loro/Loro) stavano

AVOID THE *Blunder*

✗ noi eramo
✗ loro eravano
✗ loro facevanno

## Uses

As mentioned above, the imperfect tense expresses past actions that were continuous (went on for a while), states and conditions that were habitual or recurring, and characteristics of people and things as they used to be or once were.

Mentre tu studiavi, tuo fratello
suonava il pianoforte.

*While you were studying, your
brother played the piano.*

Da giovane, mio cugino ci
    visitava ogni settimana.
Da bambina, lei aveva i capelli
    biondi.

*As a youth, my cousin used to
    visit us every week.*
*As a child, she had blonde hair.*

AVOID THE *Blunder*

✗ Mentre io leggevo, mio fratello ha guardato la TV.
✗ Da ragazza, lei ha avuto i capelli lunghi.
✗ Da bambino, lui ha giocato spesso al calcio.

The imperfect tense is a major source of blunders, because English
sometimes uses a perfect tense to translate the Italian imperfect.

Mentre dormivo, tu guardavi
    la TV.

*While I slept / was sleeping, you
    watched / were watching TV.*

You must therefore always look for clues among the other words in a
sentence to determine whether the imperfect should or should not be
used. Words such as the following generally indicate the necessity of
using the imperfect.

mentre     *while*
sempre     *always*
di solito  *usually*

Da bambino, mio fratello giocava
    sempre col computer.
Alcuni anni fa, guardavo sempre
    le partite di calcio in televisione.

*As a child, my brother always
    played on the computer.*
*A few years ago, I used to always
    watch soccer matches on
    television.*

AVOID THE *Blunder*

✗ Mio fratello ha giocato di solito a calcio anni fa.
✗ Io ho guardato sempre la televisione da bambina.

# Exercises

**A** Write the imperfect form of the verb according to the pronoun in parentheses.

ESEMPIO    (io) cantare    _io cantavo_

1. (io) leggere          _____
2. (io) capire           _____
3. (io) bere             _____
4. (tu) mangiare         _____
5. (tu) vedere           _____
6. (tu) dormire          _____
7. (tu) essere           _____
8. (lui) cominciare      _____
9. (lei) avere           _____
10. (lui) fare           _____
11. (lei) dire           _____
12. (noi) pagare         _____
13. (noi) sapere         _____
14. (noi) dare           _____
15. (voi) mangiare       _____
16. (voi) potere         _____
17. (voi) uscire         _____
18. (voi) essere         _____
19. (loro) arrivare      _____
20. (loro) avere         _____
21. (loro) venire        _____

**B** Choose the present perfect or imperfect form of the verb, as appropriate.

1. Quando mia sorella era giovane, _____ il pianoforte.

    a. ha suonato

    b. suonava

2. Da giovane, lei _____ i capelli lunghi.

    a. ha avuto

    b. aveva

3. Ieri, mentre mio fratello dormiva, io _____ la TV.

    a. ho guardato

    b. guardavo

4. Ieri _____ tutta la giornata (*all day long*).

    a. ho dormito

    b. dormivo

5. Mentre tu studiavi, lui _____ al computer.

    a. ha giocato

    b. giocava

6. Da giovane, nostro cugino _____ una sola volta (*only once*) in Italia.

    a. è andato

    b. andava

7. Da bambina, lei non _____ mangiare la pasta.

    a. ha voluto

    b. voleva

8. Da bambino, lui _____ quattro volte in Italia.

    a. è andato

    b. andava

9. Alcuni anni fa, io _____ spesso al cinema, ma non più.

    a. sono andata

    b. andavo

# VERBS
## the past absolute

The past absolute (also called the preterit) covers many of the same uses as the present perfect. Unlike the present perfect, however, it can express actions that occurred in the distant past.

| | |
|---|---|
| Ieri loro sono andati in Italia. (PRESENT PERFECT) | *Yesterday they went to Italy.* |
| Andarono in Italia molti anni fa. (PAST ABSOLUTE) | *They went to Italy many years ago.* |

## Conjugation

The past absolute is formed by dropping the infinitive ending and adding the following endings according to conjugation.

**FIRST-CONJUGATION ENDINGS** -ai, -asti, -ò, -ammo, -aste, -arono

cantare *to sing*

| | |
|---|---|
| (io) cantai | *I sang* |
| (tu) cantasti | *you* (familiar singular) *sang* |
| (lui/lei/Lei) cantò | *he/she/you* (polite singular) *sang* |
| (noi) cantammo | *we sang* |
| (voi) cantaste | *you* (familiar plural) *sang* |
| (loro/Loro) cantarono | *they/you* (polite plural) *sang* |

---

AVOID THE *Blunder*

✗ lui cantà
✗ noi cantiammo
✗ loro cantaronno

---

**SECOND-CONJUGATION ENDINGS** -ei/-etti, -esti, -é/-ette,
                              -emmo, -este, -erono/-ettero

vendere *to sell*

| | |
|---|---|
| (io) vendei/vendetti | *I sold* |
| (tu) vendesti | *you* (familiar singular) *sold* |
| (lui/lei/Lei) vendé/vendette | *he/she/you* (polite singular) *sold* |
| (noi) vendemmo | *we sold* |
| (voi) vendeste | *you* (familiar plural) *sold* |
| (loro/Loro) venderono/vendettero | *they/you* (polite plural) *sold* |

AVOID THE *Blunder*

✗ lui vendò
✗ noi vendammo

**THIRD-CONJUGATION ENDINGS** -ii, -isti, -ì, -immo, -iste, -irono

finire *to finish*

| | |
|---|---|
| (io) finii | *I finished* |
| (tu) finisti | *you* (familiar singular) *finished* |
| (lui/lei/Lei) finì | *he/she/you* (polite singular) *finished* |
| (noi) finimmo | *we finished* |
| (voi) finiste | *you* (familiar plural) *finished* |
| (loro/Loro) finirono | *they/you* (polite plural) *finished* |

AVOID THE *Blunder*

✗ io fini
✗ loro finironno

## Irregular Forms

Irregular verb forms are a source of many blunders. Following are the
most troublesome irregular past absolute forms.

**avere** *to have*

  (io) ebbi, (tu) avesti, (lui/lei/Lei) ebbe,
  (noi) avemmo, (voi) aveste, (loro/Loro) ebbero

**bere** *to drink*

  (io) bevvi/bevetti, (tu) bevesti, (lui/lei/Lei) bevve/bevette,
  (noi) bevemmo, (voi) beveste, (loro/Loro) bevvero/bevettero

## cadere *to fall*

(io) caddi, (tu) cadesti, (lui/lei/Lei) cadde,
(noi) cademmo, (voi) cadeste, (loro/Loro) caddero

## chiedere *to ask for*

(io) chiesi, (tu) chiedesti, (lui/lei/Lei) chiese,
(noi) chiedemmo, (voi) chiedeste, (loro/Loro) chiesero

## chiudere *to close*

(io) chiusi, (tu) chiudesti, (lui/lei/Lei) chiuse,
(noi) chiudemmo, (voi) chiudeste, (loro/Loro) chiusero

## conoscere *to know (someone), be familiar with*

(io) conobbi, (tu) conoscesti, (lui/lei/Lei) conobbe,
(noi) conoscemmo, (voi) conosceste, (loro/Loro) conobbero

## dare *to give*

(io) diedi, (tu) desti, (lui/lei/Lei) diede,
(noi) demmo, (voi) deste, (loro/Loro) diedero

## decidere *to decide*

(io) decisi, (tu) decidesti, (lui/lei/Lei) decise,
(noi) decidemmo, (voi) decideste, (loro/Loro) decisero

## dire *to say, tell*

(io) dissi, (tu) dicesti, (lui/lei/Lei) disse,
(noi) dicemmo, (voi) diceste, (loro/Loro) dissero

## essere *to be*

(io) fui, (tu) fosti, (lui/lei/Lei) fu,
(noi) fummo, (voi) foste, (loro/Loro) furono

## fare *to do, make*

(io) feci, (tu) facesti, (lui/lei/Lei) fece,
(noi) facemmo, (voi) faceste, (loro/Loro) fecero

## leggere *to read*

(io) lessi, (tu) leggesti, (lui/lei/Lei) lesse,
(noi) leggemmo, (voi) leggeste, (loro/Loro) lessero

## mettere *to put*

(io) misi, (tu) mettesti, (lui/lei/Lei) mise,
(noi) mettemmo, (voi) metteste, (loro/Loro) misero

**nascere** *to be born*

(io) nacqui, (tu) nascesti, (lui/lei/Lei) nacque,
(noi) nascemmo, (voi) nasceste, (loro/Loro) nacquero

**perdere** *to lose*

(io) persi, (tu) perdesti, (lui/lei/Lei) perse,
(noi) perdemmo, (voi) perdeste, (loro/Loro) persero

**prendere** *to take*

(io) presi, (tu) prendesti, (lui/lei/Lei) prese,
(noi) prendemmo, (voi) prendeste, (loro/Loro) presero

**sapere** *to know*

(io) seppi, (tu) sapesti, (lui/lei/Lei) seppe,
(noi) sapemmo, (voi) sapeste, (loro/Loro) seppero

**scegliere** *to choose, select*

(io) scelsi, (tu) scegliesti, (lui/lei/Lei) scelse,
(noi) scegliemmo, (voi) sceglieste, (loro/Loro) scelsero

**scendere** *to descend, go down*

(io) scesi, (tu) scendesti, (lui/lei/Lei) scese,
(noi) scendemmo, (voi) scendeste, (loro/Loro) scesero

**scrivere** *to write*

(io) scrissi, (tu) scrivesti, (lui/lei/Lei) scrisse,
(noi) scrivemmo, (voi) scriveste, (loro/Loro) scrissero

**stare** *to stay*

(io) stetti, (tu) stesti, (lui/lei/Lei) stette,
(noi) stemmo, (voi) steste, (loro/Loro) stettero

**vedere** *to see*

(io) vidi, (tu) vedesti, (lui/lei/Lei) vide,
(noi) vedemmo, (voi) vedeste, (loro/Loro) videro

**venire** *to come*

(io) venni, (tu) venisti, (lui/lei/Lei) venne,
(noi) venimmo, (voi) veniste, (loro/Loro) vennero

**volere** *to want*

(io) volli, (tu) volesti, (lui/lei/Lei) volle,
(noi) volemmo, (voi) voleste, (loro/Loro) vollero

X loro averono
X loro berono
X io cadi
X loro chiederono
X lui chiudè
X io conoscei
X loro decidero
X loro dicerono

X io leggei
X loro metterono
X loro nascettero
X loro prenderono
X loro saperono
X loro scriverono
X loro volerono

## Uses

As mentioned above, the past absolute can be used in place of the present perfect in many cases. It is, however, the only tense that can express historical events, as well as events that occurred in the distant past.

| | |
|---|---|
| I miei genitori tornarono in Italia nel 2004. | *My parents returned to Italy in 2004.* |
| Marco Polo portò tanti tesori indietro. | *Marco Polo brought back many treasures.* |
| Finirono quel lavoro tanto tempo fa. | *They finished that job a long time ago.* |

The past absolute cannot be used with temporal adverbs such as the following.

| | |
|---|---|
| già | *already* |
| poco fa | *a little while ago* |

These limit the action to the immediate past (occurring within the last 24 hours). Only the present perfect can be used in such cases.

| | |
|---|---|
| Alessandro è arrivato poco tempo fa. | *Alexander arrived a little while ago.* |
| Ho già telefonato a lei. | *I have already phoned her.* |

Aside from this restriction, the past absolute can be used (judiciously) as an alternative to the present perfect.

Maria è venuta in America nel 2004. }
Maria venne in America nel 2004. } *Mary came to America in 2004.*

Ieri ti ho telefonato alle due. }
Ieri ti telefonai alle due. } *Yesterday I phoned you at two.*

The past absolute is essentially a literary past tense. It is used in particular in the narration of historical events.

Colombo arrivò nel Nuovo Mondo nel 1492.      *Columbus arrived in the New World in 1492.*

Verdi morì molto vecchio.      *Verdi died at a very old age.*

Whichever tense you decide to use, you must use it consistently, especially with verbs in subordinate clauses.

AVOID THE *Blunder*

✗ Entrarono dieci minuti fa.
✗ Galileo ha inventato il telescopio.

# Exercises

**A** *For each present perfect form, write the corresponding past absolute form.*

1. ho mangiato _____

2. ho venduto _____

3. sono partita _____

4. ho avuto _____

5. sei andato _____

6. hai venduto _____

7. sei uscito _____

8. hai fatto _____

9. è arrivato _____

10. ha potuto _____

11. ha preferito _____

12. è stata _____

13. abbiamo pagato _____

14. abbiamo dovuto _____

15. abbiamo dormito _____

16. abbiamo detto _____

17. avete cantato _____

18. avete potuto _____

19. siete partiti _____

20. avete dato _____

21. hanno cominciato _____

22. hanno dovuto _____

23. hanno capito _____

24. sono nati _____

**B** *Choose the present perfect, imperfect, or past absolute form of the verb, as appropriate.*

1. I miei genitori _____ in Italia molti anni fa.

   a. sono tornati

   b. tornavano

   c. tornarono

2. I miei genitori _____ per l'Italia due ore fa.

 a. sono partiti

 b. partivano

 c. partirono

3. I miei genitori _____ spesso in Italia alcuni anni fa.

 a. sono andati

 b. andavano

 c. andarono

4. Marco Polo _____ in Cina per la prima volta quando era molto giovane.

 a. è andato

 b. andava

 c. andò

5. Michele _____ poco tempo fa.

 a. è uscito

 b. usciva

 c. uscì

6. Non ho fame perché _____ già.

 a. ho mangiato

 b. mangiavo

 c. mangiai

7. Rossini _____ a Parigi da vecchio.

 a. è andato

 b. andava

 c. andò

# VERBS
## the pluperfect

The pluperfect is a compound tense. As such, it is conjugated with an auxiliary verb, either *avere* or *essere,* and the past participle of the verb. (To review the formation of compound tenses, see the unit on the present perfect.)

## Conjugation

The pluperfect is formed with the imperfect of the auxiliary verb plus the past participle of the verb, in that order.

Following are the complete conjugations of two verbs in the pluperfect tense, one verb conjugated with *avere* and the other conjugated with *essere.*

### parlare *to speak*

| | |
|---|---|
| (io) avevo parlato | *I had spoken* |
| (tu) avevi parlato | *you* (familiar singular) *had spoken* |
| (lui/lei/Lei) aveva parlato | *he/she/you* (polite singular) *had spoken* |
| (noi) avevamo parlato | *we had spoken* |
| (voi) avevate parlato | *you* (familiar plural) *had spoken* |
| (loro/Loro) avevano parlato | *they/you* (polite plural) *had spoken* |

AVOID THE

✗ noi aveviamo parlato
✗ loro avevanno parlato

### partire *to leave*

| | |
|---|---|
| (io) ero partito(-a) | *I had left* |
| (tu) eri partito(-a) | *you* (familiar singular) *had left* |
| (lui/lei/Lei) era partito(-a) | *he/she/you* (polite singular) *had left* |
| (noi) eravamo partiti(-e) | *we had left* |
| (voi) eravate partiti(-e) | *you* (familiar plural) *had left* |
| (loro/Loro) erano partiti(-e) | *they/you* (polite plural) *had left* |

**147**

## Uses

The pluperfect tense (literally, "more than perfect" or "more than past") expresses an action that occurred before a simple past action (as expressed by the present perfect, imperfect, or past absolute).

| | |
|---|---|
| Dopo che era arrivata, mi ha telefonato. | *After she had arrived, she phoned me.* |
| Lui mi ha detto che aveva già parlato al professore. | *He told me that he had already talked to the professor.* |

Essentially, this tense corresponds to the English pluperfect ("had" + past participle). But be careful! Sometimes the pluperfect is only implied in English colloquial usage.

| | |
|---|---|
| Sono andati in Italia dopo che avevano finito gli esami. | *They went to Italy after they finished (= had finished) their exams.* |

## Exercises

**A** *For each present perfect form, write the corresponding pluperfect form.*

1. ho mangiato _____
2. ho venduto _____
3. sono partita _____
4. ho avuto _____
5. sei andato _____
6. hai venduto _____
7. sei uscito _____
8. hai fatto _____
9. è arrivato _____
10. ha potuto _____
11. ha preferito _____
12. è stata _____
13. abbiamo pagato _____
14. abbiamo dovuto _____
15. abbiamo dormito _____
16. abbiamo detto _____
17. avete cantato _____
18. avete potuto _____
19. siete partiti _____
20. avete dato _____
21. hanno cominciato _____
22. hanno dovuto _____
23. hanno capito _____
24. sono nati _____

**B** *Choose the present perfect, imperfect, or pluperfect form of the verb, as appropriate.*

1. Loro _____ già quando mi hai chiamato.

 a. sono rientrati

 b. rientravano

 c. erano rientrati

2. Loro _____ per l'Italia ieri.

 a. sono partiti

 b. partivano

 c. erano partiti

3. Loro _____ spesso quando erano giovani.

 a. sono usciti

 b. uscivano

 c. erano usciti

4. Lui mi ha detto che tu _____ già quel libro.

 a. hai letto

 b. leggevi

 c. avevi letto

5. Lui _____ poco tempo fa.

 a. è uscito

 b. usciva

 c. era uscito

6. Ieri non avevo fame perché _____ già.

 a. ho mangiato

 b. mangiavo

 c. avevo mangiato

7. Dopo che Rossini _____ a Parigi, compose della bellissima musica sacra. *(After Rossini went to Paris, he composed some very beautiful sacred music.)*

 a. è andato

 b. andava

 c. era andato

# VERBS
## the future tenses

The simple future tense, as its name implies, expresses an action that will occur in the future. The future perfect expresses an action that will have occurred before a simple future action.

| | |
|---|---|
| Domani andremo in centro. | *Tomorrow we will be going downtown.* |
| Dopo che saremo andati in centro, ti chiameremo. | *After having gone downtown, we'll call you.* |

## The Simple Future

### Conjugation

The simple future is formed by dropping the final *-e* of the infinitive in all three conjugations, changing the *-ar* of first-conjugation verbs to *-er*, and adding these endings: *-ò, -ai, -à, -emo, -ete, -anno*.

| INFINITIVE | FUTURE STEM |
|---|---|
| parlare | parler- |
| scrivere | scriver- |
| finire | finir- |

Following are complete conjugations of three verbs in the future tense.

**parlare** *to speak*

| | |
|---|---|
| (io) parlerò | *I will speak* |
| (tu) parlerai | *you* (familiar singular) *will speak* |
| (lui/lei/Lei) parlerà | *he/she/you* (polite singular) *will speak* |
| (noi) parleremo | *we will speak* |
| (voi) parlerete | *you* (familiar plural) *will speak* |
| (loro/Loro) parleranno | *they/you* (polite plural) *will speak* |

AVOID THE *Blunder*

✗ io parlarò
✗ loro parlaranno

**151**

## scrivere *to write*

| | |
|---|---|
| (io) scriverò | *I will write* |
| (tu) scriverai | *you* (familiar singular) *will write* |
| (lui/lei/Lei) scriverà | *he/she/you* (polite singular) *will write* |
| (noi) scriveremo | *we will write* |
| (voi) scriverete | *you* (familiar plural) *will write* |
| (loro/Loro) scriveranno | *they/you* (polite plural) *will write* |

AVOID THE *Blunder*

✗ noi scrivemo
✗ loro scrivanno

## finire *to finish*

| | |
|---|---|
| (io) finirò | *I will finish* |
| (tu) finirai | *you* (familiar singular) *will finish* |
| (lui/lei/Lei) finirà | *he/she/you* (polite singular) *will finish* |
| (noi) finiremo | *we will finish* |
| (voi) finirete | *you* (familiar plural) *will finish* |
| (loro/Loro) finiranno | *they/you* (polite plural) *will finish* |

AVOID THE *Blunder*

✗ noi finiramo
✗ loro finirano

To indicate that the hard /c/ and /g/ sounds of verbs ending in -*care* and -*gare* are to be retained, the following spelling adjustments are made.

| INFINITIVE | FUTURE STEM |
|---|---|
| cercare *to search for* | cercher- |
| pagare *to pay* | pagher- |

| | |
|---|---|
| (io) cercherò | *I will search* |
| (tu) cercherai | *you* (familiar singular) *will search* |
| (lui/lei/Lei) cercherà | *he/she/you* (polite singular) *will search* |
| (noi) cercheremo | *we will search* |
| (voi) cercherete | *you* (familiar plural) *will search* |
| (loro/Loro) cercheranno | *they/you* (polite plural) *will search* |

| | |
|---|---|
| (io) pagherò | *I will pay* |
| (tu) pagherai | *you* (familiar singular) *will pay* |
| (lui/lei/Lei) pagherà | *he/she/you* (polite singular) *will pay* |

| (noi) pagheremo | *we will pay* |
| (voi) pagherete | *you* (familiar plural) *will pay* |
| (loro/Loro) pagheranno | *they/you* (polite plural) *will pay* |

✗ io cercarò
✗ loro pagaranno

The *-i* of verbs ending in *-ciare* or *-giare* is not retained in the conjugation of the future tense.

| INFINITIVE | FUTURE STEM |
|---|---|
| cominciare *to begin* | comincer- |
| mangiare *to eat* | manger- |

| (io) comincerò | *I will begin* |
| (tu) comincerai | *you* (familiar singular) *will begin* |
| (lui/lei/Lei) comincerà | *he/she/you* (polite singular) *will begin* |
| (noi) cominceremo | *we will begin* |
| (voi) comincerete | *you* (familiar plural) *will begin* |
| (loro/Loro) cominceranno | *they/you* (polite plural) *will begin* |

| (io) mangerò | *I will eat* |
| (tu) mangerai | *you* (familiar singular) *will eat* |
| (lui/lei/Lei) mangerà | *he/she/you* (polite singular) *will eat* |
| (noi) mangeremo | *we will eat* |
| (voi) mangerete | *you* (familiar plural) *will eat* |
| (loro/Loro) mangeranno | *they/you* (polite plural) *will eat* |

✗ io cominciarò
✗ lui mangierà

## Irregular Forms

Irregular verb forms are a source of many blunders. Following are the most problematic irregular verbs in the future. Note that many irregular forms involve dropping both vowels of the infinitive.

| INFINITIVE | FUTURE STEM |
|---|---|
| andare *to go* | andr- |
| avere *to have* | avr- |

## andare *to go*

(io) andrò, (tu) andrai, (lui/lei/Lei) andrà,
(noi) andremo, (voi) andrete, (loro/Loro) andranno

## avere *to have*

(io) avrò, (tu) avrai, (lui/lei/Lei) avrà,
(noi) avremo, (voi) avrete, (loro/Loro) avranno

## bere *to drink*

(io) berrò, (tu) berrai, (lui/lei/Lei) berrà,
(noi) berremo, (voi) berrete, (loro/Loro) berranno

## cadere *to fall*

(io) cadrò, (tu) cadrai, (lui/lei/Lei) cadrà,
(noi) cadremo, (voi) cadrete, (loro/Loro) cadranno

## dare *to give*

(io) darò, (tu) darai, (lui/lei/Lei) darà,
(noi) daremo, (voi) darete, (loro/Loro) daranno

## dovere *to have to, must*

(io) dovrò, (tu) dovrai, (lui/lei/Lei) dovrà,
(noi) dovremo, (voi) dovrete, (loro/Loro) dovranno

## essere *to be*

(io) sarò, (tu) sarai, (lui/lei/Lei) sarà,
(noi) saremo, (voi) sarete, (loro/Loro) saranno

## fare *to do, make*

(io) farò, (tu) farai, (lui/lei/Lei) farà,
(noi) faremo, (voi) farete, (loro/Loro) faranno

## potere *to be able to, can*

(io) potrò, (tu) potrai, (lui/lei/Lei) potrà,
(noi) potremo, (voi) potrete, (loro/Loro) potranno

## sapere *to know*

(io) saprò, (tu) saprai, (lui/lei/Lei) saprà,
(noi) sapremo, (voi) saprete, (loro/Loro) sapranno

## stare *to stay*

(io) starò, (tu) starai, (lui/lei/Lei) starà,
(noi) staremo, (voi) starete, (loro/Loro) staranno

**tenere** *to hold, keep*

(io) terrò, (tu) terrai, (lui/lei/Lei) terrà,
(noi) terremo, (voi) terrete, (loro/Loro) terranno

**vedere** *to see*

(io) vedrò, (tu) vedrai, (lui/lei/Lei) vedrà,
(noi) vedremo, (voi) vedrete, (loro/Loro) vedranno

**venire** *to come*

(io) verrò, (tu) verrai, (lui/lei/Lei) verrà,
(noi) verremo, (voi) verrete, (loro/Loro) verranno

**volere** *to want*

(io) vorrò, (tu) vorrai, (lui/lei/Lei) vorrà,
(noi) vorremo, (voi) vorrete, (loro/Loro) vorranno

AVOID THE *Blunder*

| | |
|---|---|
| ✗ io anderò | ✗ io saperò |
| ✗ loro averanno | ✗ io tenerò |
| ✗ loro caderanno | ✗ loro vederanno |
| ✗ io doverò | ✗ io venirò |
| ✗ loro poteranno | ✗ io volerò |

## Uses

The Italian future tense corresponds, generally, to the English future—
*I will go, you will write,* etc. It also conveys the idea expressed in English *going to write* and *will be writing.*

| | |
|---|---|
| Manderò un'email al mio amico domani. | *I will send / am going to send / will be sending an e-mail to my friend tomorrow.* |
| Partiranno tra un mese. | *They will leave / are going to leave / will be leaving in a month.* |

The Italian future is also used to express probability.

| | |
|---|---|
| Sai quanto costa quell'orologio? | *Do you know how much that watch costs?* |
| Costerà mille euro. | *It probably costs 1,000 euros.* |
| Chi sarà? | *Who can that (possibly) be?* |
| A quest'ora sarà tua sorella. | *At this hour, it is probably your sister.* |

## The Future Perfect

### Conjugation

Like the present perfect and pluperfect tenses, the future perfect is a compound tense. It is formed with the future of the auxiliary verb plus the past participle of the verb, in that order. Following are complete conjugations of two verbs in the future perfect tense, one verb conjugated with *avere* and the other conjugated with *essere*.

**mangiare** *to eat*

| | |
|---|---|
| (io) avrò mangiato | *I will have eaten* |
| (tu) avrai mangiato | *you (familiar singular) will have eaten* |
| (lui/lei/Lei) avrà mangiato | *he/she/you (polite singular) will have eaten* |
| (noi) avremo mangiato | *we will have eaten* |
| (voi) avrete mangiato | *you (familiar plural) will have eaten* |
| (loro/Loro) avranno mangiato | *they/you (polite plural) will have eaten* |

**partire** *to leave*

| | |
|---|---|
| (io) sarò partito(-a) | *I will have left* |
| (tu) sarai partito(-a) | *you (familiar singular) will have left* |
| (lui/lei/Lei) sarà partito(-a) | *he/she/you (polite singular) will have left* |
| (noi) saremo partiti(-e) | *we will have left* |
| (voi) sarete partiti(-e) | *you (familiar plural) will have left* |
| (loro) saranno partiti(-e) | *they/you (polite plural) will have left* |

## Uses

In general, the Italian future perfect corresponds to its English counter-part. It indicates actions that will have occurred before simple future actions.

| | |
|---|---|
| Andremo al cinema, dopo che avrai finito di lavorare. | *We will go to the movies after you (will) have finished working.* |

In conversational Italian, however, the simple future can often be used instead.

| | |
|---|---|
| Andremo al cinema, appena finirai di lavorare. | *We will go to the movies as soon as you finish working.* |

**AVOID THE** *Blunder*

✗ Usciremo dopo che finisci di lavorare.
✗ Andremo al cinema, dopo che finisci di lavorare.

Like the simple future, the future perfect can also be used to express probability.

| | |
|---|---|
| Quanto sarà costata quella macchina? | *How much did that car probably cost?* |
| Sarà costata molto. | *It must have cost a lot.* |
| A che ora ha telefonato? | *At what time did he phone?* |
| Avrà telefonato alle sei. | *He must have phoned at six.* |

**AVOID THE** *Blunder*

✗ Quanto è costata probabilmente quella macchina?
✗ Quella macchina è costata probabilmente molto.

## Exercises

**A** *For each present tense form, write the corresponding future and future perfect forms.*

| | SIMPLE FUTURE | FUTURE PERFECT |
|---|---|---|
| 1. io arrivo | | |
| 2. io vendo | | |
| 3. io preferisco | | |
| 4. io vado | | |
| 5. io ho | | |
| 6. tu mangi | | |
| 7. tu metti | | |
| 8. tu apri | | |
| 9. tu bevi | | |
| 10. tu cadi | | |
| 11. lui comincia | | |
| 12. lei chiede | | |
| 13. lui capisce | | |
| 14. Lei dà | | |
| 15. lei è | | |
| 16. noi paghiamo | | |
| 17. noi chiudiamo | | |
| 18. noi finiamo | | |
| 19. noi facciamo | | |
| 20. noi possiamo | | |
| 21. voi cercate | | |
| 22. voi mettete | | |
| 23. voi preferite | | |
| 24. voi sapete | | |
| 25. voi tenete | | |
| 26. loro mangiano | | |
| 27. loro chiedono | | |
| 28. loro preferiscono | | |

29. loro vedono _____   _____

30. loro vengono _____   _____


**B** *Express the following English sentences in Italian.*

1. *I am going to send an e-mail to my brother tomorrow.*

   _____

2. *They will be going to Italy in a month.*

   _____

3. *That car must have cost a lot, don't you think?*

   _____

4. *Who can that (possibly) be?*

   _____

5. *We will be going to the movies after we have finished studying.*

   _____

6. *How much did that car probably cost?*

   _____

7. *It must have cost a lot.*

   _____

# VERBS
## the conditional tenses

The conditional mood basically expresses a condition: *I would go if . . . , We would do it, but. . . .*

| | |
|---|---|
| Uscirei oggi, ma devo studiare. | *I would go out today, but I have to study.* |
| Vorrei andare in Italia, ma non ho soldi. | *I would like to go to Italy, but I do not have the money.* |

## The Simple Conditional
### Conjugation
The simple conditional is formed like the simple future: The final *-e* of the infinitive in all three conjugations is dropped, the *-ar* of first-conjugation verbs is changed to *-er,* and these endings are added: *-ei, -esti, -ebbe, -emmo, -este, -ebbero.*

**parlare** *to speak*

| | |
|---|---|
| (io) parlerei | *I would speak* |
| (tu) parleresti | *you* (familiar singular) *would speak* |
| (lui/lei/Lei) parlerebbe | *he/she/you* (polite singular) *would speak* |
| (noi) parleremmo | *we would speak* |
| (voi) parlereste | *you* (familiar plural) *would speak* |
| (loro/Loro) parlerebbero | *they/you* (polite plural) *would speak* |

AVOID THE *Blunder*

✗ io parlarei
✗ loro arrivarebbero

## scrivere *to write*

| | |
|---|---|
| (io) scriverei | *I would write* |
| (tu) scriveresti | *you* (familiar singular) *would write* |
| (lui/lei/Lei) scriverebbe | *he/she/you* (polite singular) *would write* |
| (noi) scriveremmo | *we would write* |
| (voi) scrivereste | *you* (familiar plural) *would write* |
| (loro/Loro) scriverebbero | *they/you* (polite plural) *would write* |

AVOID THE *Blunder*

✗ io scrivrei
✗ lui scrivebbe

## finire *to finish*

| | |
|---|---|
| (io) finirei | *I would finish* |
| (tu) finiresti | *you* (familiar singular) *would finish* |
| (lui/lei/Lei) finirebbe | *he/she/you* (polite singular) *would finish* |
| (noi) finiremmo | *we would finish* |
| (voi) finireste | *you* (familiar plural) *would finish* |
| (loro/Loro) finirebbero | *they/you* (polite plural) *would finish* |

AVOID THE *Blunder*

✗ io finerei
✗ loro finebbero

As in the case of the simple future, to indicate that the hard /c/ and /g/ sounds of verbs ending in *-care* and *-gare* are to be retained, the following spelling adjustments are made.

| INFINITIVE | CONDITIONAL STEM |
|---|---|
| cercare *to search (for)* | cercher- |
| pagare *to pay* | pagher- |

| | |
|---|---|
| (io) cercherei | *I would search* |
| (tu) cercheresti | *you* (familiar singular) *would search* |
| (lui/lei/Lei) cercherebbe | *he/she/you* (polite singular) *would search* |
| (noi) cercheremmo | *we would search* |
| (voi) cerchereste | *you* (familiar plural) *would search* |
| (loro/Loro) cercherebbero | *they/you* (polite plural) *would search* |

| | |
|---|---|
| (io) pagherei | *I would pay* |
| (tu) pagheresti | *you* (familiar singular) *would pay* |
| (lui/lei/Lei) pagherebbe | *he/she/you* (polite singular) *would pay* |

| (noi) pagheremmo | *we would pay* |
|---|---|
| (voi) paghereste | *you* (familiar plural) *would pay* |
| (loro/Loro) pagherebbero | *they/you* (polite plural) *would pay* |

AVOID THE *Blunder*

✗ io cercarei
✗ loro pagarebbero

And as in the case of the simple future, the *-i* of verbs ending in *-ciare* or *-giare* is not retained in the conjugation of the conditional tense.

| INFINITIVE | CONDITIONAL STEM |
|---|---|
| cominciare *to begin* | comincer- |
| mangiare *to eat* | manger- |

| (io) comincerei | *I would begin* |
|---|---|
| (tu) cominceresti | *you* (familiar singular) *would begin* |
| (lui/lei/Lei) comincerebbe | *he/she/you* (polite singular) *would begin* |
| (noi) cominceremmo | *we would begin* |
| (voi) comincereste | *you* (familiar plural) *would begin* |
| (loro/Loro) comincerebbero | *they/you* (polite plural) *would begin* |

| (io) mangerei | *I would eat* |
|---|---|
| (tu) mangeresti | *you* (familiar singular) *would eat* |
| (lui/lei/Lei) mangerebbe | *he/she/you* (polite singular) *would eat* |
| (noi) mangeremmo | *we would eat* |
| (voi) mangereste | *you* (familiar plural) *would eat* |
| (loro/Loro) mangerebbero | *they/you* (polite plural) *would eat* |

AVOID THE *Blunder*

✗ io comincierei
✗ loro mangiarebbero

The very same verbs that are irregular in the future are also irregular in the conditional, and in the same way. For example, to conjugation *andare* in the irregular future and conditional tenses, both vowels are dropped from the infinitive ending, and then the appropriate endings are added. In other words, the verb stem is the same, but the endings are different. The following chart compares future and conditional forms.

| FUTURE | | CONDITIONAL | |
|---|---|---|---|
| io andrò | *I will go* | io andrei | *I would go* |
| noi saremo | *we will be* | noi saremmo | *we would be* |
| lui potrà | *he will be able to* | lui potrebbe | *he would be able to* |
| loro verranno | *they will come* | loro verrebbero | *they would come* |

AVOID THE *Blunder*

✗ io andarei
✗ loro venirebbero

## Uses

In general, the Italian conditional tense corresponds to its English counter-part—*I would go, you would write*, etc.

| | |
|---|---|
| Pagherei il conto, ma non ho soldi. | *I would pay the bill, but I have no money.* |
| Comprerebbe la macchina, ma non ha ancora la patente. | *He would buy the car, but he doesn't yet have a license.* |

It is also used in the following cases:

- To make a polite request

| | |
|---|---|
| Potrei parlare? | *May I speak?* |
| Mi darebbe la sua penna? | *Could you give me your pen?* |

- To indicate that something is an opinion rather than a fact

| | |
|---|---|
| Secondo lui, quella ragazza sarebbe intelligente. | *According to him, that girl must be / is intelligent.* |
| Nella loro opinione, l'Italia sarebbe il miglior paese del mondo. | *In their opinion, Italy is the best country in the world.* |

AVOID THE *Blunder*

✗ Pago il conto, ma non ho abbastanza soldi.
✗ Posso dire qualcosa (**something**)?
✗ Secondo mio fratello, l'Italia è un bel paese.
✗ Nella sua opinione, gli italiani sono tutti simpatici.

# The Conditional Perfect

## Conjugation

The conditional perfect is a compound tense, formed with the simple conditional of the auxiliary verb plus the past participle of the verb, in that order. Following are complete conjugations of two verbs in the conditional perfect tense, one verb conjugated with *avere* and the other with *essere*.

### mangiare *to eat*

| | |
|---|---|
| (io) avrei mangiato | *I would have eaten* |
| (tu) avresti mangiato | *you* (familiar singular) *would have eaten* |
| (lui/lei/Lei) avrebbe mangiato | *he/she/you* (polite singular) *would have eaten* |
| (noi) avremmo mangiato | *we would have eaten* |
| (voi) avreste mangiato | *you* (familiar plural) *would have eaten* |
| (loro/Loro) avrebbero mangiato | *they/you* (polite plural) *would have eaten* |

AVOID THE *Blunder*

✗ io averei mangiato
✗ loro averebbero mangiato

### partire *to leave*

| | |
|---|---|
| (io) sarei partito(-a) | *I would have left* |
| (tu) saresti partito(-a) | *you* (familiar singular) *would have left* |
| (lui/lei/Lei) sarebbe partito(-a) | *he/she/you* (polite singular) *would have left* |
| (noi) saremmo partiti(-e) | *we would have left* |
| (voi) sareste partiti(-e) | *you* (familiar plural) *would have left* |
| (loro/Loro) sarebbero partiti(-e) | *they/you* (polite plural) *would have left* |

AVOID THE *Blunder*

✗ io avrei partito
✗ loro serebbero andati

## Uses

In general, the Italian conditional perfect corresponds to the English past conditional—*I would have* . . . , *you would have* . . . , etc. It indicates conditional (hypothetical) actions that can only be logically expressed in a perfect tense, as shown in the following examples.

| | |
|---|---|
| Mi ha detto che sarebbe venuto. | *He told me that he would / would have come.* |
| Sapeva che io avrei capito. | *He knew that I would have understood.* |
| Avrei voluto comprare quella macchina, ma non avevo soldi. | *I would have wanted to buy that car, but I didn't have the money.* |

AVOID THE *Blunder*

✗ Mi ha detto che avrà chiamato.
✗ Secondo mio fratello, noi abbiamo dovuto studiare di più.

Like the simple conditional, the conditional perfect tense is also used to indicate that something was an opinion rather than a fact.

| | |
|---|---|
| Secondo lui, quella ragazza avrebbe dovuto studiare di più. | *According to him, that girl should have studied more.* |
| Nella loro opinione, l'Italia avrebbe dovuto vincere. | *In their opinion, Italy should have won.* |

# Exercises

**A** *For each future tense form, write the corresponding conditional and conditional perfect forms.*

|  | SIMPLE CONDITIONAL | CONDITIONAL PERFECT |
|---|---|---|
| 1. io arriverò | | |
| 2. io venderò | | |
| 3. io preferirò | | |
| 4. io andrò | | |
| 5. io avrò | | |
| 6. tu mangerai | | |
| 7. tu metterai | | |
| 8. tu aprirai | | |
| 9. tu berrai | | |
| 10. tu cadrai | | |
| 11. lui comincerà | | |
| 12. lei chiederà | | |
| 13. lui capirà | | |
| 14. Lei darà | | |
| 15. lei sarà | | |
| 16. noi pagheremo | | |
| 17. noi chiuderemo | | |
| 18. noi finiremo | | |
| 19. noi faremo | | |
| 20. noi potremo | | |
| 21. voi cercherete | | |
| 22. voi metterete | | |
| 23. voi preferirete | | |
| 24. voi saprete | | |
| 25. voi terrete | | |
| 26. loro mangeranno | | |
| 27. loro chiederanno | | |
| 28. loro preferiranno | | |

29. loro vedranno   _____   _____
30. loro verranno   _____   _____

**B** Choose the future, future perfect, conditional, or conditional perfect form of the verb, as appropriate.

1. Lui _____ il conto, ma non ha soldi.
   a. pagherà
   b. avrà pagato
   c. pagherebbe
   d. avrebbe pagato

2. Mia sorella _____ la macchina, ma non ha ancora la patente.
   a. comprerà
   b. avrà comprato
   c. comprerebbe
   d. avrebbe comprato

3. Domani lui _____ il conto di sicuro (for sure).
   a. pagherà
   b. avrà pagato
   c. pagherebbe
   d. avrebbe pagato

4. _____ dire qualcosa, per favore?
   a. Potrò
   b. Avrò potuto
   c. Potrei
   d. Avrei potuto

5. Mi _____ la sua matita, professore?
   a. darà
   b. avrà dato
   c. darebbe
   d. avrebbe dato

6. Dopo che _____ di mangiare, usciremo.

   a. finiremo

   b. avremo finito

   c. finiremmo

   d. avremmo finito

7. Secondo lui, quella ragazza _____ italiana.

   a. sarà

   b. sarà stata

   c. sarebbe

   d. sarebbe stata

8. Quella ragazza _____ l'italiano l'anno prossimo.

   a. studierà

   b. avrà studiato

   c. studierebbe

   d. avrebbe studiato

9. Mi ha detto che sua sorella _____ alla festa, ma deve studiare.

   a. verrà

   b. sarà venuta

   c. verrebbe

   d. sarebbe venuta

10. Io sapevo che lui _____ quella macchina.

   a. comprerà

   b. avrà comprato

   c. comprerebbe

   d. avrebbe comprato

11. Anche loro _____ comprare quella macchina, ma non avevano soldi.

   a. vorranno

   b. avranno voluto

   c. vorrebbero

   d. avrebbero voluto

12. Secondo lui, quella ragazza _____ studiare di più ieri.

    a. dovrà

    b. avrà dovuto

    c. dovrebbe

    d. avrebbe dovuto

13. Quella ragazza _____ per l'esame domani.

    a. studierà

    b. avrà studiato

    c. studierebbe

    d. avrebbe studiato

14. Nella loro opinione, l'Italia _____ vincere l'anno scorso.

    a. dovrà

    b. avrà dovuto

    c. dovrebbe

    d. avrebbe dovuto

15. Nella loro opinione, l'Italia _____ vincere l'anno prossimo.

    a. dovrà

    b. avrà dovuto

    c. dovrebbe

    d. avrebbe dovuto

# VERBS
## the imperative

The imperative is used to give commands, advice, orders, instructions, and so on.

| | |
|---|---|
| Marco, mangia la pesca! | *Mark, eat the peach!* |
| Signor Verdi, legga il giornale! | *Mr. Verdi, read the newspaper!* |

## Formation

The imperative is formed by dropping the infinitive ending of the verb, then adding the following endings according to conjugation.

**FIRST-CONJUGATION ENDINGS** —, -a, -i, -iamo, -ate, -ino

aspettare  *to wait (for)*

| | |
|---|---|
| (io) — | |
| (tu) aspetta | *wait* (familiar singular) |
| (Lei) aspetti | *wait* (polite singular) |
| (noi) aspettiamo | *let's wait* |
| (voi) aspettate | *wait* (familiar plural) |
| (Loro) aspettino | *wait* (polite plural) |

AVOID THE *Blunder*

✗ Marco, aspetti!
✗ Signor Verdi, aspetta!

**SECOND-CONJUGATION ENDINGS** —, -i, -a, -iamo, -ete, -ano

chiudere  *to close*

| | |
|---|---|
| (io) — | |
| (tu) chiudi | *close* (familiar singular) |
| (Lei) chiuda | *close* (polite singular) |
| (noi) chiudiamo | *let's close* |
| (voi) chiudete | *close* (familiar plural) |
| (Loro) chiudano | *close* (polite plural) |

**171**

✗ Maria, chiuda la porta!
✗ Signora Verdi, chiudi la porta!

**THIRD-CONJUGATION ENDINGS (TYPE I)** —, -i, -a, -iamo, -ite, -ano
aprire *to open*

(io) —
(tu) apri          *open* (familiar singular)
(Lei) apra        *open* (polite singular)
(noi) apriamo    *let's open*
(voi) aprite       *open* (familiar plural)
(Loro) aprano    *open* (polite plural)

✗ Marco, apra la porta!
✗ Signor Verdi, apri la porta!

**THIRD-CONJUGATION ENDINGS (TYPE II)** —, -isci, -isca, -iamo, -ite, -iscano
finire *to finish*

(io) —
(tu) finisci         *finish* (familiar singular)
(Lei) finisca       *finish* (polite singular)
(noi) finiamo      *let's finish*
(voi) finite         *finish* (familiar plural)
(Loro) finiscano  *finish* (polite plural)

✗ Ragazzi, finiscete!
✗ Signori, finiscono!

To indicate that the hard /c/ and /g/ sounds of verbs ending in *-care* and *-gare* are to be retained, *h* must be inserted before the *-i*, *-iamo*, and *-ino* endings.

## cercare *to search (for)*

| (io) — | |
|---|---|
| (tu) cerca | *search* (familiar singular) |
| (Lei) cerchi | *search* (polite singular) |
| (noi) cerchiamo | *let's search* |
| (voi) cercate | *search* (familiar plural) |
| (Loro) cerchino | *search* (polite plural) |

## pagare *to pay*

| (io) — | |
|---|---|
| (tu) paga | *pay* (familiar singular) |
| (Lei) paghi | *pay* (polite singular) |
| (noi) paghiamo | *let's pay* |
| (voi) pagate | *pay* (familiar plural) |
| (Loro) paghino | *pay* (polite plural) |

### AVOID THE *Blunder*

✗ Marco, cerchi la penna!
✗ Signor Verdi, cerca la penna!

The *-i* of verbs ending in *-ciare* or *-giare* is dropped before the *-i, -iamo,* and *-ino* endings.

## cominciare *to begin*

| (io) — | |
|---|---|
| (tu) comincia | *begin* (familiar singular) |
| (Lei) cominci | *begin* (polite singular) |
| (noi) cominciamo | *let's begin* |
| (voi) cominciate | *begin* (familiar plural) |
| (Loro) comincino | *begin* (polite plural) |

## mangiare *to eat*

| (io) — | |
|---|---|
| (tu) mangia | *eat* (familiar singular) |
| (Lei) mangi | *eat* (polite singular) |
| (noi) mangiamo | *let's eat* |
| (voi) mangiate | *eat* (familiar plural) |
| (Loro) mangino | *eat* (polite plural) |

## The Negative Imperative

To form the negative imperative, *non* is added before the verb in the usual way. However, an adjustment is required in this case—the second-person singular imperative form must be changed to the infinitive. This, of course, is a frequent source of blunders.

| AFFIRMATIVE | | NEGATIVE | |
|---|---|---|---|
| Aspetta! | *Wait!* | Non aspettare! | *Don't wait!* |
| Scrivi! | *Write!* | Non scrivere! | *Don't write!* |
| Finisci! | *Finish!* | Non finire! | *Don't finish!* |

**OTHER NEGATIVE IMPERATIVE FORMS**

| | | | |
|---|---|---|---|
| Aspetti! | *Wait!* (polite singular) | Non aspetti! | *Don't wait!* |
| Scriviamo! | *Let's write!* | Non scriviamo! | *Let's not write!* |
| Finite! | *Finish!* (familiar plural) | Non finite! | *Don't finish!* |
| Aspettino! | *Wait!* (polite plural) | Non aspettino! | *Don't wait!* |

## Irregular Forms

Irregular imperative forms are the source of many blunders. Following are the most irregular verbs in the imperative.

**andare** *to go*

(tu) va', (Lei) vada, (noi) andiamo, (voi) andate, (Loro) vadano

**avere** *to have*

(tu) abbi, (Lei) abbia, (noi) abbiamo, (voi) abbiate, (Loro) abbiano

**bere** *to drink*

(tu) bevi, (Lei) beva, (noi) beviamo, (voi) bevete, (Loro) bevano

**dare** *to give*

(tu) da', (Lei) dia, (noi) diamo, (voi) date, (Loro) diano

**dire** *to say, tell*

(tu) di', (Lei) dica, (noi) diciamo, (voi) dite, (Loro) dicano

**essere** *to be*

(tu) sii, (Lei) sia, (noi) siamo, (voi) siate, (Loro) siano

**fare** *to do, make*

(tu) fa', (Lei) faccia, (noi) facciamo, (voi) fate, (Loro) facciano

**salire** *to go up, climb*

(tu) sali, (Lei) salga, (noi) saliamo, (voi) salite, (Loro) salgano

**sapere** *to know*

(tu) sappi, (Lei) sappia, (noi) sappiamo, (voi) sappiate, (Loro) sappiano

**scegliere** *to choose, select*

(tu) scegli, (Lei) scelga, (noi) scegliamo, (voi) scegliete, (Loro) scelgano

**stare** *to stay*

(tu) sta', (Lei) stia, (noi) stiamo, (voi) state, (Loro) stiano

**tenere** *to hold, keep*

(tu) tieni, (Lei) tenga, (noi) teniamo, (voi) tenete, (Loro) tengano

**uscire** *to go out*

(tu) esci, (Lei) esca, (noi) usciamo, (voi) uscite, (Loro) escano

**venire** *to come*

(tu) vieni, (Lei) venga, (noi) veniamo, (voi) venite, (Loro) vengano

AVOID THE *Blunder*

✗ vadi
✗ dicete
✗ siete
✗ facci
✗ sapi
✗ usci
✗ veni

## Uses

As in English, the imperative is used to issue commands, give orders, make requests, and so on.

| | |
|---|---|
| Marco, aspetta qui! | *Mark, wait here!* |
| Signora Verdi, scriva il Suo nome qui! | *Mrs. Verdi, write your name here!* |
| Studenti, aprite i vostri libri! | *Students, open your books!* |
| Signora Verdi e Signor Rossi, aspettino qui! | *Mrs. Verdi and Mr. Rossi, wait here!* |
| Signor Dini, cerchi i Suoi occhiali! | *Mr. Dini, look for your glasses!* |
| Paghiamo il conto. | *Let's pay the bill.* |
| E ora, mangiamo! | *And now, let's eat!* |

Pay close attention to the differences between the familiar and polite forms. This area is a frequent source of blunders.

### FAMILIAR SINGULAR (tu FORMS)

| | |
|---|---|
| Maria, mangia la mela! | *Mary, eat the apple!* |
| Alessandro, finisci di studiare! | *Alexander, finish studying!* |

### FAMILIAR PLURAL (voi FORMS)

| | |
|---|---|
| Marco e Maria, mangiate la mela! | *Mark and Mary, eat the apple!* |
| Alessandro e Sara, finite di studiare! | *Alexander and Sarah, finish studying!* |

### POLITE SINGULAR (Lei FORMS)

| | |
|---|---|
| Signora Verdi, mangi la mela! | *Mrs. Verdi, eat the apple!* |
| Signor Rossi, finisca di studiare! | *Mr. Rossi, finish studying!* |

### POLITE PLURAL (Loro FORMS)

| | |
|---|---|
| Signora Verdi e Signor Rossi, mangino la mela! | *Mrs. Verdi and Mr. Rossi, eat the apple!* |
| Signora Verdi e Signor Rossi, finiscano di studiare! | *Mrs. Verdi and Mr. Rossi, finish studying!* |

AVOID THE *Blunder*

✗ Maria, mangi la pesca!
✗ Signor Rossi, apri la porta!
✗ Ragazzi, chiudano la porta!
✗ Signori, chiudete la porta!

## Exercises

**A** Complete the following chart by rewriting the commands, substituting the polite equivalent for the familiar imperative form and the familiar equivalent for the polite imperative form.

| FAMILIAR | POLITE |
|---|---|
| 1. Mangia la mela! | _____ |
| 2. _____ | Cominci a mangiare! |
| 3. Aspetta qui! | _____ |
| 4. _____ | Apra la porta! |
| 5. Finisci la mela! | _____ |
| 6. _____ | Cerchi la chiave! |
| 7. Paga il conto! | _____ |
| 8. _____ | Scriva l'email! |
| 9. Chiudi la porta! | _____ |
| 10. _____ | Dorma! |
| 11. Aprite le porte! | _____ |
| 12. _____ | Chiudano le porte! |
| 13. Finite di studiare! | _____ |
| 14. _____ | Abbia pazienza! |
| 15. Va' a dormire! | _____ |

**B** Complete the following chart by rewriting the commands, substituting the negative equivalent for the affirmative imperative form and the affirmative equivalent for the negative imperative form.

| AFFIRMATIVE | NEGATIVE |
|---|---|
| 1. Mangia la pesca! | _____ |
| 2. _____ | Non guardi la televisione! |
| 3. Finiamo di mangiare! | _____ |
| 4. _____ | Non chiudere la porta! |
| 5. Bevi tutta l'acqua! | _____ |
| 6. _____ | Non dica questo! |
| 7. Usciamo stasera! | _____ |

**C** *Issue the following commands in Italian.*

Tell Mary to . . .

1. *eat the apple*

   _____

2. *not drink the water*

   _____

3. *close the door*

   _____

4. *open the door*

   _____

Now, tell both Mary and Mark to . . .

5. *eat the apple*

   _____

6. *not drink the water*

   _____

7. *close the door*

   _____

8. *open the door*

   _____

Now, tell Mrs. Verdi to . . .

9. *eat the apple*

   _____

10. *not drink the water*

   _____

11. *close the door*

   _____

12. *open the door*

   _____

Finally, tell both Mrs. Verdi and Mr. Rossi to . . .

13. *eat the apple*

   _____

14. *not drink the water*

    _____

15. *close the door*

    _____

16. *open the door*

    _____

# VERBS
## the present subjunctive

The subjunctive mood is used to express a point of view, fear, doubt, hope, possibility—that is, anything that is not a fact. The subjunctive is, thus, a counterpoint to the indicative, which is the mood that is used to convey facts and information.

## Conjugation

The present subjunctive is formed by dropping the infinitive ending of the verb, then adding the following endings according to conjugation.

**FIRST-CONJUGATION ENDINGS** -i, -i, -i, -iamo, -iate, -ino
aspettare *to wait (for)*

| | |
|---|---|
| (io) aspetti | *I wait* |
| (tu) aspetti | *you wait* (familiar singular) |
| (lui/lei/Lei) aspetti | *he/she waits / you* (polite singular) *wait* |
| (noi) aspettiamo | *we wait* |
| (voi) aspettiate | *you* (familiar plural) *wait* |
| (loro/Loro) aspettino | *they/you* (polite plural) *wait* |

AVOID THE *Blunder*

✗ lui aspetta
✗ loro aspettano

**SECOND-CONJUGATION ENDINGS** -a, -a, -a, -iamo, -iate, -ano
chiudere *to close*

| | |
|---|---|
| (io) chiuda | *I close* |
| (tu) chiuda | *you* (familiar singular) *close* |
| (lui/lei/Lei) chiuda | *he/she closes / you* (polite singular) *close* |
| (noi) chiudiamo | *we close* |
| (voi) chiudiate | *you* (familiar plural) *close* |
| (loro/Loro) chiudano | *they/you* (polite plural) *close* |

**THIRD-CONJUGATION ENDINGS (TYPE I)** -a, -a, -a, -iamo, -iate, -ano
aprire *to open*

| | |
|---|---|
| (io) apra | *I open* |
| (tu) apra | *you* (familiar singular) *open* |
| (lui/lei/Lei) apra | *he/she opens / you* (polite singular) *open* |
| (noi) apriamo | *we open* |
| (voi) apriate | *you* (familiar plural) *open* |
| (loro/Loro) aprano | *they/you* (polite plural) *open* |

**THIRD-CONJUGATION ENDINGS (TYPE II)** -isca, -isca, -isca,
-iamo, -iate, -iscano
finire *to finish*

| | |
|---|---|
| (io) finisca | *I finish* |
| (tu) finisca | *you* (familiar singular) *finish* |
| (lui/lei/Lei) finisca | *he/she finishes / you* (polite singular) *finish* |
| (noi) finiamo | *we finish* |
| (voi) finiate | *you* (familiar plural) *finish* |
| (loro/Loro) finiscano | *they/you* (polite plural) *finish* |

To indicate that the hard /c/ and /g/ sounds of verbs ending in -*care*
and -*gare* are to be retained, *h* is inserted before all the endings.

## cercare *to search (for)*

| | |
|---|---|
| (io) cerchi | *I search* |
| (tu) cerchi | *you* (familiar singular) *search* |
| (lui/lei/Lei) cerchi | *he/she searches / you* (polite singular) *search* |
| (noi) cerchiamo | *we search* |
| (voi) cerchiate | *you* (familiar plural) *search* |
| (loro/Loro) cerchino | *they/you* (polite plural) *search* |

## pagare *to pay*

| | |
|---|---|
| (io) paghi | *I pay* |
| (tu) paghi | *you* (familiar singular) *pay* |
| (lui/lei/Lei) paghi | *he/she pays / you* (polite singular) *pay* |
| (noi) paghiamo | *we pay* |
| (voi) paghiate | *you* (familiar plural) *pay* |
| (loro/Loro) paghino | *they/you* (polite plural) *pay* |

AVOID THE *Blunder*

✗ lui cerca
✗ loro pagano

The *-i* of verbs ending in *-ciare* or *-giare* is dropped before all the endings.

## cominciare *to begin*

| | |
|---|---|
| (io) cominci | *I begin* |
| (tu) cominci | *you* (familiar singular) *begin* |
| (lui/lei/Lei) cominci | *he/she begins / you* (polite singular) *begin* |
| (noi) cominciamo | *we begin* |
| (voi) cominciate | *you* (familiar plural) *begin* |
| (loro/Loro) comincino | *they/you* (polite plural) *begin* |

## mangiare *to eat*

| | |
|---|---|
| (io) mangi | *I eat* |
| (tu) mangi | *you* (familiar singular) *eat* |
| (lui/lei/Lei) mangi | *he/she eats / you* (polite singular) *eat* |
| (noi) mangiamo | *we eat* |
| (voi) mangiate | *you* (familiar plural) *eat* |
| (loro/Loro) mangino | *they/you* (polite plural) *eat* |

Because the singular endings of the present subjunctive are the same within a conjugation, subject pronouns are used much more frequently with this tense.

| | |
|---|---|
| È necessario che tu finisca quel lavoro. | *It is necessary that you finish that job.* |
| È necessario che lui finisca quel lavoro. | *It is necessary that he finish that job.* |

## Irregular Forms

Verbs that are irregular in the present indicative are also irregular in the present subjunctive. The following verbs are irregular in the present subjunctive and are a constant source of blunders.

### andare *to go*

(io) vada, (tu) vada, (lui/lei/Lei) vada,
(noi) andiamo, (voi) andiate, (loro/Loro) vadano

### avere *to have*

(io) abbia, (tu) abbia, (lui/lei/Lei) abbia,
(noi) abbiamo, (voi) abbiate, (loro/Loro) abbiano

### bere *to drink*

(io) beva, (tu) beva, (lui/lei/Lei) beva,
(noi) beviamo, (voi) beviate, (loro/Loro) bevano

### dare *to give*

(io) dia, (tu) dia, (lui/lei/Lei) dia,
(noi) diamo, (voi) diate, (loro/Loro) diano

### dire *to say, tell*

(io) dica, (tu) dica, (lui/lei/Lei) dica,
(noi) diciamo, (voi) diciate, (loro/Loro) dicano

### dovere *to have to, must*

(io) deva/debba, (tu) deva/debba, (lui/lei/Lei) deva/debba,
(noi) dobbiamo, (voi) dobbiate, (loro/Loro) devano/debbano

**essere** *to be*

(io) sia, (tu) sia, (lui/lei/Lei) sia,
(noi) siamo, (voi) siate, (loro/Loro) siano

**fare** *to do, make*

(io) faccia, (tu) faccia, (lui/lei/Lei) faccia,
(noi) facciamo, (voi) facciate, (loro/Loro) facciano

**morire** *to die*

(io) muoia, (tu) muoia, (lui/lei/Lei) muoia,
(noi) moriamo, (voi) moriate, (loro/Loro) muoiano

**potere** *to be able to, can*

(io) possa, (tu) possa, (lui/lei/Lei) possa,
(noi) possiamo, (voi) possiate, (loro/Loro) possano

**salire** *to go up, climb*

(io) salga, (tu) salga, (lui/lei/Lei) salga,
(noi) saliamo, (voi) saliate, (loro/Loro) salgano

**sapere** *to know*

(io) sappia, (tu) sappia, (lui/lei/Lei) sappia,
(noi) sappiamo, (voi) sappiate, (loro/Loro) sappiano

**scegliere** *to choose, select*

(io) scelga, (tu) scelga, (lui/lei/Lei) scelga,
(noi) scegliamo, (voi) scegliate, (loro/Loro) scelgano

**stare** *to stay*

(io) stia, (tu) stia, (lui/lei/Lei) stia,
(noi) stiamo, (voi) stiate, (loro/Loro) stiano

**tenere** *to hold, keep*

(io) tenga, (tu) tenga, (lui/lei/Lei) tenga,
(noi) teniamo, (voi) teniate, (loro/Loro) tengano

**uscire** *to go out*

(io) esca, (tu) esca, (lui/lei/Lei) esca,
(noi) usciamo, (voi) usciate, (loro/Loro) escano

**venire** *to come*

(io) venga, (tu) venga, (lui/lei/Lei) venga,
(noi) veniamo, (voi) veniate, (loro/Loro) vengano

## volere *to want*

(io) voglia, (tu) voglia, (lui/lei/Lei) voglia,
(noi) vogliamo, (voi) vogliate, (loro/Loro) vogliano

---

AVOID THE *Blunder*

| | |
|---|---|
| ✗ tu vadi | ✗ tu sei **(as subjunctive)** |
| ✗ tu abbi | ✗ tu facci |
| ✗ tu bevi | ✗ tu possi |
| ✗ tu dai | ✗ tu sappi |
| ✗ tu dici | ✗ tu veni |
| ✗ tu devi | ✗ tu voli |

---

## Main Uses

The subjunctive is used mainly in subordinate clauses introduced by *che* "that/which." When a verb in the main clause (the verb preceding *che*) expresses doubt, an opinion, etc., the verb in the subordinate clause (the verb following *che*) must be in the subjunctive.

| | |
|---|---|
| Spero che loro parlino italiano. | *I hope that they speak Italian.* |
| Penso che lui cominci a lavorare alle nove. | *I think that he starts working at nine.* |
| Crede che loro arrivino domani. | *He believes (that) they are arriving tomorrow.* |
| Immagino che lei capisca tutto. | *I imagine (that) she understands everything.* |
| Dubitiamo che voi finiate in tempo. | *We doubt that you will finish in time.* |

---

AVOID THE *Blunder*

✗ Spero che lui parla italiano.
✗ Credo che loro arrivano domani.

---

Not all verbs in subordinate clauses must be subjunctive—only those connected to a main clause whose verb expresses a nonfact (opinion, fear, supposition, anticipation, wish, hope, doubt, etc.).

**INDICATIVE**

| | |
|---|---|
| Sa che è vero. | *He knows it is true.* |
| È certo che paga lui. | *It is certain that he will pay.* |

## SUBJUNCTIVE

Pensa che sia vero.       *He thinks it is true.*
È improbabile che paghi lui.       *It is improbable that he will pay.*

Note that *che* is always used in Italian, whereas "that" is often omitted in English. This is a frequent source of blunders.

AVOID THE *Blunder*

✗ Penso lui parla italiano.
✗ Spero loro arrivano domani.

Following is a list of common main-clause verbs that require the use of the subjunctive in subordinate clauses.

| | | | |
|---|---|---|---|
| credere | *to believe* | pensare | *to think* |
| desiderare | *to desire* | sembrare | *to seem* |
| dubitare | *to doubt* | sperare | *to hope* |
| immaginare | *to imagine* | volere | *to want* |

AVOID THE *Blunder*

✗ Dubito che lei parla italiano.
✗ Immagino che chiudono alle sei.

## Other Uses

Impersonal verbs and expressions, which have only third-person forms, also require that the subordinate-clause verb be in the subjunctive.

È probabile che lui non venga       *It is probable that he will not*
   alla festa.                    *come to the party.*
Bisogna che loro studino di più.       *It is necessary that they study*
                                     *more.*

AVOID THE *Blunder*

✗ Spero che lui arriva domani.
✗ Credo che loro partono domani.

Superlative expressions also require that the verb in the subordinate clause be in the subjunctive.

| | |
|---|---|
| Lei è la persona più intelligente che io conosca. | *She is the most intelligent person I know.* |
| Tu sei la persona più elegante che io conosca. | *You are the most elegant person I know.* |

AVOID THE *Blunder*

✗ Alessandro è la persona più intelligente che io conosco.
✗ Lei è la persona più elegante che loro conoscono.

Certain conjunctions and indefinite constructions also require a subjunctive verb in the clauses they introduce.

| | |
|---|---|
| Dovunque tu vada, io ti seguirò. | *Wherever you go, I will follow you.* |
| Benché piova, esco lo stesso. | *Although it is raining, I'm going out just the same.* |

The most common of these conjunctions are the following.

| | |
|---|---|
| a meno che | *unless* |
| affinché | *so that* |
| benché | *although* |
| chiunque | *whoever* |
| come se | *as if* |
| dovunque | *wherever* |
| nel caso che | *in the event that* |
| nonostante che | *despite* |
| prima che | *before* |
| purché | *provided that* |
| sebbene | *although* |
| senza che | *without* |

AVOID THE *Blunder*

✗ Benché piove, esco lo stesso.
✗ Vengo alla festa, purché vieni anche lei.

Finally, the subjunctive is used in wishes.

| | |
|---|---|
| Che piova se vuole! | *Let it rain if it wants to!* |
| Che Dio ce la mandi buona! | *May God help us!* |

AVOID THE *Blunder*

✗ Che piovi se vuole!
✗ Che Dio ci aiuta!

## Exercises

**A** *Write the present subjunctive form of the verb according to the pronoun in parentheses.*

ESEMPIO   (io) cantare   _io canti_____

1. (io) leggere   _____
2. (io) capire   _____
3. (io) bere   _____
4. (tu) mangiare   _____
5. (tu) vedere   _____
6. (tu) dormire   _____
7. (tu) essere   _____
8. (lui) cominciare   _____
9. (lei) avere   _____
10. (lui) fare   _____
11. (lei) dire   _____
12. (noi) pagare   _____
13. (noi) sapere   _____
14. (noi) dare   _____
15. (voi) mangiare   _____
16. (voi) potere   _____
17. (voi) uscire   _____
18. (voi) essere   _____
19. (loro) arrivare   _____
20. (loro) avere   _____
21. (loro) venire   _____
22. (loro) capire   _____
23. (loro) chiudere   _____

**B** *Choose the present indicative or present subjunctive form of the verb, as appropriate.*

1. Immaginiamo che loro _____ domani.

   a. arrivano

   b. arrivino

2. Penso che loro _____ di lavorare alle sei.

   a. finiscono

   b. finiscano

3. Pensiamo che loro _____ domani per l'Italia.

   a. partono

   b. partano

4. È probabile che lei non _____ l'italiano.

   a. capisce

   b. capisca

5. Dubitiamo che voi _____ prima delle sei.

   a. uscite

   b. usciate

6. Io so che lui _____ una brava persona.

   a. è

   b. sia

7. È certo che _____ anche lui alla festa.

   a. viene

   b. venga

8. È probabile che lui non _____ dov'è la festa.

   a. sa

   b. sappia

9. Bisogna che loro _____ di più.

   a. lavorano

   b. lavorino

10. Lui è il professore più intelligente che io _____.

    a. conosco

    b. conosca

11. Tu sei la persona più simpatica che _____ in quella città.

   a. vive

   b. viva

12. Dovunque tu _____, io ti seguirò.

   a. vai

   b. vada

13. Benché _____, lui vuole uscire lo stesso.

   a. piove

   b. piova

14. Che _____ se vuole!

   a. piove

   b. piova

# VERBS
## other subjunctive tenses

Three subjunctive tenses are used to express past actions: the past, imperfect, and pluperfect.

| | |
|---|---|
| Penso che lui abbia già mangiato. | *I think he has already eaten.* |
| Pensavo che mangiasse quando l'ho chiamato ieri. | *I thought he was eating when I called him yesterday.* |
| Pensavo che lui avesse già mangiato. | *I thought he had already eaten.* |

## The Past Subjunctive
### Conjugation

Like the present perfect indicative, the past subjunctive is a compound tense. It is formed with the present subjunctive of the auxiliary verb plus the past participle of the verb, in that order. Following are complete conjugations of two verbs in the past subjunctive tense, one verb conjugated with *avere* and the other with *essere*.

**parlare** *to speak*

| | |
|---|---|
| (io) abbia parlato | *I have spoken, I spoke* |
| (tu) abbia parlato | *you* (familiar singular) *have spoken, you spoke* |
| (lui/lei/Lei) abbia parlato | *he/she has / you* (polite singular) *have spoken, he/she/you spoke* |
| (noi) abbiamo parlato | *we have spoken, we spoke* |
| (voi) abbiate parlato | *you* (familiar plural) *have spoken, you spoke* |
| (loro/Loro) abbiano parlato | *they/you* (polite plural) *have spoken, they/you spoke* |

AVOID THE *Blunder*

✗ tu abbi parlato
✗ voi aviate parlato

## arrivare *to arrive*

| | |
|---|---|
| (io) sia arrivato(-a) | *I have arrived, I arrived* |
| (tu) sia arrivato(-a) | *you* (familiar singular) *have arrived, you arrived* |
| (lui/lei/Lei) sia arrivato(-a) | *he/she has / you* (polite singular) *have arrived, he/she/you arrived* |
| (noi) siamo arrivati(-e) | *we have arrived, we arrived* |
| (voi) siate arrivati(-e) | *you* (familiar plural) *have arrived, you arrived* |
| (loro/Loro) siano arrivati(-e) | *they/you* (polite plural) *have arrived, they/you arrived* |

AVOID THE *Blunder*

✗ tu sei arrivato (**as subjunctive**)
✗ voi siete arrivati (**as subjunctive**)

## Uses

The Italian past subjunctive corresponds to the present perfect. Essentially, it expresses a past action with respect to the main-clause verb.

| | |
|---|---|
| Non credo che lui abbia capito. | *I don't believe he understood.* |
| Non è possibile che loro siano già partiti. | *It's not possible that they have already left.* |
| Benché abbia piovuto ieri, è uscito lo stesso. | *Although it rained yesterday, he went out just the same.* |

AVOID THE *Blunder*

✗ Penso che lui mangi già.
✗ Sebbene piova ieri, noi siamo andati al cinema lo stesso.

# The Imperfect Subjunctive
## Conjugation
The imperfect subjunctive is formed by dropping the infinitive ending, then adding the following endings according to conjugation.

**FIRST-CONJUGATION ENDINGS** -assi, -assi, -asse, -assimo, -aste, -assero
parlare *to speak*

| | |
|---|---|
| (io) parlassi | *I was speaking, I used to speak* |
| (tu) parlassi | *you (familiar singular) were speaking, you used to speak* |
| (lui/lei/Lei) parlasse | *he/she was / you (polite singular) were speaking, he/she/you used to speak* |
| (noi) parlassimo | *we were speaking, we used to speak* |
| (voi) parlaste | *you (familiar plural) were speaking, you used to speak* |
| (loro/Loro) parlassero | *they/you (polite plural) were speaking, they/you used to speak* |

AVOID THE *Blunder*

✗ voi parlasse
✗ loro parlasseno

**SECOND-CONJUGATION ENDINGS** -essi, -essi, -esse, -essimo, -este, -essero
scrivere *to write*

| | |
|---|---|
| (io) scrivessi | *I was writing, I used to write* |
| (tu) scrivessi | *you (familiar singular) were writing, you used to write* |
| (lui/lei/Lei) scrivesse | *he/she was / you (polite singular) were writing, he/she/you used to write* |
| (noi) scrivessimo | *we were writing, we used to write* |
| (voi) scriveste | *you (familiar plural) were writing, you used to write* |
| (loro/Loro) scrivessero | *they/you (polite plural) were writing, they/you used to write* |

AVOID THE *Blunder*

✗ voi scrivesse
✗ loro scrivesseno

**THIRD-CONJUGATION ENDINGS** -issi, -issi, -isse, -issimo, -iste, -issero
finire *to finish*

| | |
|---|---|
| (io) finissi | *I was finishing, I used to finish* |
| (tu) finissi | *you (familiar singular) were finishing, you used to finish* |
| (lui/lei/Lei) finisse | *he/she was / you (polite singular) were finishing, he/she/you used to finish* |
| (noi) finissimo | *we were finishing, we used to finish* |
| (voi) finiste | *you (familiar plural) were finishing, you used to finish* |
| (loro/Loro) finissero | *they/you (polite plural) were finishing, they/you used to finish* |

AVOID THE

✗ voi finisse
✗ loro finisseno

## Irregular Verbs

Verbs that are irregular in the imperfect indicative are also irregular in the imperfect subjunctive. The following verbs are irregular in the imperfect subjunctive and are a constant source of blunders.

**bere *to drink***

(io) bevessi, (tu) bevessi, (lui/lei/Lei) bevesse,
(noi) bevessimo, (voi) beveste, (loro/Loro) bevessero

**dare *to give***

(io) dessi, (tu) dessi, (lui/lei/Lei) desse,
(noi) dessimo, (voi) deste, (loro/Loro) dessero

**dire *to say, tell***

(io) dicessi, (tu) dicessi, (lui/lei/Lei) dicesse,
(noi) dicessimo, (voi) diceste, (loro/Loro) dicessero

**essere *to be***

(io) fossi, (tu) fossi, (lui/lei/Lei) fosse,
(noi) fossimo, (voi) foste, (loro/Loro) fossero

**fare *to do, make***

(io) facessi, (tu) facessi, (lui/lei/Lei) facesse,
(noi) facessimo, (voi) faceste, (loro/Loro) facessero

**stare** *to stay*

(io) stessi, (tu) stessi, (lui/lei/Lei) stesse,
(noi) stessimo, (voi) steste, (loro/Loro) stessero

AVOID THE *Blunder*

✗ io dassi
✗ io dissi

## Uses

As in the case of the imperfect indicative, the imperfect subjunctive expresses repeated action in the past. Generally, if the main-clause verb is in a past tense, the verb in the subordinate clause is in the imperfect subjunctive.

| | |
|---|---|
| Spero che tu abbia capito. | *I hope that you have understood.* |
| Sembra che lui abbia detto la verità. | *It seems that he told the truth.* |

BUT

| | |
|---|---|
| Speravo che tu avessi capito. | *I was hoping that you understood.* |
| Sembrava che lui dicesse la verità. | *It seemed that he was telling the truth.* |

AVOID THE *Blunder*

✗ Speravo che lui abbia capito.
✗ Sembrava che loro abbiano detto la verità.
✗ Pensavo che lei sia venuta alla festa.

The imperfect subjunctive is also used after *se* "if" in counterfactual sentences when the main-clause verb is in the conditional.

| | |
|---|---|
| Se tu andassi a Roma, vedresti il Colosseo. | *If you were to go to Rome, you would see the Colosseum.* |
| Se potessimo, andremmo in Italia subito. | *If we could, we would go to Italy right away.* |

✗ Se lui studiava di più, sarebbe più intelligente.
✗ Se potremmo, andremmo in Italia.

The imperfect subjunctive is also used after *magari* "if only / I wish" to express a wish or desire.

| | |
|---|---|
| Magari non piovesse! | *If only it wouldn't rain!* |
| Magari vincessi la lotteria! | *If only I would win the lottery!* |

✗ Magari vinco la lotteria!
✗ Magari vengono anche loro!

## The Pluperfect Subjunctive

### Conjugation

The Italian pluperfect subjunctive corresponds to the pluperfect indicative. It is formed with the imperfect subjunctive of the auxiliary verb plus the past participle of the verb, in that order. Following are complete conjugations of two verbs in the pluperfect subjunctive tense, one verb conjugated with *avere* and the other with *essere*.

**parlare** *to speak*

| | |
|---|---|
| (io) avessi parlato | *I had spoken* |
| (tu) avessi parlato | *you* (familiar singular) *had spoken* |
| (lui/lei/Lei) avesse parlato | *he/she/you* (polite singular) *had spoken* |
| (noi) avessimo parlato | *we had spoken* |
| (voi) aveste parlato | *you* (familiar plural) *had spoken* |
| (loro/Loro) avessero parlato | *they/you* (polite plural) *had spoken* |

✗ tu avesse parlato
✗ voi avesse parlato

## partire *to leave*

| | |
|---|---|
| (io) fossi partito(-a) | *I had left* |
| (tu) fossi partito(-a) | *you* (familiar singular) *had left* |
| (lui/lei/Lei) fosse partito(-a) | *he/she/you* (polite singular) *had left* |
| (noi) fossimo partiti(-e) | *we had left* |
| (voi) foste partiti(-e) | *you* (familiar plural) *had left* |
| (loro/Loro) fossero partiti(-e) | *they/you* (polite plural) *had left* |

AVOID THE *Blunder*

✗ tu fosse partito
✗ voi fosse partiti

## Uses

The Italian pluperfect subjunctive corresponds to the pluperfect indicative in usage. It expresses a past action in the subordinate clause that occurred before a past action in the main clause.

| | |
|---|---|
| Sembrava che lui fosse già arrivato. | *It seemed that he had already arrived.* |
| Eravamo contenti che voi foste venuti. | *We were happy that you had come.* |

Like the imperfect subjunctive, the pluperfect subjunctive is also used after *se* "if" in counterfactual sentences when the main-clause verb is in the conditional perfect.

| | |
|---|---|
| Se avessi avuto i soldi, l'avrei comprata. | *If I had had the money, I would have bought it.* |
| Se tu avessi studiato ieri, saresti potuto uscire. | *If you had studied yesterday, you could have gone out.* |

AVOID THE *Blunder*

✗ Pensavo che lei arrivasse già.
✗ Se avessi i soldi, avrei comprata quella macchina.

# Exercises

**A** *For each indicative form (past, imperfect, pluperfect), write the corresponding subjunctive form (past, imperfect, or pluperfect).*

1. io sono arrivato _____

2. io vendevi _____

3. io avevo preferito _____

4. io andavo _____

5. io ho avuto _____

6. tu mangiavi _____

7. tu avevi messo _____

8. tu hai messo _____

9. tu bevevi _____

10. tu eri caduto _____

11. lui cominciava _____

12. lei ha chiesto _____

13. lui aveva capito _____

14. Lei dava _____

15. lei era _____

16. noi pagavamo _____

17. noi abbiamo chiuso _____

18. noi avevamo finito _____

19. noi facevamo _____

20. noi potevamo _____

21. voi cercavate _____

22. voi mettevate _____

23. voi avete preferito _____

24. voi sapevate _____

25. voi avevate tenuto _____

26. loro mangiavano _____

27. loro hanno chiesto _____

28. loro avevano preferito _____

29. loro vedevano _____

30. loro venivano _____

**B** *Choose the past, imperfect, or pluperfect subjunctive form of the verb, as appropriate.*

1. Dubito che lui _____ già.

   a. abbia mangiato

   b. mangiasse

   c. avesse mangiato

2. Credevo che _____ quando l'ho chiamato ieri.

   a. abbia mangiato

   b. mangiasse

   c. avesse mangiato

3. Pensavo che lui _____ già, quando abbiamo chiamato.

   a. abbia mangiato

   b. mangiasse

   c. avesse mangiato

4. È impossibile che loro _____ già.

   a. siano partiti

   b. partissero

   c. fossero partiti

5. Benché _____ ieri, è uscito lo stesso.

   a. abbia piovuto

   b. piovesse

   c. avesse piovuto

6. Spero che voi _____.

   a. abbiate capito

   b. capiste

   c. aveste capito

7. Penso che lui _____ la verità.

   a. abbia detto

   b. dicesse

   c. avesse detto

8. Speravo che voi _____.

   a. abbiate capito

   b. capiste

   c. aveste capito

9. Sembrava che lui _____ la verità.

   a. abbia detto

   b. dicesse

   c. avesse detto

10. Se tu _____ a Firenze, saresti molto contenta.

    a. sia andata

    b. andassi

    c. fossi andata

11. Se tu _____ a Firenze, saresti stata molto contenta.

    a. sia andata

    b. andassi

    c. fossi andata

12. Magari non _____ sempre in aprile!

    a. abbia piovuto

    b. piovesse

    c. avesse piovuto

13. Se io _____ i soldi, la comprerei.

    a. abbia avuto

    b. avessi

    c. avessi avuto

14. Se io _____ i soldi, l'avrei comprata.

    a. abbia avuto

    b. avessi

    c. avessi avuto

15. Benché _____ i soldi, non l'ha comprata.

    a. abbia avuto

    b. avesse

    c. avesse avuto

# VERBS
## the progressive tenses

The progressive tenses express an ongoing action in the present or past.

| | |
|---|---|
| In questo momento lui sta guardando la TV. | *At this moment, he is watching TV.* |
| Mentre stava guardando la TV, io ho chiamato. | *While he was watching TV, I called.* |
| Penso che in questo momento lui stia guardando la TV. | *I think that, at this moment, he is watching TV.* |
| Pensavo che stesse guardando la TV, quando ho chiamato. | *I thought he was watching TV when I called.* |

There are four progressive tenses in Italian, the present indicative and subjunctive and the imperfect indicative and subjunctive.

## The Present Progressive Tenses

Progressive tenses are formed with the verb *stare* plus the gerund, both of which have been treated in previous units. The present indicative progressive tense is conjugated with the present indicative of *stare*; the present subjunctive progressive tense is conjugated with the present subjunctive of *stare*. Following are complete conjugations of two verbs in the present progressive tense, one verb conjugated in the indicative and the other in the subjunctive.

INDICATIVE

guardare  *to watch*

| | |
|---|---|
| (io) sto guardando | *I am watching* |
| (tu) stai guardando | *you (familiar singular) are watching* |
| (lui/lei/Lei) sta guardando | *he/she is / you (polite singular) are watching* |
| (noi) stiamo guardando | *we are watching* |
| (voi) state guardando | *you (familiar plural) are watching* |
| (loro/Loro) stanno guardando | *they/you (polite plural) are watching* |

**AVOID THE** *Blunder*

✗ tu sta parlando
✗ loro stano parlando

**SUBJUNCTIVE**

finire *to finish*

| | |
|---|---|
| (io) stia finendo | *I am finishing* |
| (tu) stia finendo | *you* (familiar singular) *are finishing* |
| (lui/lei/Lei) stia finendo | *he/she is / you* (polite singular) *are finishing* |
| (noi) stiamo finendo | *we are finishing* |
| (voi) stiate finendo | *you* (familiar plural) *are finishing* |
| (loro/Loro) stiano finendo | *they/you* (polite plural) *are finishing* |

**AVOID THE** *Blunder*

✗ tu stai finendo (as subjunctive)
✗ voi state finendo (as subjunctive)

The present progressive tenses are alternatives to the present indicative and subjunctive and express an ongoing action.

| | |
|---|---|
| In questo momento, mia sorella sta mangiando. | *At this moment, my sister is eating.* |
| Penso che in questo momento, mia sorella stia mangiando. | *I think that, at this moment, my sister is eating.* |

**AVOID THE** *Blunder*

The following examples are more blunders of usage than of grammar; it is better to use the progressive than the nonprogressive form of the verb.

✗ In questo momento, mio fratello mangia.
✗ Penso che in questo momento, mio fratello mangi.

## The Imperfect Progressive Tenses

The imperfect indicative progressive tense is conjugated with the imperfect indicative of *stare*; the imperfect subjunctive progressive tense is conjugated with the imperfect subjunctive of *stare*. Following are complete conjugations of two verbs in the imperfect progressive tense, one verb conjugated in the indicative and the other in the subjunctive.

### INDICATIVE

guardare *to watch*

| | |
|---|---|
| (io) stavo guardando | *I was watching* |
| (tu) stavi guardando | *you* (familiar singular) *were watching* |
| (lui/lei/Lei) stava guardando | *he/she was / you* (polite singular) *were watching* |
| (noi) stavamo guardando | *we were watching* |
| (voi) stavate guardando | *you* (familiar plural) *were watching* |
| (loro/Loro) stavano guardando | *they/you* (polite plural) *were watching* |

AVOID THE *Blunder*

✗ tu stava guardando
✗ voi stavete guardando

### SUBJUNCTIVE

finire *to finish*

| | |
|---|---|
| (io) stessi finendo | *I was finishing* |
| (tu) stessi finendo | *you* (familiar singular) *were finishing* |
| (lui/lei/Lei) stesse finendo | *he/she was / you* (polite singular) *were finishing* |
| (noi) stessimo finendo | *we were finishing* |
| (voi) steste finendo | *you* (familiar plural) *were finishing* |
| (loro/Loro) stessero finendo | *they/you* (polite plural) *were finishing* |

AVOID THE *Blunder*

✗ tu stesse finendo
✗ voi stesse finendo

The imperfect progressive tenses are alternatives to the imperfect indicative and subjunctive and express an ongoing action in the past.

| | |
|---|---|
| Mentre lei stava mangiando, io guardavo la TV. | *While she was eating, I was watching TV.* |
| Penso che ieri mia sorella stesse mangiando, quando è arrivata la zia. | *I think my sister was eating yesterday when our aunt arrived.* |
| Non so cosa stesse facendo ieri, quando le ho telefonato. | *I do not know what she was doing yesterday when I phoned her.* |

AVOID THE *Blunder*

✗ Mentre lei ha dormito, io guardavo la TV.
✗ Penso che ieri lui mangiava, quando ho chiamato.

# Exercises

**A** *For each nonprogressive verb form, write the equivalent progressive form.*

1. io arrivo _____

2. io venda _____

3. io preferivo _____

4. io andassi _____

5. io ho _____

6. tu mangi _____

7. tu metta _____

8. tu aprivi _____

9. tu bevessi _____

10. tu cadi _____

11. lui comincia _____

12. lei chieda _____

13. lui capiva _____

14. Lei desse _____

15. lei faceva _____

16. noi paghiamo _____

17. noi chiudevamo _____

18. noi finiamo _____

19. noi facessimo _____

20. noi cerchiamo _____

21. voi cercate _____

22. voi mettiate _____

23. voi preferivate _____

24. voi uscite _____

25. voi teniate _____

26. loro mangiano _____

27. loro chiedano _____

28. loro preferivano _____

29. loro vedessero _____

30. loro vengono _____

**B** *Rewrite each sentence, replacing the verb with its corresponding progressive form.*

1. Noi non studiamo l'italiano.

_____

2. Penso che loro partino per l'Italia.

_____

3. Maria, con chi parli?

_____

4. Marco, che cosa cerchi?

_____

5. Mio fratello guarda la TV in questo momento.

_____

6. Credo che mia sorella guardi la TV.

_____

7. Cosa leggete?

_____

**C** *Choose the indicative or subjunctive form of the progressive, as appropriate.*

1. Dubito che lui _____ ieri, quando ho chiamato.

   a. stava mangiando

   b. stesse mangiando

2. Mentre lui _____, io ho chiamato.

   a. stava mangiando

   b. stesse mangiando

3. Pensavo che lui _____, quando voi avete chiamato.

   a. stava studiando

   b. stesse studiando

4. Marco, che cosa _____ ieri quando ti ho chiamato?

   a. stavi facendo

   b. stessi facendo

5. Non so cosa _____ ieri Marco, quando l'ho chiamato.

   a. stava facendo

   b. stesse facendo

# VERBS
## reflexive verbs

A reflexive verb is a verb, in any tense or mood, that requires a reflexive pronoun. Technically, it has an identical subject and direct object, as in *She dressed herself.*

A reflexive infinitive in Italian is identifiable by the ending *-si* "oneself" attached to the infinitive (minus the final *-e*).

alzare + si → alzarsi    *to get up*

Following is a list of common reflexive verbs.

| | |
|---|---|
| alzarsi | *to get up* |
| annoiarsi | *to become bored* |
| arrabbiarsi | *to become angry* |
| chiamarsi | *to be called* |
| dimenticarsi | *to forget* |
| divertirsi | *to enjoy oneself, have fun* |
| lamentarsi | *to complain* |
| lavarsi | *to wash oneself* |
| mettersi | *to put on, wear; set about, begin to* |
| preoccuparsi | *to worry* |
| prepararsi | *to prepare oneself* |
| sentirsi | *to feel* |
| sposarsi | *to marry, get married* |
| svegliarsi | *to wake up* |
| vergognarsi | *to be ashamed* |
| vestirsi | *to get dressed* |

AVOID THE *Blunder*

✗ alzaresi
✗ metteresi

## Conjugation

Reflexive verbs are conjugated in exactly the same manner as non-reflexive verbs, with, of course, the addition of reflexive pronouns. These are *mi, ti, si, ci, vi, si.*

| | |
|---|---|
| (Io) mi alzo presto ogni giorno. (PRESENT INDICATIVE) | *I get up early every day.* |
| Sembra che tu ti diverta sempre in Italia. (PRESENT SUBJUNCTIVE) | *It seems that you always enjoy yourself in Italy.* |
| Lui si sposerà l'anno prossimo. (SIMPLE FUTURE) | *He is getting married next year.* |
| Lei si sposerebbe se avesse più soldi. (CONDITIONAL) | *She would get married if she had more money.* |
| Come si chiama suo fratello? (PRESENT INDICATIVE) | *What's her brother's name?* |
| (Noi) ci divertivamo sempre da bambini. (IMPERFECT INDICATIVE) | *We always used to have fun as children.* |
| Penso che voi vi siate annoiati ieri. (PAST SUBJUNCTIVE) | *I think that you became bored yesterday.* |
| Anche loro si divertirono in Italia. (PAST ABSOLUTE) | *They also had fun in Italy.* |

Note that some verbs are reflexive in Italian, but not in English. This is a common source of errors.

AVOID THE *Blunder*

✗ Marco sposerà l'anno prossimo.
✗ Lui non mette mai la giacca.
✗ Perché voi diventate annoiati?
✗ Loro sentono bene.

## Compound Tenses

In compound tenses, all reflexive verbs are conjugated with *essere.*

| | |
|---|---|
| Io mi sono alzato tardi ieri. (PRESENT PERFECT) | *I got up late yesterday.* |
| Perché non ti sei messa la maglia? (PRESENT PERFECT) | *Why didn't you put a sweater on?* |
| Loro si sono divertiti molto in Italia. (PRESENT PERFECT) | *They had a lot of fun in Italy.* |
| Dopo che ci saremo alzati, andremo in centro. (FUTURE PERFECT) | *After getting up, we'll be going downtown.* |

| | |
|---|---|
| Quando si saranno sposati, andranno a vivere in Italia. (FUTURE PERFECT) | *When they will have gotten married, they will go and live in Italy.* |
| Se lui si fosse svegliato più presto, non sarebbe arrivato in ritardo. (PLUPERFECT SUBJUNCTIVE) | *If he had woken up earlier, he would not have arrived late.* |

AVOID THE *Blunder*

✗ Lui si ha alzato tardi ieri.
✗ Lei non si ha messo la maglia ieri.

## Imperative Forms

The reflexive pronouns are attached to the familiar and first-person plural forms of the affirmative imperative.

| FAMILIAR | POLITE |
|---|---|
| **tu FORMS** | **Lei FORMS** |
| Marco, vestiti! | Signor Verdi, si vesta! |
| *Mark, get dressed!* | *Mr. Verdi, get dressed!* |
| Maria, alzati! | Signora Rossi, si alzi! |
| *Mary, get up!* | *Mrs. Rossi, get up!* |
| **noi FORMS** | |
| Divertiamoci! | |
| *Let's have fun!* | |
| Sposiamoci! | |
| *Let's get married!* | |
| **voi FORMS** | **Loro FORMS** |
| Divertitevi! | Si divertano! |
| *Enjoy yourselves!* | *Enjoy yourselves!* |
| Alzatevi! | Si alzino! |
| *Get up!* | *Get up!* |

AVOID THE *Blunder*

✗ Marco, ti vesti!
✗ Signor Verdi, vestasi!

In the negative imperative, the pronouns are attached in the same way, as a general rule. However, in the case of the second-person singular form, remember that the infinitive is required (see the unit on the imperative). In this case, the pronoun may be attached as an ending or placed before the verb. If attached, the final -e of the infinitive is dropped.

| AFFIRMATIVE tu FORMS | NEGATIVE tu FORMS |
|---|---|
| Marco, alzati! | Marco, non ti alzare! |
| *Mark, get up!* | *Mark, don't get up!* |
| Maria, alzati! | Maria, non alzarti! |
| *Mary, get up!* | *Mary, don't get up!* |

The imperative of reflexive verbs is complicated, and for this reason it is a constant source of blunders.

AVOID THE *Blunder*

X Alessandro, non ti alza!
X Marco, non ti preoccupi!

## Reciprocal Forms

Some nonreflexive verbs can be turned into reflexives; these are called reciprocal verbs.

| VERB | | RECIPROCAL | |
|---|---|---|---|
| parlare | *to speak* | parlarsi | *to speak to one another* |
| telefonare | *to phone* | telefonarsi | *to phone one another* |
| vedere | *to see* | vedersi | *to see one another* |
| capire | *to understand* | capirsi | *to understand one another* |

| | |
|---|---|
| Loro non si parlano più. | *They do not speak to each other anymore.* |
| Noi ci telefoniamo spesso. | *We phone each other often.* |
| Voi non vi vedete da molti anni, vero? | *You haven't seen each other for many years, isn't that right?* |
| Loro non si capiscono mai. | *They never understand each other.* |

AVOID THE *Blunder*

X Noi parliamo a noi spesso.
X Loro vedono loro stessi spesso.

# Exercises

**A** Write the present indicative, future, and present perfect forms of the reflexive verb according to the pronoun in parentheses.

| PRESENT INDICATIVE | FUTURE | PRESENT PERFECT |
|---|---|---|

1. (tu) alzarsi

2. (lei) annoiarsi

3. (lui) arrabbiarsi

4. (io) alzarsi

5. (noi) dimenticarsi

6. (voi) divertirsi

7. (io) lamentarsi

8. (loro) lavarsi

9. (tu) mettersi

10. (lei) preoccuparsi

11. (lui) prepararsi

12. (noi) sentirsi

13. (voi) sposarsi

14. (loro) svegliarsi

15. (lui) vestirsi

**B**   *Write the affirmative equivalent of the negative commands and the negative equivalent of the affirmative commands. As an example, for* Marco, alzati! *you would write* Marco, non ti alzare! *or* Marco, non alzarti!

1. Marco e Maria, non vergognatevi!

2. Signor Bruni, si alzi!

3. Sara, alzati!

4. Signorina Dorelli, si preoccupi!

5. Alessandro, non arrabbiarti!

**C**   *Express the following English sentences in Italian.*

1. We get up early every day.

2. It seems that he always enjoys himself in Italy.

3. She would get married if she meets the right person.

4. I always used to have fun as a child.

5. She got up late yesterday.

6. We do not speak to each other anymore.

7. They phone each other often.

8. Mark and Maria, you haven't seen each other for many years, isn't that right?

9. We never understand each other.

# VERBS
## the verbs *piacere* and *esserci*

### *piacere*

The verb *piacere* is used to express likes and dislikes. But it is a tricky verb, because it literally means "to be pleasing to," not "like."

Mi piace la pizza.

*I like pizza.* (literally, *"To me is pleasing the pizza."*)

Non gli è piaciuta la pizza.

*He didn't like the pizza.* (literally, *"To him was not pleasing the pizza."*)

Because of this difference, *piacere* is a constant source of blunders. Before discussing this verb, it is necessary to know the indirect object pronouns; these are as follows.

| SINGULAR | | PLURAL | |
|---|---|---|---|
| mi | *to me* | ci | *to us* |
| a me | *to me* | a noi | *to us* |
| ti | *to you* (familiar) | vi | *to you* (familiar) |
| a te | *to you* (familiar) | a voi | *to you* (familiar) |
| gli | *to him* | gli | *to them* |
| a lui | *to him* | a loro | *to them* |
| le | *to her* | gli | *to them* |
| a lei | *to her* | a loro | *to them* |
| Le | *to you* (polite) | Loro | *to you* (polite) |
| a Lei | *to you* (polite) | a Loro | *to you* (polite) |

### Conjugation

The verb *piacere* is regular in all tenses except the following three.

#### PRESENT INDICATIVE

(io) piaccio, (tu) piaci, (lui/lei/Lei) piace,
(noi) piacciamo, (voi) piacete, (loro/Loro) piacciono

#### PAST ABSOLUTE

(io) piacqui, (tu) piacesti, (lui/lei/Lei) piacque,
(noi) piacemmo, (voi) piaceste, (loro/Loro) piacquero

**PRESENT SUBJUNCTIVE**
(io) piaccia, (tu) piaccia, (lui/lei/Lei) piaccia,
(noi) piacciamo, (voi) piacciate, (loro/Loro) piacciano

AVOID THE *Blunder*

✗ io piacio
✗ loro piacettero

*Piacere* is conjugated with *essere* in the compound tenses.

| | |
|---|---|
| Non mi è piaciuta la pasta. | *I didn't like the pasta.* |
| Non gli sono piaciuti gli spaghetti. | *He didn't like the spaghetti.* |

AVOID THE *Blunder*

✗ Non mi ha piaciuto il caffè.
✗ Non vi hanno piaciuto le caramelle.

## Uses

When saying that you or someone else likes something, translate the English expression into your mind as "to be pleasing to" and then follow the word order in the formula below.

| EXPRESSION | TRANSLATE TO | ITALIAN EXPRESSION |
|---|---|---|
| *I like that book.* | "To me is pleasing that book." | Mi piace quel libro. |
| *We like those books.* | "To us are pleasing those books." | Ci piacciono quei libri. |
| *She likes her brothers.* | "To her are pleasing her brothers." | Le piacciono i suoi fratelli. |
| *The brothers like her.* | "She is pleasing to her brothers." | Lei piace ai suoi fratelli. |

AVOID THE *Blunder*

✗ Mi piaccio quel libro.
✗ Mi piace quei libri.

If you think in this way, you will always be correct. Note that the real subject is usually put at the end, although this is not necessary.

| Mary likes John. | "To Mary is pleasing John." | A Maria piace Giovanni. |

OR

| | "John is pleasing to Mary." | Giovanni piace a Maria. |

Since *piacere* is conjugated with *essere* in the compound tenses, the past participle agrees with the subject.

| *I didn't like her.* | "*Not to me was she pleasing.*" | (Lei) non mi è piaciuta. |
| *She didn't like us.* | "*Not to her were we pleasing.*" | (Noi) non le siamo piaciuti. |

---

**AVOID THE** *Blunder*

✗ Non mi è piaciuto quella rivista.
✗ Non mi è piaciuto quelle riviste.

---

The object pronouns are sometimes placed after the verb for emphasis or clarity. (See the chart on page 215.)

| La musica piace a me, non a te! | *I like the music, not you!* (literally, *The music is pleasing to me, not to you!*) |

---

**AVOID THE** *Blunder*

✗ Io non mi piace lei.
✗ La musica mi piace, non gli piace.

---

**A HANDY RULE OF THUMB**

*Piacere* can be very confusing for someone accustomed to the English verb "to like." The following rule of thumb may help you use this important verb more readily.

Since the verb is often used with an indirect object pronoun, think of the pronoun as the subject, then make the verb agree in number with the predicate.

| Mi piace quella rivista. | *I like that magazine. (That magazine is pleasing to me.)* |
| Ti piacciono quelle riviste. | *You like those magazines. (Those magazines are pleasing to you.)* |
| Gli piace quella rivista. | *He likes that magazine. (That magazine is pleasing to him.)* |

| | |
|---|---|
| Le piacciono quelle riviste. | *She likes those magazines. (Those magazines are pleasing to her.)* |
| Ci piace la pizza. | *We like the pizza. (The pizza is pleasing to us.)* |
| Vi piacciono gli spaghetti. | *You like the spaghetti. (The spaghetti is pleasing to you.)* |
| Gli piace la pizza. | *They like the pizza. (The pizza is pleasing to them.)* |

AVOID THE *Blunder*

✗ Io piaccio la rivista.
✗ Lui piace le caramelle.

## Expressing Dislike

To express dislike for something, *non* is placed before the verb in the normal fashion.

| | |
|---|---|
| Non mi piace quella rivista. | *I do not like that magazine.* *(= I dislike that magazine.)* |
| Non le piacciono i ravioli. | *She doesn't like ravioli.* *(= She dislikes ravioli.)* |

Be careful! The verb *dispiacere* is not used to express the same notion; it means "to regret, be sorry."

| | |
|---|---|
| Mi dispiace. | *I am sorry.* |
| Ti dispiace. | *You are sorry.* |
| Gli dispiace. | *He is sorry.* |

AVOID THE *Blunder*

✗ Io dispiaccio.
✗ Lui dispiace la pizza.

## esserci

The verb *essere* + *ci* produces the expression *esserci* "to be here/there."
It is conjugated like *essere* with *ci* before it. Note, however, that it can
only be used in the third person.

| | |
|---|---|
| C'è poco tempo. | *There is little time.* |
| Ci sarà molta gente alla festa. | *There will be a lot of people at the party.* |
| Penso che non ci sia tanta gente. | *I think that there are not a lot of people.* |
| Ci sono stato tante volte. | *I have been there many times.* |

**AVOID THE** *Blunder*

✗ Ci è poco tempo.
✗ C'è tante cose da fare.

*Ecco* also means "here is, there are," but it is used to indicate or point
out someone or something. *Essere, esserci,* and *ecco* are often confused
by learners. The following chart indicates the differences between
them.

| SINGULAR | PLURAL |
|---|---|
| Che cosa è? | Che cosa sono? |
| *What is it?* | *What are they?* |
| È un libro. | Sono dei libri. |
| *It's a book.* | *They are books.* |
| C'è Marco? | Ci sono Marco e Maria? |
| *Is Mark there?* | *Are Mark and Mary there?* |
| Sì, c'è. | Sì, ci sono. |
| *Yes, he is (here/there).* | *Yes, they are (here/there).* |
| Dov'è Marco? | Dove sono Marco e Maria? |
| *Where is Mark?* | *Where are Mark and Mary?* |
| Ecco Marco. | Ecco Marco e Maria. |
| *Here/There is Mark.* | *Here/There are Mark and Mary.* |

**AVOID THE** *Blunder*

✗ Che cosa è? C'è un libro.
✗ Dov'è Marco? C'è Marco.

# Exercises

**A** *Choose the appropriate form of the verb.*

1. Maria, ti _____ quel film?

   a. piace

   b. piaccio

2. Maria, io ti _____?

   a. piace

   b. piaccio

3. A lui non _____ quei libri.

   a. piacerà

   b. piaceranno

4. A Maria non sono _____ gli spaghetti.

   a. piaciuta

   b. piaciuti

5. Da bambini, ci _____ guardare spesso la TV.

   a. piaceva

   b. piacevano

6. Noi non siamo _____ a tua sorella.

   a. piaciuta

   b. piaciuti

7. A chi _____ quelle riviste?

   a. piace

   b. piacciono

**B** *Each of the following items contains one or more errors. Rewrite the item, correcting the error(s).*

1. Che cosa è? C'è una nuova macchina.

   _____

2. Dov'è la macchina nuova? C'è la macchina nuova.

   _____

3. C'è Maria? Sì, è.

   _____

4. Io dispiaccio che tu non sei venuto alla festa.

_____

5. Mi dispiace quella pizza.

_____


**C** *Express the following English sentences in Italian.*

1. *We like that book.*

_____

2. *But we don't like those other books.*

_____

3. *She likes him.*

_____

4. *And he likes her.*

_____

5. *Mary likes me.*

_____

6. *I didn't like them.*

_____

7. *He didn't like us.*

_____

8. *He likes that music, not she.*

_____

# VERBS
## the passive

Verbs are marked not only for mood and tense, but also for voice, which can be active or passive. In the active voice, the subject acts on the object.

Il ragazzo ha mangiato la pizza.    *The boy ate the pizza.*

Many nonreflexive verbs also have a passive form, in which the subject is acted on.

La pizza è mangiata dal ragazzo.    *The pizza is eaten by the boy.*

## Formation

An active sentence can be turned into a passive sentence by the following three steps.

- Change the order of the subject and the object.

Marco mangia la mela.    *Mark is eating the apple.*
→ La mela [mangia] Marco.

- Change the verb into the passive form by using the auxiliary verb *essere* in the same tense and mood as the original verb and changing the verb itself into the past participle, which must agree with the new subject in gender and number.

La mela [mangia] Marco.
→ La mela è mangiata [Marco].

- Insert *da* before the new object.

La mela è mangiata [Marco].
→ La mela è mangiata da Marco.    *The apple is eaten by Mark.*

AVOID THE *Blunder*

A common blunder is to use *di* instead of *da*.

✗ La mela è mangiata di Marco.

223

Following are examples of active and passive forms of the same sentence.

| ACTIVE | PASSIVE |
|--------|---------|
| La ragazza legge quel libro. *The girl reads that book.* | Quel libro è letto dalla ragazza. *That book is being read by the girl.* |
| Quell'uomo comprerà la FIAT. *That man will buy the FIAT.* | La FIAT sarà comprata da quell'uomo. *The FIAT will be bought by that man.* |
| Io scrissi quell'email. *I wrote that e-mail.* | Quell'email fu scritta da me. *That e-mail was written by me.* |

Common blunders in this area are the use of *di* instead of *da* (as mentioned) and the use of the wrong auxiliary verb.

AVOID THE *Blunder*

✗ Quella casa ha comprata dai miei amici.
✗ Quelle caramelle hanno state mangiate da lei.

Note that the preposition *da* contracts with the definite article as follows.

- da + il → dal

  Quella macchina è stata comprata dal cugino di Maria.
  *That car was bought by Mary's cousin.*

- da + lo → dallo

  Quella casa sarà comprata dallo zio.
  *That house will be bought by my uncle.*

- da + la → dalla

  Quel libro è letto dalla gente che ama i libri.
  *That book is read by people who love books.*

- da + i → dai

  Quella casa è stata comprata dai miei genitori.
  *That house was bought by my parents.*

- da + gli → dagli

  Quel programma sarà guardato dagli studenti.
  *That program will be watched by the students.*

■  da + le → dalle

Quelle scarpe sono state
comprate dalle mie amiche.

*Those shoes were bought by my
friends.*

AVOID THE *Blunder*

✗ Quel libro è letto da la gente che ama i libri.
✗ Quel programma sarà guardato da gli studenti.

## General Passives

The passive form of the verb is used to express ideas and situations that
are communicated more appropriately in this form.

La lezione è finita alle sei.
I negozi sono chiusi a quest'ora.

*The class finished at six.*
*Stores are closed at this hour.*

AVOID THE *Blunder*

✗ La lezione ha finito alle sei.
✗ I negozi hanno chiuso a quest'ora.

A similar general expression involves the use of the impersonal *si,*
meaning "one," "we," "they," etc. It has the following characteristics.

■  The verb agrees with what appears to be the predicate—not with the
sentence subject—because, as you can see in the following pairs of
examples, the construction is really a type of passive.

Si beve quel caffè solo in Italia.
Quel caffè è bevuto solo in Italia.

*One drinks that coffee only
in Italy.*
*That coffee is drunk only
in Italy.*

Si mangiano quegli spaghetti
solo in Italia.
Quegli spaghetti sono mangiati
solo in Italia.

*One eats that spaghetti only
in Italy.*
*That spaghetti is eaten only
in Italy.*

AVOID THE *Blunder*

✗ Si mangia quegli spaghetti solo in Italia.
✗ Si compra quelle scarpe solo in Italia.

- In compound tenses, the auxiliary verb is *essere*.

Si è vista quella cosa solo
in Italia.
Quella cosa è stata vista solo
in Italia.

> *One saw that thing only in Italy.*
> *That thing was seen only in Italy.*

Si sono viste quelle cose solo
in Italia.
Quelle cose sono state viste
solo in Italia.

> *One saw those things only in Italy.*
> *Those things were seen only*
> *in Italy.*

**AVOID THE** *Blunder*

✗ Si ha visto quella cosa solo in Italia.
✗ Si hanno visto quelle cose solo in Italia.

---

- When followed by a predicate adjective, the adjective is always plural (even if the verb is singular).

Si è contenti in Italia.        *One is happy in Italy.*

**AVOID THE** *Blunder*

✗ Si è contento in Italia.

---

- Direct object pronouns are placed before *si*.

Si deve dire sempre la verità.     *One must always tell the truth.*
La si deve dire sempre.           *One must always tell it.*

**AVOID THE** *Blunder*

✗ Si la deve dire sempre.

---

- Before the reflexive pronoun *si,* the impersonal *si* is changed to *ci*.

Ci si diverte in Italia.         *One enjoys oneself in Italy.*

**AVOID THE** *Blunder*

✗ Si si diverte sempre in Italia.

# Exercises

**A** *If a sentence is active, rewrite it as passive; if it is passive, rewrite it as active.*

1. Mio fratello non ha mangiato la pizza ieri.

2. Gli spaghetti sono mangiati solo da mia sorella.

3. Marco mangia sempre le patate a cena.

4. Quel libro è letto da tutti.

5. Quella donna comprerà la macchina giapponese.

6. Quell'email fu scritta da mio fratello.

7. Maria ha comprato quella macchina.

8. Quella casa è stata comprata dai miei amici.

9. Gli studenti studieranno quella lezione per domani.

**B** *Express the following English sentences in Italian.*

1. *The class began at nine.*

2. *Stores are open at this hour.*

3. *One drinks that coffee only in Italy.*

4. *One eats those potatoes only in Italy.*

5. *One saw that thing only in Italy.*

6. *One is happy in Italy.*

_____

7. *One always enjoys oneself in Italy.*

_____

# SUBORDINATE CLAUSES

Sentences are organized sequences of words that constitute statements, questions, and so on.

A simple sentence has two basic parts: a subject and a predicate. A subject is "who" or "what" the sentence is about; it is often the first element in a simple sentence. A predicate is the part of a sentence that expresses what is said about the subject.

Maria studia il francese.     *Mary is studying French.*

**SUBJECT** Maria
**PREDICATE** studia il francese

A sentence can have more than one subject or predicate. In this case, the subject and predicate constructions are called clauses. Typically, there is a main clause and a subordinate clause, united by elements such as relative pronouns or conjunctions, of which *che* is the most common.

Maria dice che il francese è     *Mary says that French is*
    una bella lingua.        *a beautiful language.*

**MAIN CLAUSE** Maria dice (qualcosa)
**SUBORDINATE CLAUSE** il francese è una bella lingua
**CONJUNCTION** che

## Subordinate Clauses

A clause is a group of related words that contains a subject and predicate and is part of a sentence.

La ragazza che legge il giornale     *The girl who is reading the*
    è francese.                 *newspaper is French.*

There are two primary types of subordinate clauses.

- A relative clause is a subordinate clause introduced by a relative pronoun.

    **MAIN CLAUSE** La ragazza è italiana. *The girl is Italian.*
    **RELATIVE CLAUSE** legge il giornale *is reading the newspaper*
    **RELATIVE PRONOUN** che

| La ragazza che legge il giornale è italiana. | *The girl (who is) reading the newspaper is Italian.* |

Note that the relative pronoun can sometimes be omitted in English. This is a major source of blunders.

AVOID THE *Blunder*

✗ La ragazza leggendo il giornale è italiana.
✗ Il ragazzo guarda quel programma è mio fratello.

- A temporal clause is a subordinate clause introduced by a conjunction that involves a time element.

| appena | *as soon as* |
| dopo che | *after* |
| mentre | *while* |
| quando | *when* |

| Andremo al cinema, dopo che avremo finito di mangiare. | *We will go to the movies after (having finished) eating.* |
| Quando arriveranno, cominceremo a mangiare. | *When they arrive, we will begin eating.* |

AVOID THE *Blunder*

✗ Andremo al cinema, dopo mangiando.

## Conjoining Elements

Words that join two sentences, two clauses, two phrases, or two words are generally called conjoining elements. In the unit on the subjunctive, conjunctions were used that require the subjunctive in the clauses they introduce.

| Benché piova, esco lo stesso. | *Although it is raining, I'm going out just the same.* |

To join two sentences, two clauses, etc., the conjunctions *e* "and," *o* "or," and *ma* "but" are used often.

| Maria studia e suo fratello guarda la TV. | *Mary is studying, and her brother is watching TV.* |
| La ragazza che ha i capelli biondi e che parla italiano molto bene è americana. | *The girl who has blonde hair and speaks Italian quite well is American.* |

| | |
|---|---|
| Vengo con la macchina o a piedi. | *I'm coming by car or on foot.* |
| Gino e Gina parlano italiano. | *Gino and Gina speak Italian.* |

**AVOID THE** Blunder

✗ Gino e Gina parla italiano.

As mentioned above, a relative clause is introduced by a relative pronoun. The relative pronouns in Italian are as follows.

| | |
|---|---|
| che | *that, which, who, whom* |
| cui (*after a preposition*) | *which, of whom, to whom,* etc. |
| chi | *he who, she who, they who* |
| quel che<br>quello che<br>ciò che | *that which, what* |

Following are examples of their uses.

### che

| | |
|---|---|
| La donna che legge il giornale<br>è mia sorella. | *The woman who is reading the*<br>*newspaper is my sister.* |
| Il vestito che hai comprato ieri<br>è molto bello. | *The dress you bought yesterday*<br>*is very beautiful.* |
| Mi piace il libro che stai leggendo. | *I like the book you are reading.* |

**AVOID THE** Blunder

✗ La donna leggendo il giornale è mia madre.

### cui

| | |
|---|---|
| Il ragazzo a cui ho dato il libro<br>è mio cugino. | *The boy to whom I gave the book*<br>*is my cousin.* |
| Non trovo lo zaino in cui ho<br>messo il tuo libro. | *I can't find the backpack in*<br>*which I put your book.* |
| Ecco la rivista di cui ho parlato. | *Here is the magazine of which*<br>*I spoke.* |

**AVOID THE** Blunder

✗ La persona a chi parlavi è mio fratello.

## chi

Chi va in Italia si divertirà.

*He/She who goes to Italy will enjoy himself/herself.*

C'è chi dorme e c'è chi lavora.

*Some sleep, some work.*

AVOID THE *Blunder*

✗ Lui chi va in Italia si divertirà.

## quel che / quello che / ciò che

Non sai quel che dici.

*You don't know what you are saying.*

Quello che dici è vero.

*What / That which you are saying is true.*

Ciò che dici non ha senso.

*What you are saying makes no sense.*

AVOID THE *Blunder*

✗ Che dici non è vero.

Both *che* and *cui* can be replaced by *il quale* if there is an antecedent. *Il quale* agrees in gender and number with the antecedent; the definite article is necessary.

L'uomo che legge il giornale
è italiano.
L'uomo il quale legge il giornale
è italiano.

*The man who is reading the newspaper is Italian.*

Gli uomini che leggono
il giornale sono italiani.
Gli uomini i quali leggono
il giornale sono italiani.

*The men who are reading the newspaper are Italian.*

La donna che legge il giornale
è italiana.
La donna la quale legge
il giornale è italiana.

*The woman who is reading the newspaper is Italian.*

Le donne che leggono
il giornale sono italiane.
Le donne le quali leggono
il giornale sono italiane.

*The women who are reading the newspaper are Italian.*

✗ Gli uomini il quale leggono il giornale sono italiani.
✗ Le donne la quale leggono il giornale sono italiane.

The form *il cui* "whose" is used to indicate possession. The article agrees in gender and number with the noun modified.

| | |
|---|---|
| Ecco i ragazzi il cui padre è professore. | *Here are the boys whose father is a professor.* |
| Ecco lo scrittore i cui romanzi sono celebri. | *Here is the writer whose novels are famous.* |
| Ecco lo studente la cui intelligenza è straordinaria. | *Here is the student whose intelligence is extraordinary.* |
| Ecco la ragazza le cui amiche sono italiane. | *Here is the girl whose friends are Italian.* |

✗ Lui è l'uomo il cui sorella è medico.

# Exercises

**A** *Choose the correct pronoun or conjunction for each item.*

1. _____ Giacomo arriva, andremo al negozio.

   a. Quando

   b. Che

2. _____ arriva la madre, ci metteremo a studiare.

   a. Quel che

   b. Appena

3. _____ sei uscito, è arrivata Sandra.

   a. Quando

   b. Dopo che

4. _____ tu dormivi, io leggevo il giornale.

   a. Mentre

   b. Dopo che

5. La persona _____ sta leggendo il giornale è una mia amica.

   a. che

   b. cui

6. Le scarpe _____ hai comprato ieri sono molto belle.

   a. le cui

   b. le quali

7. La persona _____ hai dato il libro è un mio amico.

   a. a cui

   b. al quale

8. _____ va a Roma si divertirà.

   a. Ciò che

   b. Chi

9. Ecco il ragazzo _____ sorella vuole essere medico.

   a. il cui

   b. la cui

**B** *Join the sentences with an appropriate conjoining element.*

1. Maria sta studiando. Suo fratello guarda la TV.

_____

2. La ragazza ha i capelli biondi. La ragazza parla italiano molto bene.
   La ragazza è americana.

_____

_____

3. Paolo parla italiano. Franca parla italiano.

_____

4. Mi piace il libro. Maria sta leggendo il libro.

_____

5. Non trovo lo zaino. Nello zaino ho messo il tuo libro.

_____

# PRONOUNS

A pronoun is a word used in place of a noun, a substantive (a word that functions as a noun), or a noun phrase (a noun accompanied by articles, demonstratives, adjectives, etc.).

| | |
|---|---|
| Giovanni è americano. | *John is American.* |
| Lui è americano. | *He is American.* |

Several types of pronouns have been discussed in previous units, including reflexive and relative pronouns. This unit is limited to personal pronouns functioning as subjects and objects and to indefinite pronoun forms. These are major sources of blunders in Italian.

## Subject Pronouns

Personal pronouns refer to a person (*I, you, we,* and so on) and are classified as subject, object, or reflexive pronouns. They are also classified according to the person(s) speaking (first person), the person(s) spoken to (second person), or the person(s) spoken about (third person). The pronoun can, of course, be singular (referring to one person) or plural (referring to more than one person).

Subject pronouns are used as the subject of a verb.

| | |
|---|---|
| Io parlo italiano e lui parla francese. | *I speak Italian and he speaks French.* |

The Italian subject pronouns are as follows.

| | |
|---|---|
| io | *I* |
| tu | *you* (familiar singular) |
| lui | *he* |
| lei | *she* |
| Lei | *you* (polite singular) |
| | |
| noi | *we* |
| voi | *you* (familiar plural) |
| loro | *they* |
| Loro | *you* (polite plural) |

Note that *io* is not capitalized unless it is the first word of a sentence.

AVOID THE *Blunder*

✗ Vengo anch'Io.

A subject pronoun is optional in a simple affirmative sentence, because it is easy to tell from the verb ending which person is the subject.

| | |
|---|---|
| Io non capisco. | *I do not understand.* |
| OR Non capisco. | |
| Loro vanno in Italia. | *They are going to Italy.* |
| OR Vanno in Italia. | |

However, subject pronouns may be used for emphasis, to avoid ambiguity, or if more than one subject pronoun is required.

| | |
|---|---|
| Devi parlare tu, non io! | *You have to speak, not I!* |
| Non è possibile che l'abbiano fatto loro. | *It's not possible that they did it.* |
| Mentre lui guarda la TV, lei ascolta la radio. | *While he watches TV, she listens to the radio.* |
| Lui e io vogliamo che tu dica la verità. | *He and I want you to tell the truth.* |

AVOID THE *Blunder*

✗ Devi parlare, non devo io!

A subject pronoun must be used after the following adverbs.

| | |
|---|---|
| anche | *also, too* |
| neanche/neppure/nemmeno | *neither, not even* |
| proprio | *really* |

| | |
|---|---|
| Anche tu devi venire alla festa. | *You too must come to the party.* |
| Non è venuto neanche lui. | *He didn't come either.* |
| Signor Rossini, è proprio Lei? | *Mr. Rossini, is it really you?* |

AVOID THE *Blunder*

✗ Anche devi venire alla festa.
✗ Non è venuto neanche.

The English subject pronoun "it" is not usually stated in Italian.

| | |
|---|---|
| È vero. | *It is true.* |
| Sembra che sia vero. | *It appears to be true.* |

However, if the subject is required, the following forms are used.

esso (*masculine singular*)  essi (*masculine plural*)
essa (*feminine singular*)  esse (*feminine plural*)

| | |
|---|---|
| È una buona scusa, ma neanche essa potrà aiutarti adesso. | *It's a good excuse, but not even it can help you now.* |
| Sono buone scuse, ma neanche esse potranno aiutarti adesso. | *They are good excuses, but not even they can help you now.* |

AVOID THE *Blunder*

✗ È una buona scusa, ma neanche potrà aiutarti adesso.
✗ Sono buone scuse, ma neanche potranno aiutarti adesso.

Note that "you" has both familiar and polite forms in Italian.

| | |
|---|---|
| Maria, anche tu studi l'italiano? | *Mary, are you studying Italian too?* |
| Signora Giusti, anche Lei studia l'italiano? | *Mrs. Giusti, are you studying Italian too?* |

In writing, the polite forms (*Lei* and *Loro*) are usually capitalized in order to distinguish them from *lei* "she" and *loro* "they," but this is not obligatory.

AVOID THE *Blunder*

✗ Signora Giusti, anche tu studia l'italiano?

In the plural, there is a strong current tendency to use *voi* as the plural of both *tu* and *Lei*. *Loro* is restricted to very formal situations (for instance, in addressing an audience or when a waiter takes an order).

The forms *lui* and *lei* are used in ordinary conversation and for most purposes. However, there are two more-formal pronouns: *egli* and *ella*. These are especially used in reference to famous people.

| | |
|---|---|
| Dante scrisse la «Divina Commedia». Egli era fiorentino. | *Dante wrote* The Divine Comedy. *He was Florentine.* |
| Chi era Natalia Ginzburg? Ella era una grande scrittrice. | *Who was Natalia Ginzburg? She was a great writer.* |

AVOID THE *Blunder*

✗ Chi era Galileo? Lui era un grande scienziato (**scientist**).
✗ Chi era Lucrezia Borgia? Lei era una duchessa.

## Object Pronouns

Object pronouns are used as objects of verbs and other elements. Their primary use is to replace direct and indirect objects.

### DIRECT OBJECT

| | |
|---|---|
| Marco sta leggendo quel libro adesso. | *Mark is reading that book now.* |
| Marco lo sta leggendo adesso. | *Mark is reading it now.* |

### INDIRECT OBJECT

| | |
|---|---|
| Marco darà quel libro a sua sorella domani. | *Mark will give that book to his sister tomorrow.* |
| Marco le darà quel libro domani. | *Mark will give her that book tomorrow.* |

Italian object pronouns generally come right before the verb. There are some exceptions, however, which are discussed later in this unit.

The Italian direct and indirect object pronouns are as follows.

| DIRECT OBJECT PRONOUNS | | INDIRECT OBJECT PRONOUNS | |
|---|---|---|---|
| mi | *me* | mi | *to me* |
| ti | *you* (familiar singular) | ti | *to you* (familiar singular) |
| lo | *him, it* | gli | *to him* |
| la | *her, it* | le | *to her* |
| La | *you* (polite singular) | Le | *to you* (polite singular) |
| ci | *us* | ci | *to us* |
| vi | *you* (familiar plural) | vi | *to you* (familiar plural) |
| li | *them/you* (polite plural) (masculine) | gli | *to them/you* (polite plural) |
| le | *them/you* (polite plural) (feminine) | gli | *to them/you* (polite plural) |

Note that, in ordinary Italian, the plural of the indirect object pronouns *gli* "to him" and *le* "to her" is *gli* "to them." In more formal situations, however, some Italians prefer to use *loro* "to them," which goes after the verb.

| | |
|---|---|
| Dove sono i tuoi amici? | *Where are your (male) friends?* |
| Gli voglio parlare. | *I want to speak to them.* |
| OR Voglio parlare loro. | |

| | |
|---|---|
| Dove sono le tue amiche? | *Where are your (female) friends?* |
| Gli voglio parlare. | *I want to speak to them.* |
| OR Voglio parlare loro. | |

AVOID THE *Blunder*

✗ Lui dà il libro a mi.
✗ Marco li dà il libro.
✗ Voglio loro parlare.

The English direct object pronoun "it" (plural: "them") is expressed by the third-person direct object pronoun. Be careful! The pronoun must agree in gender and number with the noun it replaces.

**MASCULINE SINGULAR**

| | |
|---|---|
| Marco comprerà il gelato domani. | *Mark will buy the ice cream tomorrow.* |
| Marco lo comprerà domani. | *Mark will buy it tomorrow.* |

**FEMININE SINGULAR**

| | |
|---|---|
| Marco comprerà la rivista domani. | *Mark will buy the magazine tomorrow.* |
| Marco la comprerà domani. | *Mark will buy it tomorrow.* |

**MASCULINE PLURAL**

| | |
|---|---|
| Marco comprerà i biglietti domani. | *Mark will buy the tickets tomorrow.* |
| Marco li comprerà domani. | *Mark will buy them tomorrow.* |

**FEMININE PLURAL**

| | |
|---|---|
| Marco comprerà le riviste domani. | *Mark will buy the magazines tomorrow.* |
| Marco le comprerà domani. | *Mark will buy them tomorrow.* |

AVOID THE *Blunder*

✗ Marco comprerà li domani.

If the verb is in a compound tense, the past participle agrees in gender and number with these four pronouns (*lo, la, li,* and *le*).

**MASCULINE SINGULAR**

| | |
|---|---|
| Marco ha comprato il gelato ieri. | *Mark bought the ice cream yesterday.* |
| Marco lo ha comprato ieri. | *Mark bought it yesterday.* |

**FEMININE SINGULAR**

| | |
|---|---|
| Marco ha comprato la rivista ieri. | *Mark bought the magazine yesterday.* |
| Marco la ha comprata ieri. | *Mark bought it yesterday.* |

**MASCULINE PLURAL**

| | |
|---|---|
| Marco ha comprato i biglietti ieri. | *Mark bought the tickets yesterday.* |
| Marco li ha comprati ieri. | *Mark bought them yesterday.* |

**FEMININE PLURAL**

| | |
|---|---|
| Marco ha comprato le riviste ieri. | *Mark bought the magazines yesterday.* |
| Marco le ha comprate ieri. | *Mark bought them yesterday.* |

AVOID THE *Blunder*

✗ Marco li ha comprato ieri.
✗ Marco le ha comprato ieri.

Note that only the singular forms *lo* and *la* can be elided with the auxiliary forms of *avere* that begin with *h*: *ho, hai, ha,* and *hanno.*

Marco lo ha comprato ieri. → Marco l'ha comprato ieri.
Marco la ha comprata ieri. → Marco l'ha comprata ieri.

AVOID THE *Blunder*

✗ Lui l'ha comprati ieri.
✗ Lei l'ha viste ieri.

The past participle may agree with the other direct object pronouns (*mi, ti, ci,* and *vi*), but this is optional.

Giovanni ci ha chiamato. ⎫
Giovanni ci ha chiamati. ⎭    *John called us.*

The past participle does not agree with indirect object pronouns.

| Giovanni gli ha scritto. | *John wrote (to) him/them.* |
| Giovanni le ha scritto. | *John wrote (to) her.* |

Note that *le* can be either a direct object pronoun or an indirect object pronoun.

### AS DIRECT OBJECT PRONOUN (AGREEMENT)

| Lui ha mangiato le patate già. | *He already ate the potatoes.* |
| Lui le ha mangiate già. | *He already ate them.* |

### AS INDIRECT OBJECT PRONOUN (NO AGREEMENT)

| Lui ha scritto a sua sorella. | *He wrote to his sister.* |
| Lui le ha scritto. | *He wrote to her.* |

AVOID THE *Blunder*

✗ Marco, hai mangiato le caramelle? Sì, le ho mangiato.
✗ Marco, hai telefonato alla tua amica? No, non le ho telefonata.

## Double Pronouns

When both direct and indirect object pronouns are required, the following rules apply.

- The indirect object pronoun always precedes the direct object pronoun, and the only possible direct object forms are *lo, la, li,* and *le.*

| Marco mi dà il libro domani. | *Mark will give me the book tomorrow.* |
| Marco me lo dà domani. | *Mark will give it to me tomorrow.* |

AVOID THE *Blunder*

✗ Marco lo mi dà domani.

- The indirect pronouns *mi, ti, ci,* and *vi* are changed to *me, te, ce,* and *ve,* respectively.

| Maria mi dà il libro domani. | *Mary will give me the book tomorrow.* |
| Maria me lo dà domani. | *Mary will give it to me tomorrow.* |
| Maria ti ha dato i suoi libri già. | *Mary has already given her books to you.* |
| Maria te li ha dati già. | *Mary has already given them to you.* |

| | |
|---|---|
| Maria vi regalerà le scarpe per Natale. | *Mary will give you shoes for Christmas.* |
| Maria ve le regalerà per Natale. | *Mary will give them to you for Christmas.* |

Note that agreement of the past participle with the direct object pronoun still holds.

| | |
|---|---|
| Maria ci ha regalato la sua bella penna ieri. | *Mary gave us her beautiful pen yesterday.* |
| Maria ce l'ha regalata ieri. | *Mary gave it to us yesterday.* |

AVOID THE *Blunder*

✗ Maria te li ha dato già.
✗ Lui vi le ha date.

- The indirect object pronouns *gli* and *le* are both changed to *glie*, then combined with the direct object pronouns *lo, la, li,* and *le* to form one word: *glielo, gliela, glieli,* and *gliele.*

| | |
|---|---|
| Marco dà il libro a Paolo domani. | *Mark will give the book to Paul tomorrow.* |
| Marco glielo dà domani. | *Mark will give it to him tomorrow.* |
| Maria regalerà quella borsa a sua sorella per Natale. | *Mary will give her sister that purse for Christmas.* |
| Maria gliela regalerà per Natale. | *Mary will give it to her for Christmas.* |
| Il nonno ha dato i suoi orologi ad Alessandro due anni fa. | *The grandfather gave Alexander his watches two years ago.* |
| Il nonno glieli ha dati due anni fa. | *The grandfather gave them to him two years ago.* |
| Io ho dato le mie chiavi a Marco poco tempo fa. | *I gave Mark my keys a little while ago.* |
| Io gliele ho date poco tempo fa. | *I gave them to him a little while ago.* |

AVOID THE *Blunder*

✗ Le lo darà domani.
✗ Gli lo regalerà a Natale.

- Reflexive pronouns are changed to *me, te, se, ce, ve,* and *se* before direct object pronouns.

| | |
|---|---|
| Marco si mette sempre la giacca. | *Mark always puts on a jacket.* |
| Marco se la mette sempre. | *Mark always puts it on.* |

**AVOID THE** *Blunder*

✗ Maria si la mette sempre.

In compound tenses, the past participle agrees with the direct object pronoun, not with the subject.

| | |
|---|---|
| Marco si è messo la giacca ieri. | *Mark put on his jacket yesterday.* |
| (AGREEMENT WITH THE SUBJECT) | |
| Marco se la è messa ieri. | *Mark put it on yesterday.* |
| (AGREEMENT WITH THE DIRECT OBJECT PRONOUN) | |

**AVOID THE** *Blunder*

✗ Lei se le è messa ieri.

## Attached Pronouns

An object pronoun is attached to an infinitive or gerund. Double pronouns are written as one word in such cases.

| | |
|---|---|
| Prima di mangiare il gelato, mangerò i ravioli. | *Before eating the ice cream, I'm going to eat the ravioli.* |
| Prima di mangiarlo, mangerò i ravioli. | *Before eating it, I'm going to eat the ravioli.* |
| Prima di dare i miei libri a voi, li voglio leggere un'altra volta. | *Before giving my books to you, I want to read them one more time.* |
| Prima di darveli, li voglio leggere un'altra volta. | *Before giving them to you, I want to read them one more time.* |
| Vedendo Maria, l'ho salutata. | *Seeing Mary, I greeted her.* |
| Vedendola, l'ho salutata. | *Seeing her, I greeted her.* |

An object pronoun is also attached to the form *ecco* (see page 219).

| | |
|---|---|
| Ecco la matita. | *Here is the pencil.* |
| Eccola. | *Here it is.* |
| | |
| Ecco Marco e Maria. | *Here are Mark and Mary.* |
| Eccoli. | *Here they are.* |
| | |
| Ecco i libri per te. | *Here are the books for you.* |
| Eccoteli. | *Here they are for you.* |

If the conjugated verb is a modal verb, the object pronoun may be attached to the infinitive or placed before the modal verb.

| | |
|---|---|
| Non posso mangiare la carne. | *I cannot eat meat.* |
| Non posso mangiarla. | |
| Non la posso mangiare. ⎫ | *I cannot eat it.* |
| | |
| Tu devi fare un bel regalo | *You must give your sister a nice* |
| a tua sorella per Natale. | *gift for Christmas.* |
| Tu devi farglielo per Natale. ⎫ | |
| Tu glielo devi fare per Natale. ⎭ | *You must give it to her for Christmas.* |
| | |
| Lui mi vuole dare la sua | *He wants to give me his car.* |
| macchina. | |
| Lui vuole darmela. | |
| Lui me la vuole dare. ⎫ | *He wants to give it to me.* |

An object pronoun is also attached to familiar forms of the imperative. They are not attached to the polite *Lei* and *Loro* forms.

**FAMILIAR FORMS**

| | |
|---|---|
| Marco, mangia la mela! | *Mark, eat the apple!* |
| Marco, mangiala! | *Mark, eat it!* |
| Maria, scrivi l'email a tuo fratello! | *Mary, write your brother the e-mail!* |
| Maria, scriviglielo! | *Mary, write it to him!* |
| Marco e Maria, date la vostra penna a me! | *Mark and Mary, give your pen to me!* |
| Marco e Maria, datemela! | *Mark and Mary, give it to me!* |

AVOID THE *Blunder*

✗ Maria, glielo scrivi!
✗ Marco e Maria, me la date!

**POLITE FORMS**

| | |
|---|---|
| Signor Verdi, mangi la mela! | *Mr. Verdi, eat the apple!* |
| Signor Verdi, la mangi! | *Mr. Verdi, eat it!* |
| Signora Rossi, scriva l'email a Suo fratello! | *Mrs. Rossi, write your brother the e-mail!* |
| Signora Rossi, glielo scriva! | *Mrs. Rossi, write it to him!* |
| Signor Verdi e Signora Rossi, diano la Loro penna a me! | *Mr. Verdi and Mrs. Rossi, give your pen to me!* |
| Signor Verdi e Signor Rossi, me la diano! | *Mr. Verdi and Mrs. Rossi, give it to me!* |

AVOID THE *Blunder*

✗ Signor Bianchi, comprimela!

When attaching an object pronoun to a familiar imperative form ending with an apostrophe (*da', di', fa', sta',* or *va'*), the first letter (sound) of the pronoun is doubled.

| | |
|---|---|
| Dammi la penna! | *Give me the pen!* |
| Dilla! | *Say it!* |
| Fallo! | *Do it!* |

AVOID THE *Blunder*

✗ Dami la penna!

There is, of course, no double *gl*.

| | |
|---|---|
| Digli la verità! | *Tell him the truth!* |
| Faglielo! | *Do it for him!* |

AVOID THE *Blunder*

✗ Fagglielo!

With the second-person singular negative infinitive form of the imperative, the object pronoun is either attached to the infinitive or else placed before it.

| | | |
|---|---|---|
| **AFFIRMATIVE** | Mangialo! | *Eat it!* |
| **NEGATIVE** | Non mangiarlo!<br>Non lo mangiare! ⎱ | *Don't eat it!* |

| | | |
|---|---|---|
| **AFFIRMATIVE** | Mandamela! | *Send it to me!* |
| **NEGATIVE** | Non mandarmela!<br>Non me la mandare! ⎱ | *Don't send it to me!* |

AVOID THE *Blunder*

✗ Non mandarmi la!

## Stressed Pronouns

There is a second type of object pronoun that goes after the verb, known as a stressed or tonic pronoun.

| BEFORE THE VERB | | AFTER THE VERB | |
|---|---|---|---|
| **DIRECT OBJECT PRONOUNS** | | | |
| mi | *me* | me | *me* |
| ti | *you* (familiar singular) | te | *you* (familiar singular) |
| lo | *him* | lui | *him* |
| la | *her* | lei | *her* |
| La | *you* (polite singular) | Lei | *you* (polite singular) |
| ci | *us* | noi | *us* |
| vi | *you* (familiar plural) | voi | *you* (familiar plural) |
| li | *them/you* (polite plural) (masculine) | loro | *them/you* (polite plural) |
| le | *them/you* (polite plural) (feminine) | loro | *them/you* (polite plural) |

### INDIRECT OBJECT PRONOUNS

| mi | *to me* | a me | *to me* |
|----|---------|------|---------|
| ti | *to you* (familiar singular) | a te | *to you* (familiar singular) |
| gli | *to him* | a lui | *to him* |
| le | *to her* | a lei | *to her* |
| Le | *to you* (polite singular) | a Lei | *to you* (polite singular) |
| ci | *to us* | a noi | *to us* |
| vi | *to you* (familiar plural) | a voi | *to you* (familiar plural) |
| gli | *to them/you* (polite plural) (masculine) | a loro | *to them/you* (polite plural) |
| gli | *to them/you* (polite plural) (feminine) | a loro | *to them/you* (polite plural) |

In most cases, the two types of pronouns can be used interchangeably. However, the stressed pronouns are more appropriate when emphasis is required or in order to avoid ambiguity. They allow you to put greater emphasis on the object.

| Marco lo darà a me, non a te! | *Mark will give it to me, not to you!* |
|---|---|
| Ieri ho scritto a te, e solo a te! | *Yesterday I wrote to you, and only you!* |

Stressed pronouns are the only object pronouns you can use after a preposition.

| Maria viene con noi. | *Mary is coming with us.* |
|---|---|
| Il professore parla di te. | *The professor is speaking of you.* |
| L'ha fatto per me. | *He did it for me.* |

AVOID THE *Blunder*

✗ Lui la darà a mi.
✗ Gli ha parlato, non le ha parlato.

## Other Pronouns

Words such as *molto* and *tanto* can also function as pronouns.

| Lui mangia assai. | *He eats quite a lot.* |
|---|---|
| Tuo fratello dorme molto, no? | *Your brother sleeps a lot, doesn't he?* |
| Ieri ho mangiato troppo. | *Yesterday I ate too much.* |

When referring to people in general, plural forms like *molti* "many," *alcuni* "some," *tanti* "a lot of," *pochi* "few," *parecchi* "quite a few," and *tutti* "all" are used.

| | |
|---|---|
| Molti vanno in Italia quest'anno. | *Many (people) are going to Italy this year.* |
| Alcuni dormono, ma parecchi lavorano già. | *Some are sleeping, but quite a few are already working.* |
| Tutti sanno quello. | *Everyone knows that.* |

The corresponding feminine forms (*molte, alcune,* etc.) are used to refer to females.

| | |
|---|---|
| Di quelle ragazze, molte sono italiane. | *Of those girls, many are Italian.* |
| Di tutte quelle donne, alcune sono americane. | *Of all those women, some are American.* |

**AVOID THE *Blunder***

✗ Di tutte quelle donne, alcuni sono americane.

Note the following useful expression.

alcuni ... altri    *some . . . others*

| | |
|---|---|
| Alcuni andranno in Italia; altri, invece, andranno in Francia. | *Some will go to Italy; others, instead, will go to France.* |

The pronoun *ne* has three main functions.

- It replaces partitive constructions.

| | |
|---|---|
| Comprerai anche delle patate? | *Will you also buy some potatoes?* |
| Sì, ne comprerò. | *Yes, I'll buy some.* |

- It replaces nouns used with numbers and expressions of quantity.

| | |
|---|---|
| Quanti libri hai letto? | *How many books did you read?* |
| Ne ho letti due. | *I read two (of them).* |

Note that the past participle agrees with the noun replaced by *ne*.

| | |
|---|---|
| Hai letto molti libri, non è vero? | *You read a lot of books, didn't you?* |
| Sì, ne ho letti molti. | *Yes, I read a lot (of them).* |

- It replaces phrases introduced by *di*.

| | |
|---|---|
| Ha parlato di matematica, vero? | *He spoke about mathematics, didn't he?* |
| Sì, ne ha parlato. | *Yes, he spoke about it.* |

Note that there is no past participle agreement in this case.

The locative (place) pronoun *ci* means "(to) there."

| | |
|---|---|
| Andate in Italia, non è vero? | *You are going to Italy, aren't you?* |
| Sì, ci andiamo domani. | *Yes, we are going there tomorrow.* |
| Marco vive a Perugia, non è vero? | *Mark lives in Perugia, doesn't he?* |
| Sì, ci vive da molti anni. | *Yes, he has been living there for many years.* |

*Ne* is used to express "from there."

| | |
|---|---|
| Sei arrivato dall'Italia ieri, non è vero? | *You arrived from Italy yesterday, didn't you?* |
| Sì, ne sono arrivato proprio ieri. | *Yes, I did indeed arrive from there yesterday.* |

Both *ci* and *ne* can occur with an object pronoun. In such a case, *ci* is changed to *ce* and is placed before the object pronoun, whereas *ne* is placed after it.

| | |
|---|---|
| Ho messo la penna nello zaino ieri. | *I put the pen in my backpack yesterday.* |
| Ce l'ho messa ieri. | *I put it there yesterday.* |
| Metticela! | *Put it there!* |
| Gli ho dato delle matite ieri. | *I gave him some pencils yesterday.* |
| Gliene ho date ieri. | *I gave him some yesterday.* |
| Dammi due matite! | *Give me two pencils!* |
| Dammene due! | *Give me two (of them)!* |

# Exercises

**A** *Choose the correct pronoun for each item.*

1. Mio fratello è andato anche _____ in Italia.

   a. lui

   b. egli

2. Dante era anche _____ un fiorentino.

   a. lui

   b. egli

3. Franco, quando _____ hai chiamato?

   a. mi

   b. me

4. Maria, è vero che _____ hai parlato già?

   a. gli

   b. lui

5. Ho parlato a suo fratello ieri. Non _____ ho detto proprio niente (*nothing*).

   a. gli

   b. le

6. Loro hanno parlato a quella donna ieri. Non _____ hanno detto proprio niente.

   a. gli

   b. le

7. Vieni con _____ in centro!

   a. mi

   b. me

**B** *Rewrite each sentence, replacing the object(s) in italics with the appropriate pronoun(s) and making all necessary changes.*

ESEMPIO    Marco mi darà *il libro* domani.

_Marco me lo darà domani._

1. Io ti ho dati *le matite* ieri.

   _____

2. Loro hanno regalato *le scarpe alla loro amica.*

   _____

3. Prima di mangiare *gli gnocchi,* voglio mangiare l'antipasto.

   _____

4. Ecco *il fratello e sua sorella.*

   _____

5. Lui si è messo *le scarpe nuove* ieri.

   _____

6. Non voglio mangiare *la carne.*

   _____

7. Marco, mangia *le patate!*

   _____

8. Maria, dammi *due matite!*

   _____

9. Marco è andato *in Italia* ieri.

   _____

10. Maria ha comprato *molte mele* ieri.

    _____

11. Ci sono *quattro matite* nello zaino.

    _____

# ADVERBS

Adverbs are words that modify verbs, adjectives, or other adverbs. They convey relations of manner, time, place, and degree of intensity.

| | |
|---|---|
| Maria guida lentamente. | *Maria drives slowly.* |
| Marco arriva oggi. | *Mark is arriving today.* |
| Pietro siede qui. | *Peter is sitting here.* |
| Questa casa è molto bella. | *This house is very beautiful.* |
| Giovanni guida troppo lentamente. | *John drives too slowly.* |

## Adverbs of Manner

Adverbs of manner are formed as follows.

- Change the *-o* ending of a descriptive adjective to *-a*.

| | | |
|---|---|---|
| certo | *certain* | certa- |
| lento | *slow* | lenta- |

- Add *-mente* (which roughly corresponds to the English ending "-ly").

| | | |
|---|---|---|
| certa- + -mente → certamente | *certainly* |
| lenta- + -mente → lentamente | *slowly* |

AVOID THE *Blunder*

✗ certomente

- If the adjective ends in *-e* instead of *-o,* simply add *-mente.*

| | | | |
|---|---|---|---|
| elegante | *elegant* | elegantemente | *elegantly* |
| semplice | *simple* | semplicemente | *simply* |

- However, if the adjective ends in *-le* or *-re* preceded by a vowel, the *-e* is dropped.

| | | | |
|---|---|---|---|
| facile | *easy* | facilmente | *easily* |
| popolare | *popular* | popolarmente | *popularly* |

There are a few exceptions to these rules.

| | | | |
|---|---|---|---|
| benevolo | *benevolent* | benevolmente | *benevolently* |
| leggero | *light* | leggermente | *lightly* |
| violento | *violent* | violentemente | *violently* |

Following is a list of some common adverbs of manner, with their corresponding adjectives.

| ADJECTIVE | | ADVERB OF MANNER | |
|---|---|---|---|
| enorme | *enormous* | enormemente | *enormously* |
| felice | *happy* | felicemente | *happily* |
| preciso | *precise* | precisamente | *precisely* |
| raro | *rare* | raramente | *rarely* |
| regolare | *regular* | regolarmente | *regularly* |
| speciale | *special* | specialmente | *specially* |
| triste | *sad* | tristemente | *sadly* |
| utile | *useful* | utilmente | *usefully* |
| vero | *true* | veramente | *truly* |

These adjectives normally follow the verb, but they may begin a sentence for emphasis.

| | |
|---|---|
| Lui scrive delle email ai suoi amici regolarmente. | *He sends his friends e-mails regularly.* |
| Regolarmente, lui scrive delle email ai suoi amici. | *Regularly, he sends his friends e-mails.* |

## Other Kinds of Adverbs

Adverbs cover a wide range of meanings, from time relations to quantity. Following are some very common adverbs and adverbial phrases, many of which have been introduced in previous units.

| | |
|---|---|
| abbastanza | *enough* |
| allora | *then* |
| anche | *also, too* |
| ancora | *again, still, yet* |
| anzi | *as a matter of fact* |
| appena | *just, barely* |
| di nuovo | *again, anew* |
| domani | *tomorrow* |
| finora | *until now* |
| fra/tra poco | *in a little while* |
| già | *already* |
| in fretta | *in a hurry* |
| insieme | *together* |
| invece | *instead* |
| lì/là | *there* |
| lontano | *far (away)* |
| male | *bad(ly)* |
| nel frattempo | *in the meantime* |
| oggi | *today* |
| oggigiorno | *nowadays* |
| ormai | *by now* |
| per caso | *by chance* |
| piuttosto | *rather* |
| poi | *after, then* |
| presto | *early* |
| prima | *first* |
| purtroppo | *unfortunately* |
| quasi | *almost* |
| qui | *here* |
| solo | *only* |
| spesso | *often* |
| stamani | *this morning* |
| stasera | *this evening* |
| subito | *right away* |
| tardi | *late* |
| vicino | *near(by)* |

Following are examples of how these adverbial expressions are used.

| | |
|---|---|
| Marco l'ha fatto ancora una volta. | *Mark did it again / one more time.* |
| Lui ha appena finito di lavorare. | *He has just finished working.* |
| Lei abita lontano, e lui vicino. | *She lives far away, and he nearby.* |
| Prima voglio mangiare e poi studierò. | *First I want to eat, and then I will study.* |
| Sono quasi le tre. | *It's almost three o'clock.* |
| Loro vanno spesso al cinema. | *They often go to the movies.* |

**AVOID THE** *Blunder*

✗ Marco l'ha fatto di nuovo una volta.

In compound tenses, some of these adverbs are placed between the auxiliary verb and the past participle. The ones most commonly placed in this way are *ancora, appena,* and *già.*

| | |
|---|---|
| Non abbiamo ancora finito di lavorare. | *We haven't yet finished working.* |
| Ha appena telefonato. | *She has just phoned.* |
| Sono già usciti. | *They went out already.* |

**AVOID THE** *Blunder*

✗ Non ancora abbiamo finito di lavorare.
✗ Ha telefonato appena.
✗ Già sono usciti.

The adjectives *molto, tanto, poco, troppo,* and *parecchio* can also be used as adverbs. In this case, there is no agreement with nouns.

**ADJECTIVE**

| | |
|---|---|
| Lei ha molti soldi. | *She has a lot of money.* |
| Ci sono pochi studenti. | *There are few students.* |

**ADVERB**

| | |
|---|---|
| Lei è molto intelligente. | *She is very intelligent.* |
| Loro studiano poco. | *They study little.* |

To determine if a word such as *molto* is an adjective or adverb, check the following word. If it is a noun, then *molto* is an adjective and agrees with the noun. Otherwise, it can be either an adverb or a pronoun; in either case, no agreement pattern is required.

AVOID THE *Blunder*

✗ Lui ha molto soldi.
✗ Mia sorella è molta intelligente.

## Comparison of Adverbs

Adverbs are compared in the same manner as adjectives (see pages 78–81).

| lentamente | *slowly* | più lentamente | *more slowly* |
| facilmente | *easily* | meno facilmente | *less easily* |
| lontano | *far* | il più lontano | *the farthest* |

Note the unusual comparative forms below.

| ADVERB | | COMPARATIVE | | SUPERLATIVE | |
|---|---|---|---|---|---|
| bene | *well* | più bene / meglio | *better* | il meglio | *the best* |
| male | *bad(ly)* | più male / peggio | *worse* | il peggio | *the worst* |

AVOID THE *Blunder*

✗ il più bene
✗ il più male

# Exercises

**A** *Change each adjective into an adverb of manner, and each adverb into an adjective.*

1. certamente _____
2. semplice _____
3. facilmente _____
4. popolare _____
5. benevolmente _____
6. leggero _____
7. enorme _____
8. felicemente _____
9. preciso _____
10. specialmente _____
11. utile _____
12. veramente _____

**B** *Choose the correct adverb for each item.*

1. Noi andiamo _____ al cinema.

   a. spesso

   b. già

2. Lui l'ha fatto _____ una volta.

   a. ancora

   b. sempre

3. Mio fratello vive _____, e mia sorella vicino.

   a. lontano

   b. sempre

4. È _____ l'una.

   a. quasi

   b. poi

5. Noi abbiamo _____ finito di lavorare.

   a. subito

   b. appena

6. Prima voglio guardare quel programma e _____ studierò.

   a. poi

   b. anzi

7. Loro mangiano _____.

   a. molti

   b. molto

8. Noi invece mangiamo _____.

   a. pochi

   b. poco

9. Ieri, Maria non stava troppo bene, ma oggi sta _____.

   a. meglio

   b. migliore

# PREPOSITIONS

A preposition is a word that comes before a noun, pronoun, substantive, or noun phrase, to show its relationship to another part of the sentence.

La borsa di Maria è nuova.　　*Mary's purse is new.*
Lui va a scuola in macchina.　　*He goes to school by car.*

## Prepositional Contractions

When the following prepositions immediately precede a definite article, they contract with it to form one word.

| a | to, at | in | in |
|---|---|---|---|
| di | of | su | on |
| da | from | | |

Examples of contractions follow.

- di + il → del (fratello)

  Questo è il libro del fratello di Francesca.

  *This is the book of Francesca's brother.*

- in + la → nella (scatola)

  Ci sono due euro nella scatola.

  *There are two euros in the box.*

- da + l' → dall' (Italia)

  Arrivano dall'Italia domani.

  *They are arriving from Italy tomorrow.*

The following chart summarizes the contracted forms.

| | il | lo | l' | la | i | gli | le |
|---|---|---|---|---|---|---|---|
| **a** | al | allo | all' | alla | ai | agli | alle |
| **da** | dal | dallo | dall' | dalla | dai | dagli | dalle |
| **di** | del | dello | dell' | della | dei | degli | delle |
| **in** | nel | nello | nell' | nella | nei | negli | nelle |
| **su** | sul | sullo | sull' | sulla | sui | sugli | sulle |

✗ Lui parlerà a il professore domani.
✗ Ecco il libro di la madre.
✗ Ho messo la penna su la tavola.
✗ Loro vivono in gli Stati Uniti.

Contraction with the preposition *con* "with" is optional. In fact, only the forms *col* (= *con* + *il*) and *coll'* (= *con* + *l'*) are found in current Italian with any degree of frequency.

| | |
|---|---|
| Lui parlerà col professore domani. | *He will speak with the professor tomorrow.* |
| Loro arriveranno coll'Alitalia. | *They will arrive on Alitalia.* |

These forms, although possible, are rarely, if ever, used. Avoid them.

✗ cogli zii
✗ colle amiche

Other prepositions do not contract.

| | |
|---|---|
| fra/tra | *between, among* |
| per | *for, through, on account of* |
| sopra | *above, on top* |
| sotto | *under, below* |

| | |
|---|---|
| L'ho messo tra la tavola e la sedia. | *I put it between the table and the chair.* |
| L'ho messo sotto la tavola. | *I put it under the table.* |

✗ L'ho fatto pella ragazza.

The article is dropped in expressions that have a high degree of usage or have become idiomatic.

| | |
|---|---|
| Sono a casa. | *I am at home.* |
| Vado in macchina. | *I'm going by car.* |

However, if the noun in such an expression is modified in any way, the article must be used.

| | |
|---|---|
| Andremo alla casa nuova di Michele. | *We will be going to Michael's new home.* |
| Vado nella macchina di Marco. | *I'm going in Mark's car.* |

AVOID THE *Blunder*

✗ Sono alla casa.
✗ Vado in macchina di Marco.

## Special Uses

Prepositions have many uses. Only the uses that are a common source of blunders are discussed here.

- *A* is used before a city name to render the idea of "in a city."

| | |
|---|---|
| Vivo a Roma. | *I live in Rome.* |

Before other geographical entities, *in* is used.

| | |
|---|---|
| Vivo in Italia. | *I live in Italy.* |
| Andiamo in Europa domani. | *We are going to Europe tomorrow.* |

- *Da* translates "to" and "from" in expressions such as the following.

| | |
|---|---|
| Vado dal medico domani. | *I'm going to the doctor tomorrow.* |
| Vengo dalla farmacia. | *I'm coming from the pharmacy.* |

- *Da* translates "since" and "for" with progressive tenses such as in the following examples.

| | |
|---|---|
| Vivo qui dal 2004. | *I have been living here since 2004.* |
| Vivo qui da venti anni. | *I have been living here for 20 years.* |

- *Da* translates the expression "as a . . .".

| | |
|---|---|
| Te lo dico da amico. | *I'm telling it to you as a friend.* |
| Da bambino, navigavo spesso Internet. | *As a child, I used to surf the Internet often.* |

- In expressions consisting of a noun + infinitive, *da* is translated in several ways.

| | |
|---|---|
| una macchina da vendere | *a car for sale* |
| un abito da sera | *an evening dress* |

- *Di* is used to indicate possession or some other relationship.

| | |
|---|---|
| È la macchina nuova di Alessandro. | *It is Alexander's new car.* |
| Come si chiama la figlia del professore? | *What is the name of the professor's daughter?* |

- *Per* is used in time expressions when future duration is implied.

| | |
|---|---|
| Abiterò in questa città per tre anni. | *I will live in this city for three years.* |

AVOID THE *Blunder*

✗ Vivo in Roma.
✗ Vado all'Italia domani.
✗ Vivo qui per dieci anni.
✗ Vado al medico domani.

## Exercises

**A** *Fill in the blank with the appropriate preposition (simple or contracted with the definite article).*

1. I soldi sono _____ scatola.

2. Ecco i libri _____ amici miei.

3. Le matite sono _____ tavola.

4. Domani mio cugino andrà _____ medico.

5. Arrivano _____ nove stasera.

6. Noi viaggeremo (*We will travel*) _____ Alitalia.

7. L'ho messo _____ sedia e la tavola.

8. Lui invece l'ha messo _____ tavola, non sotto.

9. Maria starà _____ casa domani tutto il giorno.

10. Preferisco andare _____ macchina a lavorare.

11. Andremo _____ casa nuova di mio fratello.

12. Andremo _____ macchina di mia sorella.

**B** *Express the following English sentences in Italian.*

1. *I live in Florence.*

_____

2. *They live in the United States.*

_____

3. *There's Sarah's new car.*

_____

4. *What's the name of your professor's daughter?*

_____

5. *Are they going to the doctor tomorrow?*

_____

6. *I'm coming from Italy.*

_____

7. *They have been living in Italy for six years.*

_____

8. *As a child, I used to surf the Internet often.*

_____

9. *She loves to put on an evening dress.*

_____

# MISCELLANEOUS TOPICS

This unit discusses the remaining areas of grammar that cause blunders for many learners of Italian.

## Negatives

Negative words are used to deny, refuse, or oppose something. Any sentence can be made negative in Italian by putting *non* before the predicate.

| | |
|---|---|
| Non conosco nessuno qui. | *I don't know anyone here.* |
| Non lo faccio più. | *I won't do it anymore.* |

### AVOID THE *Blunder*

✗ Conosco non nessuno qui.

Following are some common negative constructions. Note that *non* is retained in all of them.

| | |
|---|---|
| non ... affatto | *not at all* |
| non ... mai | *never* |
| non ... mica | *not really, quite* |
| non ... né ... né | *neither . . . nor* |
| non ... neanche/nemmeno/neppure | *not even* |
| non ... nessuno | *no one* |
| non ... niente/nulla | *nothing* |
| non ... più | *no more, no longer* |

| AFFIRMATIVE | NEGATIVE |
|---|---|
| Lui canta sempre. | Lui non canta mai. |
| *He always sings.* | *He never sings.* |
| Ci vado spesso. | Non ci vado mai. |
| *I go there a lot.* | *I never go there.* |

**269**

| | |
|---|---|
| Parlo e scrivo bene. | Non parlo né scrivo bene. |
| *I speak and write well.* | *I neither speak nor write well.* |
| Lui conosce tutti. | Lui non conosce nessuno. |
| *He knows everyone.* | *He doesn't know anyone.* |

AVOID THE *Blunder*

✗ Lui ha capito affatto.
✗ Lui va mai in centro.

A negative word can be put at the beginning of a sentence for emphasis. In this case, the *non* is omitted.

| | |
|---|---|
| Nessuno parla! | *No one is speaking!* |
| Mai capirò i verbi! | *Never will I understand verbs!* |

AVOID THE *Blunder*

✗ Non mai capirò i verbi!

## Other Topics

■ The verb *fare* can be used in causative constructions ("to have someone do something").

| | |
|---|---|
| Maria fa lavare i piatti a suo fratello. | *Mary has her brother wash the dishes.* |
| Maria li fa lavare a lui. | *Mary has him wash them.* |

AVOID THE *Blunder*

✗ Maria ha lavare i piatti a lui.
✗ Maria lui fa lavare.

■ In the present conditional tense, the modal verbs *potere, volere,* and *dovere* are translated in English as "could," "would," and "should," respectively; in the past conditional, they are translated as "could have," "would have," and "should have," respectively.

| | |
|---|---|
| Lo potrei fare. | *I could do it.* |
| Lo avrei potuto fare. | *I could have done it.* |

| | |
|---|---|
| Lo vorrei fare. | *I would want to do it.* |
| Lo avrei voluto fare. | *I would have wanted to do it.* |
| Lo dovrei fare. | *I should do it.* |
| Lo avrei dovuto fare. | *I should have done it.* |

AVOID THE *Blunder*

✗ Lo posso fare.
✗ Lo farei.

■ Whether an object is direct or indirect depends on the verb. Some verbs are followed only by one type of object or the other. Fortunately, most verbs in Italian match their English equivalents when it comes to whether or not a direct or indirect object should follow.

| | |
|---|---|
| Maria mangia la mela. | *Mary eats the apple.* |
| Marco guida una macchina italiana. | *Mark drives an Italian car.* |

However, there are differences! Following are the verbs that produce the greatest number of blunders for learners.

## Verbs Requiring a Direct Object

### ascoltare *to listen (to)*

| | |
|---|---|
| Mia madre ascolta la radio ogni sera. | *My mother listens to the radio every evening.* |

### aspettare *to wait (for)*

| | |
|---|---|
| Maria sta aspettando l'autobus. | *Mary is waiting for the bus.* |

### cercare *to search/look (for)*

| | |
|---|---|
| Lei sta cercando la sua borsa. | *She is looking for her purse.* |

## Verbs Requiring an Indirect Object

### chiedere (a) *to ask (someone)*

| | |
|---|---|
| Marco chiede al professore di venire. | *Mark asks the professor to come.* |

### rispondere (a) *to answer*

| | |
|---|---|
| La studentessa risponde sempre alle domande. | *The student always answers the questions.* |

## telefonare (a) *to phone*

Daniela telefona spesso a sua madre.

*Daniela phones her mother often.*

**AVOID THE** *Blunder*

✗ Maria ascolta sempre alla radio.
✗ Lui sta aspettando per l'autobus.
✗ Marco chiede il suo amico di venire.
✗ Noi rispondiamo sempre le domande.
✗ Daniela telefona spesso sua madre.

## Exercises

**A** *Rewrite each sentence in the negative.*

1. Lui mangia sempre gli spaghetti.

2. Ieri ho mangiato la carne e le patate.

3. Marco conosce tutti in quella scuola.

4. Lui vuole qualcosa.

5. Quello è proprio vero.

**B** *Express the following English sentences in Italian.*

1. *Mary has her sister wash the dishes.*

2. *I could call her.*

3. *He could have called her.*

4. *I would want to do it, but I can't.*

5. *I would have wanted to do it.*

6. *I should do it more often.*

7. *My mother listens to the radio every evening.*

8. *Mary is waiting for the bus.*

9. *I am looking for my purse.*

10. *He asked the professor to come.*

   _____

11. *She phones her mother often.*

   _____

12. *Mary always answers the questions.*

   _____

# TRICKY WORDS AND EXPRESSIONS

Certain Italian words and expressions constitute a constant source of blunders; some of these are so-called *falsi amici*. A "false friend" is an Italian word that has a common historical source with (and therefore looks like) an English word, but has a different meaning. For example, *libreria* and "library" come from the same Latin word, but *libreria* does not mean "library." It means "bookstore."

This unit discusses the most common tricky words and expressions.

## Knowing

The verbs *conoscere* and *sapere* both mean "to know." But they are used in specific, mutually exclusive ways.

- "To know someone" is rendered by *conoscere*.

  | | |
  |---|---|
  | Maria non conosce quell'avvocato. | *Mary doesn't know that lawyer.* |
  | Chi conosce la dottoressa Verdi? | *Who knows Dr. Verdi?* |

- "To be familiar with something" is also rendered by *conoscere*.

  | | |
  |---|---|
  | Conosci Roma? | *Are you familiar with Rome?* |
  | Conosco un bel ristorante qui vicino. | *I know a good restaurant nearby.* |

- "To know something" is rendered by *sapere*.

  | | |
  |---|---|
  | Marco non sa la verità. | *Mark doesn't know the truth.* |
  | Chi sa come si chiama quella donna? | *Who knows what that woman's name is?* |

- "To know how to do something" is also rendered by *sapere*.

  | | |
  |---|---|
  | Mia sorella sa parlare italiano. | *My sister knows how to speak Italian.* |
  | Sai cantare? | *Do you know how to sing?* |

AVOID THE *Blunder*

✗ Io so Maria.
✗ Sai Roma?
✗ Chi conosce come si chiama?
✗ Mia sorella conosce parlare italiano.

## Cognates

Cognates are Italian and English words that look alike. This is because they have a common origin; they are, so to speak, "friends." But just like friends, they can be "good" or "false." False friends are a constant source of blunders. Following are the most common ones.

| ENGLISH WORD | FALSE FRIEND | MEANING OF FALSE FRIEND | CORRECT ITALIAN WORD |
|---|---|---|---|
| *accident* | accidente | *unexpected event* | incidente |
| *argument* | argomento | *topic* | discussione |
| *assist* | assistere | *to attend* | aiutare |
| *brave* | bravo | *good* | coraggioso |
| *conductor (music)* | conduttore | *bus/train conductor* | direttore |
| *confront* | confrontare | *to compare* | affrontare |
| *effective* | effettivo | *actual* | efficace |
| *factory* | fattoria | *farm* | fabbrica |
| *firm* | firma | *signature* | ditta |
| *large* | largo | *wide* | grande |
| *lecture* | lettura | *reading* | conferenza/ lezione |
| *library* | libreria | *bookstore* | biblioteca |
| *magazine* | magazzino | *department store* | rivista |
| *sensible* | sensibile | *sensitive* | sensato |
| *stamp* | stampa | *the press* | francobollo |

AVOID THE *Blunder*

✗ Io lavoro in una fattoria.
✗ Ho bisogno di due stampe.
✗ Vuoi che io ti assisti?
✗ Quello che hai fatto non è molto sensibile.

## Idiomatic Expressions with *avere*

An idiomatic expression is a phrase that is fixed in form and whose meaning cannot always be determined by the meanings of its constituent words.

The following expressions with *avere* are a constant source of blunders.

| | |
|---|---|
| Ho fame. | *I am hungry.* (literally, *I have hunger.*) |
| Non ha paura. | *He is not afraid.* (literally, *He does not have fear.*) |
| Ho caldo. | *I am hot.* (literally, *I have heat.*) |
| Ho freddo. | *I am cold.* (literally, *I have cold.*) |
| Ho fretta. | *I am in a hurry.* (literally, *I have haste.*) |
| Ho ragione. | *I am right.* (literally, *I have rightness.*) |
| Ho torto. | *I am wrong.* (literally, *I have wrongness.*) |
| Ho sonno. | *I am sleepy.* (literally, *I have sleepiness.*) |

AVOID THE *Blunder*

✗ Sono caldo.
✗ È freddo.

## Exercises

**A** *Fill in the blank with the appropriate present indicative form of* sapere *or* conoscere.

1. Lui _____ l'italiano molto bene.
2. Tutti _____ Alessandro.
3. Voi _____ parlare bene.
4. Chi _____ il professor Verdi?
5. Io non _____ Roma affatto.
6. Loro _____ un bel ristorante qui vicino.
7. Mia sorella _____ parlare italiano.
8. Marco non _____ la verità.

**B** *Write the Italian equivalent of each English word.*

1. *accident* _____
2. *argument* _____
3. *assist* _____
4. *brave* _____
5. *conductor (music)* _____
6. *confront* _____
7. *effective* _____
8. *factory* _____
9. *firm* _____
10. *large* _____
11. *lecture* _____
12. *magazine* _____
13. *sensible* _____
14. *stamp* _____

**C** *Express the following English sentences in Italian.*

1. *Yesterday we were hungry, so we ate a lot.*

   _____

2. *Excuse me, but I'm in a hurry.*

   _____

3. *I believe you are wrong.*

   _____

4. *She is always hot.*

   _____

5. *He is always cold.*

   _____

6. *Mr. Verdi is right.*

   _____

7. *Mrs. Verdi is wrong.*

   _____

8. *I am very sleepy.*

   _____

# CATCH THE BLUNDERS

**A** *Rewrite each sentence, correcting the spelling and capitalization errors.*

1. Marco è un Cattolico.

_____

2. Maria ha molti amichi.

_____

3. Oggi è Martedì, il venti febbraio.

_____

4. Marco arriva a Gennaio.

_____

5. Perche dici questo?

_____

6. Loro sono a schuola.

_____


**B** *Rewrite each sentence, correcting the grammar errors.*

1. Che bello film!

_____

2. Ho un mal di stomaco.

_____

3. Loro hanno un cane e uno gatto.

_____

4. Sono la zia e il zio dall'Italia.

_____

5. Io amo una carne.

_____

6. La gente amano l'Italia.

   _____

7. Io mangio sempre i meli.

   _____

8. Preferisco i pani.

   _____

9. Lui porta il baffo.

   _____

10. Oggi è tre marzo.

    _____

11. Oggi è l'uno ottobre.

    _____

12. La camicia e la borsa sono nuovi.

    _____

13. È una bianca camicia.

    _____

14. Lei è una molto intelligente studentessa.

    _____

15. Ho mangiato molto patate ieri.

    _____

16. Questo è il sua libro.

    _____

17. Non ho degli zii.

    _____

18. Prendo qualche zucchero.

    _____

19. I miei amici vivono in gli Stati Uniti.

    _____

20. Tu fini alle sei?

    _____

21. Noi non capisciamo il francese.

    _____

22. Quando mia sorella era giovane, aveva suonato il pianoforte.

_____

23. Da giovane, lei ha avuto i capelli biondi.

_____

24. Ieri, mentre lui dormiva, io ho guardato la TV.

_____

25. Marco, la mangia!

_____

26. Maria, non mangiala!

_____

27. Dammilo!

_____

28. Signorina Dorelli, alzati!

_____

29. Che cosa è? C'è una nuova borsa.

_____

30. Io ti le ho date già.

_____

31. Loro gli le hanno date.

_____

32. Prima di le mangiare, voglio mangiare l'antipasto.

_____

33. Maria starà nella casa domani tutto il giorno.

_____

34. Preferisco andare nella macchina a lavorare.

_____

35. Andremo con macchina di mia sorella.

_____

**C**   *Rewrite each sentence, correcting the vocabulary errors.*

1. Io non so Roma affatto.

   _____

2. Loro sanno un bel ristorante qui vicino.

   _____

3. Noi abbiamo avuto un accidente ieri.

   _____

4. Io la assisto sempre, quando ha bisogno.

   _____

5. Lui non ha paura di niente. È molto bravo.

   _____

6. Lui è un bravo conduttore d'orchestra.

   _____

7. Studiare è molto effettivo.

   _____

8. Lei lavora in una fattoria di motociclette.

   _____

9. Per quale firma lavori?

   _____

10. Ieri non sono andato alla lettura di italiano.

    _____

11. Quando hai letto quel magazzino, fammelo avere.

    _____

12. Quante stampe hai messo sulla busta (*envelope*)?

    _____

# ANSWER KEY

## Spelling (pages 17–18)

**A**

1. a. ca
   b. co
   c. cu
   d. che
   e. chi
2. a. cia
   b. cio
   c. ciu
   d. ce
   e. ci
3. a. ga
   b. go
   c. gu
   d. ghe
   e. ghi
4. a. gia
   b. gio
   c. giu
   d. ge
   e. gi
5. a. sca
   b. sco
   c. scu
   d. sche
   e. schi
6. a. scia
   b. scio
   c. sciu
   d. sce
   e. sci

**B**

1. anche
2. questo
3. cena
4. luoghi
5. guanto
6. giovane
7. giugno
8. scuola
9. schiena
10. scarpa OR sciarpa
11. occhio
12. faccia
13. bugie
14. amiche
15. perché

## Capitalization (page 22)

**A**

1. Signora (signora)
3. Martedì (martedì)
6. Febbraio (febbraio)
9. Russo (russo)
11. Buddista (buddista)

**B**

1. Giovanni è un protestante.
2. «Il significato della matematica nella vita moderna»
3. Oggi è lunedì, il venti marzo.
4. Maria arriva a gennaio.

285

## Nouns (pages 38–39)

**A**
1. la ragazza
2. il padre
3. l'americana
4. il cantante
5. la nipote
6. il cameriere
7. la pianista
8. la persona
9. l'autore/l'autrice
10. il dottore

**B**
1. i problemi
2. il programma
3. le tesi
4. il brindisi
5. le mani
6. la radio
7. i caffè
8. la città
9. gli sport
10. il greco
11. i luoghi
12. l'amico
13. le amiche
14. il bacio
15. le farmacie
16. l'orologio
17. le camicie
18. il labbro
19. gli uomini
20. la ferrovia
21. i cacciavite

**C**
1. La gente ama l'italiano.
2. Io mangio sempre le mele.
3. Amo il pane.
4. Lui porta i baffi.
5. Il professor Rossi è molto bravo.

## Numbers (pages 52–53)

**A**
1. sette
2. dodici
3. diciassette
4. diciotto
5. diciannove
6. ventiquattro
7. trentuno
8. quarantatré
9. cinquantotto
10. trecento novantotto
11. duemila dodici
12. trentaquattromila cinquecento novantanove

**B** 1. quattromila euro
2. cinque milioni di dollari
3. ventuna ragazze
4. Ho trentun anni.
5. nessuno zio
6. nessuna zia
7. un altro ragazzo
8. un'altra ragazza
9. mezzo litro
10. sedici diviso per quattro fa quattro

**C** 1. primo, prima
2. secondo, seconda
3. terzo, terza
4. quarto, quarta
5. quinto, quinta
6. quindicesimo, quindicesima
7. ventunesimo, ventunesima
8. cinquantaseiesimo, cinquantaseiesima
9. novantatreesimo, novantatreesima

**D** 1. una ventina
2. Che ora è? / Che ore sono?
3. le due e venti
4. le ventitré
5. le nove e tre quarti
6. Sono le dieci precise.
7. Oggi è il quattro dicembre.
8. Oggi è il primo maggio.
9. Sono nata nel 1998.

## Articles and Demonstratives (pages 66–67)

**A** 1. il ragazzo
2. la ragazza
3. l'americano
4. l'italiana
5. lo studente
6. lo psicologo
7. l'orologio
8. l'amica
9. la zia

**B** 1. i ragazzi
2. la madre
3. gli americani
4. la cantante
5. gli studenti
6. l'italiano
7. i cani
8. l'orologio
9. gli gnocchi
10. l'ora
11. questi gatti
12. questa zia
13. questi amici
14. quello psicologo
15. quei ragazzi
16. quell'amico
17. quelle amiche
18. quella ragazza

**C**
| | |
|---|---|
| 1. X | 8. La |
| 2. X | 9. lo |
| 3. un | 10. Il |
| 4. lo | 11. il |
| 5. la | 12. la |
| 6. Gli | 13. la |
| 7. in | 14. a |

**D**
| | |
|---|---|
| 1. f | 5. b |
| 2. e | 6. c |
| 3. a | 7. d |
| 4. g | |

## Descriptive Adjectives (pages 82–84)

**A**
1. la ragazza intelligente
2. l'amico elegante
3. la zia alta
4. l'uomo alto
5. la sorella simpatica
6. l'amico italiano
7. la ragazza francese
8. un buon amico
9. una buona zia
10. un bel ragazzo
11. una bell'amica
12. San Mario

**B**
1. i vestiti rosa
2. la sciarpa rossa
3. gli uomini alti
4. lo zaino marrone
5. i fratelli simpatici
6. la camicia blu
7. le ragazze francesi
8. il bel ragazzo
9. le belle amiche
10. il bell'amico
11. i grandi ragazzi
12. il bell'orologio

**C**
1. La maglia e la borsa sono nuove.
2. Il vestito e la camicia sono nuovi.
3. È una sciarpa bianca.
4. Lui è uno studente molto intelligente.
5. Ho mangiato molta carne.
6. Maria è la ragazza più intelligente della classe.
7. Marco è intelligentissimo.

**D**
| | |
|---|---|
| 1. b | 6. a |
| 2. b | 7. b |
| 3. a | 8. a |
| 4. b | 9. a |
| 5. b | |

## Possessives (pages 91–92)

**A**
1. i miei orologi
2. la nostra amica
3. le mie camicie
4. il nostro libro
5. i tuoi cani
6. la vostra amica
7. le tue macchine
8. il vostro amico
9. i suoi gatti
10. la sua amica
11. i loro amici
12. la loro casa

**B**
1. X
2. la
3. il
4. la
5. X
6. il
7. un
8. una
9. il

**C**
1. il suo
2. il suo
3. le sue
4. le sue
5. Sua
6. Sua
7. la Loro

## Partitives (page 97)

**A**
1. alcune penne, qualche penna
2. degli zii, alcuni zii
3. delle mele, qualche mela
4. alcuni amici, qualche amico
5. delle ragazze, alcune ragazze

**B**
1. b
2. b
3. b
4. b
5. a
6. a

## Questions (pages 103–104)

**A**
1. Maria è italiana? / È italiana Maria?
2. Loro prendono dello zucchero? / Prendono dello zucchero loro?
3. Marco parla italiano (molto) bene? / Parla italiano (molto) bene Marco?
4. Lui è andato al cinema ieri? / È andato al cinema ieri lui?

**B**
1. Che / Cosa / Che cosa leggi/legge?
2. Chi è?
3. Di chi è la penna?
4. Come si chiama il tuo/Suo amico?
5. Dove vivono i tuoi/Suoi amici?
6. Perché non vai/va alla festa?
7. Quale rivista ti/Le piace?
8. Quando vai/va a Roma?
9. Quanto zucchero prendi/prende?

**C** 1. Prendi molto zucchero nel caffè, non è vero / vero / no?
2. Ti piace quel programma, non è vero / vero / no?
3. L'italiano è una bella lingua, non pensi?
4. Tuo fratello è francese, non è vero / vero / no?

## Infinitives and Gerunds (pages 110–111)

**A** 1. arrivare, arrivando, essendo arrivato(-a)
2. cadere, essere caduto(-a), essendo caduto(-a)
3. vendere, avere venduto, vendendo
4. avere dormito, dormendo, avendo dormito
5. partire, essere partito(-a), partendo
6. avere prodotto, producendo, avendo prodotto
7. trarre, avere tratto, traendo
8. tradurre, avere tradotto, avendo tradotto
9. avere posto, ponendo, avendo posto

**B** 1. a 5. b
2. b 6. a
3. a 7. b
4. a

## The Present Indicative (pages 121–122)

**A** 1. io parlo 10. tu cominci
2. tu apri 11. tu vendi
3. Lei apre 12. Lei parla
4. loro capiscono 13. Lei preferisce
5. voi mangiate 14. voi pagate
6. noi preferiamo 15. loro parlano
7. io vendo 16. loro vendono
8. io dormo 17. loro dormono
9. tu capisci 18. loro finiscono

**B** 1. Io finisco alle sei.
2. Noi non capiamo l'italiano.
3. Loro partono per l'Italia domani.
4. Dottor Marchi, capisce l'inglese?
5. Maria, parli italiano anche tu?
6. Maria, che cosa cerchi?
7. Noi non paghiamo mai.
8. A che ora cominciate a lavorare?
9. Noi andiamo al cinema domani.
10. Noi dobbiamo studiare l'italiano oggi.

**C** 1. Maria, studi l'italiano?
2. (Lui) finisce di lavorare alle sei.
3. In questo momento mia sorella mangia una pizza.
4. Il lunedì studio sempre l'italiano.
5. Domani mangio la pasta.
6. Dormo da ieri.
7. Anche lui dorme da otto ore.

## The Present Perfect (pages 130–131)

**A** 1. ho mangiato
2. ha pagato
3. abbiamo venduto
4. avete letto
5. hanno scritto
6. è nata
7. ho capito
8. hai finito
9. è venuto
10. hanno detto
11. avete dato
12. abbiamo fatto
13. ho chiesto
14. ha aperto

**B** 1. ha venduto
2. ha venduta
3. è andata
4. ha comprato
5. ha comprate
6. sono andati
7. sono andate
8. hanno visto
9. avete mangiato
10. siamo andati
11. è uscito
12. è uscita

**C** 1. Lo spettacolo è durato tre ore.
2. Quanto è costata la carne?
3. Mia sorella ha venduto la sua macchina.
4. Ieri abbiamo parlato al signor Verdi.
5. (Lui) ha dormito troppo ieri.
6. (Io) ho già mangiato.
7. (Il) nostro nonno è arrivato ieri.
8. La loro nonna è arrivata la settimana scorsa.

## The Imperfect (pages 137–138)

**A** 1. io leggevo
2. io capivo
3. io bevevo
4. tu mangiavi
5. tu vedevi
6. tu dormivi
7. tu eri
8. lui cominciava
9. lei aveva
10. lui faceva
11. lei diceva
12. noi pagavamo
13. noi sapevamo
14. noi davamo
15. voi mangiavate
16. voi potevate
17. voi uscivate
18. voi eravate
19. loro arrivavano
20. loro avevano
21. loro venivano

**B** 1. b
2. b
3. b
4. a
5. b

6. a
7. b
8. a
9. b

## The Past Absolute (pages 145–146)

**A** 1. mangiai
2. vendei/vendetti
3. partii
4. ebbi
5. andasti
6. vendesti
7. uscisti
8. facesti
9. arrivò
10. poté/potette
11. preferì
12. fu

13. pagammo
14. dovemmo
15. dormimmo
16. dicemmo
17. cantaste
18. poteste
19. partiste
20. deste
21. cominciarono
22. doverono/dovettero
23. capirono
24. nacquero

**B** 1. c
2. a
3. b
4. c

5. a
6. a
7. c

## The Pluperfect (pages 149–150)

**A** 1. avevo mangiato
2. avevo venduto
3. ero partita
4. avevo avuto
5. eri andato
6. avevi venduto
7. eri uscito
8. avevi fatto
9. era arrivato
10. aveva potuto
11. aveva preferito
12. era stata

13. avevamo pagato
14. avevamo dovuto
15. avevamo dormito
16. avevamo detto
17. avevate cantato
18. avevate potuto
19. eravate partiti
20. avevate dato
21. avevano cominciato
22. avevano dovuto
23. avevano capito
24. erano nati

**B** 1. c
2. a
3. b
4. c

5. a
6. c
7. c

## The Future Tenses (pages 158–159)

 1. io arriverò, io sarò arrivato(-a)
2. io venderò, io avrò venduto
3. io preferirò, io avrò preferito
4. io andrò, io sarò andato(-a)
5. io avrò, io avrò avuto
6. tu mangerai, tu avrai mangiato
7. tu metterai, tu avrai messo
8. tu aprirai, tu avrai aperto
9. tu berrai, tu avrai bevuto
10. tu cadrai, tu sarai caduto(-a)
11. lui comincerà, lui avrà cominciato
12. lei chiederà, lei avrà chiesto
13. lui capirà, lui avrà capito
14. Lei darà, Lei avrà dato
15. lei sarà, lei sarà stata
16. noi pagheremo, noi avremo pagato
17. noi chiuderemo, noi avremo chiuso
18. noi finiremo, noi avremo finito
19. noi faremo, noi avremo fatto
20. noi potremo, noi avremo potuto
21. voi cercherete, voi avrete cercato
22. voi metterete, voi avrete messo
23. voi preferirete, voi avrete preferito
24. voi saprete, voi avrete saputo
25. voi terrete, voi avrete tenuto
26. loro mangeranno, loro avranno mangiato
27. loro chiederanno, loro avranno chiesto
28. loro preferiranno, loro avranno preferito
29. loro vedranno, loro avranno visto
30. loro verranno, loro saranno venuti(-e)

 1. (Io) manderò un'email a mio fratello domani.
2. (Loro) andranno in Italia fra/tra un mese.
3. Quella macchina sarà costata molto, non pensi?
4. Chi sarà?
5. (Noi) andremo al cinema, dopo che avremo studiato.
6. Quanto sarà costata quella macchina?
7. Sarà costata molto.

# The Conditional Tenses (pages 167–170)

**A**
1. io arriverei, io sarei arrivato(-a)
2. io venderei, io avrei venduto
3. io preferirei, io avrei preferito
4. io andrei, io sarei andato(-a)
5. io avrei, io avrei avuto
6. tu mangeresti, tu avresti mangiato
7. tu metteresti, tu avresti messo
8. tu apriresti, tu avresti aperto
9. tu berresti, tu avresti bevuto
10. tu cadresti, tu saresti caduto(-a)
11. lui comincerebbe, lui avrebbe cominciato
12. lei chiederebbe, lei avrebbe chiesto
13. lui capirebbe, lui avrebbe capito
14. Lei darebbe, Lei avrebbe dato
15. lei sarebbe, lei sarebbe stata
16. noi pagheremmo, noi avremmo pagato
17. noi chiuderemmo, noi avremmo chiuso
18. noi finiremmo, noi avremmo finito
19. noi faremmo, noi avremmo fatto
20. noi potremmo, noi avremmo potuto
21. voi cerchereste, voi avreste cercato
22. voi mettereste, voi avreste messo
23. voi preferireste, voi avreste preferito
24. voi sapreste, voi avreste saputo
25. voi terreste, voi avreste tenuto
26. loro mangerebbero, loro avrebbero mangiato
27. loro chiederebbero, loro avrebbero chiesto
28. loro preferirebbero, loro avrebbero preferito
29. loro vedrebbero, loro avrebbero visto
30. loro verrebbero, loro sarebbero venuti(-e)

**B**
1. c
2. c
3. a
4. c
5. c
6. b
7. c
8. a
9. c
10. d
11. d
12. d
13. a
14. d
15. c

## The Imperative (pages 178–180)

**A**
1. Mangi la mela!
2. Comincia a mangiare!
3. Aspetti qui!
4. Apri la porta!
5. Finisca la mela!
6. Cerca la chiave!
7. Paghi il conto!
8. Scrivi l'email!
9. Chiuda la porta!
10. Dormi!
11. Aprano le porte!
12. Chiudete le porte!
13. Finiscano di studiare!
14. Abbi pazienza!
15. Vada a dormire!

**B**
1. Non mangiare la pesca!
2. Guardi la televisione!
3. Non finiamo di mangiare!
4. Chiudi la porta!
5. Non bere tutta l'acqua!
6. Dica questo!
7. Non usciamo stasera!

**C**
1. Maria, mangia la mela!
2. Maria, non bere l'acqua!
3. Maria, chiudi la porta!
4. Maria, apri la porta!
5. Maria e Marco, mangiate la mela!
6. Maria e Marco, non bevete l'acqua!
7. Maria e Marco, chiudete la porta!
8. Maria e Marco, aprite la porta!
9. Signora Verdi, mangi la mela!
10. Signora Verdi, non beva l'acqua!
11. Signora Verdi, chiuda la porta!
12. Signora Verdi, apra la porta!
13. Signora Verdi e Signor Rossi, mangino la mela!
14. Signora Verdi e Signor Rossi, non bevano l'acqua!
15. Signora Verdi e Signor Rossi, chiudano la porta!
16. Signora Verdi e Signor Rossi, aprano la porta!

## The Present Subjunctive (pages 190–192)

**A**
1. io legga
2. io capisca
3. io beva
4. tu mangi
5. tu veda
6. tu dorma
7. tu sia
8. lui cominci
9. lei abbia
10. lui faccia
11. lei dica
12. noi paghiamo
13. noi sappiamo
14. noi diamo
15. voi mangiate
16. voi possiate
17. voi usciate
18. voi siate
19. loro arrivino
20. loro abbiano
21. loro vengano
22. loro capiscano
23. loro chiudano

■ 1. b
2. b
3. b
4. b
5. b
6. a
7. a

8. b
9. b
10. b
11. b
12. b
13. b
14. b

## Other Subjunctive Tenses (pages 200-202)

**A** 1. io sia arrivato
2. io vendessi
3. io avessi preferito
4. io andassi
5. io abbia avuto
6. tu mangiassi
7. tu avessi messo
8. tu abbia messo
9. tu bevessi
10. tu fossi caduto
11. lui cominciasse
12. lei abbia chiesto
13. lui avesse capito
14. Lei desse
15. lei fosse

16. noi pagassimo
17. noi abbiamo chiuso
18. noi avessimo finito
19. noi facessimo
20. noi potessimo
21. voi cercaste
22. voi metteste
23. voi abbiate preferito
24. voi sapeste
25. voi aveste tenuto
26. loro mangiassero
27. loro abbiano chiesto
28. loro avessero preferito
29. loro vedessero
30. loro venissero

**B** 1. a
2. b
3. c
4. a
5. a OR b
6. a
7. a
8. b

9. b OR c
10. b
11. c
12. b
13. b
14. c
15. b

## The Progressive Tenses (pages 207–208)

**A**
1. io sto arrivando
2. io stia vendendo
3. io stavo preferendo
4. io stessi andando
5. io sto avendo
6. tu stai mangiando
7. tu stia mettendo
8. tu stavi aprendo
9. tu stessi bevendo
10. tu stai cadendo
11. lui sta cominciando
12. lei stia chiedendo
13. lui stava capendo
14. Lei stesse dando
15. lei stava facendo
16. noi stiamo pagando
17. noi stavamo chiudendo
18. noi stiamo finendo
19. noi stessimo facendo
20. noi stiamo cercando
21. voi state cercando
22. voi stiate mettendo
23. voi stavate preferendo
24. voi state uscendo
25. voi stiate tenendo
26. loro stanno mangiando
27. loro stiano chiedendo
28. loro stavano preferendo
29. loro stessero vedendo
30. loro stanno venendo

**B**
1. Noi non stiamo studiando l'italiano.
2. Penso che loro stiano partendo per l'Italia.
3. Maria, con chi stai parlando?
4. Marco, che cosa stai cercando?
5. Mio fratello sta guardando la TV in questo momento.
6. Credo che mia sorella stia guardando la TV.
7. Cosa state leggendo?

**C**
1. b
2. a
3. b
4. a
5. b

## Reflexive Verbs (pages 213–214)

**A**
1. tu ti alzi, tu ti alzerai, tu ti sei alzato(-a)
2. lei si annoia, lei si annoierà, lei si è annoiata
3. lui si arrabbia, lui si arrabbierà, lui si è arrabbiato
4. io mi alzo, io mi alzerò, io mi sono alzato(-a)
5. noi ci dimentichiamo, noi ci dimenticheremo, noi ci siamo dimenticati(-e)
6. voi vi divertite, voi vi divertirete, voi vi siete divertiti(-e)
7. io mi lamento, io mi lamenterò, io mi sono lamentato(-a)
8. loro si lavano, loro si laveranno, loro si sono lavati(-e)
9. tu ti metti, tu ti metterai, tu ti sei messo(-a)
10. lei si preoccupa, lei si preoccuperà, lei si è preoccupata
11. lui si prepara, lui si preparerà, lui si è preparato
12. noi ci sentiamo, noi ci sentiremo, noi ci siamo sentiti(-e)
13. voi vi sposate, voi vi sposerete, voi vi siete sposati(-e)
14. loro si svegliano, loro si sveglieranno, loro si sono svegliati(-e)
15. lui si veste, lui si vestirà, lui si è vestito

**B** 1. Marco e Maria, vergognatevi!
2. Signor Bruni, non si alzi!
3. Sara, non ti alzare! OR Sara, non alzarti!
4. Signorina Dorelli, non si preoccupi!
5. Alessandro, arrabbiati!

**C** 1. (Noi) ci alziamo presto ogni giorno.
2. Sembra che lui si diverta sempre in Italia.
3. Lei si sposerebbe se conoscesse/incontrasse la persona giusta/adatta.
4. (Io) mi divertivo sempre da bambino(-a).
5. Lei si è alzata tardi ieri.
6. (Noi) non ci parliamo più.
7. (Loro) si telefonano spesso.
8. Marco e Maria, non vi vedete da molti anni, non è vero?
9. (Noi) non ci capiamo mai.

## The Verbs *piacere* and *esserci* (pages 220–221)

**A** 1. a      5. a
2. b      6. b
3. b      7. b
4. b

**B** 1. Che cosa è? È una nuova macchina.
2. Dov'è la macchina nuova? Ecco la macchina nuova.
3. C'è Maria? Sì, c'è.
4. Mi dispiace che tu non sei venuto alla festa.
5. Non mi piace quella pizza.

**C** 1. Ci piace quel libro.
2. Ma non ci piacciono quegli altri libri.
3. Lui piace a lei. OR Le piace.
4. E lei piace a lui. OR E gli piace.
5. Io piaccio a Maria.
6. (Loro) non mi sono piaciuti(-e).
7. Noi non siamo piaciuti a lui. OR Non gli siamo piaciuti.
8. Quella musica piace a lui, non a lei.

## The Passive (pages 227–228)

**A** 1. La pizza non è stata mangiata ieri da mio fratello.
2. Mia sorella mangia solo gli spaghetti.
3. Le patate sono sempre mangiate da Marco a cena.
4. Tutti leggono quel libro.
5. La macchina giapponese sarà comprata da quella donna.
6. Mio fratello scrisse quell'email.
7. Quella macchina è stata comprata da Maria.
8. I miei amici hanno comprato quella casa.
9. Quella lezione sarà studiata dagli studenti per domani.

**B** 1. La lezione è cominciata alle nove.
    2. I negozi sono aperti a quest'ora.
    3. Si beve quel caffè solo in Italia.
    4. Si mangiano quelle patate solo in Italia.
    5. Si è vista quella cosa solo in Italia.
    6. Si è contenti in Italia.
    7. Ci si diverte sempre in Italia.

## Subordinate Clauses (pages 234–235)

**A** 1. a            6. b
    2. b            7. a
    3. b            8. b
    4. a            9. b
    5. a

**B** 1. Mentre Maria sta studiando, suo fratello guarda la TV.
    2. La ragazza che ha i capelli biondi e che parla italiano molto bene è americana.
    3. Paolo e Franca parlano italiano.
    4. Mi piace il libro che sta leggendo Maria.
    5. Non trovo lo zaino in cui / nel quale ho messo il tuo libro.

## Pronouns (pages 252–253)

**A** 1. a            5. a
    2. b            6. b
    3. a            7. b
    4. a

**B** 1. Io te le ho date ieri.
    2. Loro gliele hanno regalate.
    3. Prima di mangiarli, voglio mangiare l'antipasto.
    4. Eccoli.
    5. Lui se le è messe ieri.
    6. Non voglio mangiarla. OR Non la voglio mangiare.
    7. Marco, mangiale!
    8. Maria, dammene due!
    9. Marco ci è andato ieri.
    10. Maria ne ha comprate molte ieri.
    11. Ce ne sono quattro nello zaino.

## Adverbs (pages 260–261)

**A**
1. certo
2. semplicemente
3. facile
4. popolarmente
5. benevolo
6. leggermente
7. enormemente
8. felice
9. precisamente
10. speciale
11. utilmente
12. vero

**B**
1. a
2. a
3. a
4. a
5. b
6. a
7. b
8. b
9. a

## Prepositions (pages 267–268)

**A**
1. nella
2. degli
3. sulla / sotto la
4. dal
5. alle
6. coll'
7. fra/tra la
8. sulla / sopra la
9. a
10. in
11. alla
12. nella / con la

**B**
1. (Io) vivo a Firenze.
2. (Loro) vivono negli Stati Uniti.
3. Ecco la nuova macchina di Sara.
4. Come si chiama la figlia del tuo/Suo professore?
5. (Loro) vanno dal medico domani?
6. Vengo dall'Italia.
7. (Loro) vivono in Italia da sei anni.
8. Da bambino(-a) navigavo spesso Internet.
9. Lei ama mettersi un vestito/abito da sera. / A lei piace mettersi un vestito/abito da sera.

## Miscellaneous Topics (pages 273–274)

**A**
1. Lui non mangia mai gli spaghetti.
2. Ieri non ho mangiato né la carne né le patate.
3. Marco non conosce nessuno in quella scuola.
4. Lui non vuole niente/nulla.
5. Quello non è affatto vero.

**B** 1. Maria fa lavare i piatti a sua sorella.
2. La potrei chiamare. / Potrei chiamarla.
3. (Lui) l'avrebbe potuta chiamare. / (Lui) avrebbe potuto chiamarla.
4. Lo vorrei fare, ma non posso. / Vorrei farlo, ma non posso.
5. Lo avrei voluto fare. / Avrei voluto farlo.
6. Lo dovrei fare più spesso.
7. Mia madre ascolta la radio ogni sera.
8. Maria sta aspettando / aspetta l'autobus.
9. (Io) sto cercando / cerco la mia borsa.
10. (Lui) ha chiesto al professore di venire.
11. (Lei) telefona a sua madre spesso. / (Lei) chiama sua madre spesso.
12. Maria risponde sempre alle domande.

## Tricky Words and Expressions (pages 278–279)

**A** 1. sa
2. conoscono
3. sapete
4. conosce
5. conosco
6. conoscono
7. sa
8. sa

**B** 1. incidente
2. discussione
3. aiutare
4. coraggioso
5. direttore
6. affrontare
7. efficace
8. fabbrica
9. ditta
10. grande
11. conferenza/lezione
12. rivista
13. sensato
14. francobollo

**C** 1. Ieri avevamo fame e allora abbiamo mangiato molto.
2. Scusa, ma ho fretta.
3. Penso che tu abbia torto.
4. Lei ha sempre caldo.
5. Lui ha sempre freddo.
6. Il signor Verdi ha ragione.
7. La signora Verdi ha torto.
8. (Io) ho molto sonno.

## Catch the Blunders (pages 281–284)

**A** 1. Marco è un cattolico.
2. Maria ha molti amici.
3. Oggi è martedì, il venti febbraio.
4. Marco arriva a gennaio.
5. Perché dici questo?
6. Loro sono a scuola.

**B** 1. Che bel film!
2. Ho mal di stomaco.
3. Loro hanno un cane e un gatto.
4. Sono la zia e lo zio dall'Italia.
5. Io amo la carne.
6. La gente ama l'Italia.
7. Io mangio sempre le mele.
8. Preferisco il pane.
9. Lui porta i baffi.
10. Oggi è il tre marzo.
11. Oggi è il primo ottobre.
12. La camicia e la borsa sono nuove.
13. È una camicia bianca.
14. Lei è una studentessa molto intelligente.
15. Ho mangiato molte patate ieri.
16. Questo è il suo libro.
17. Non ho zii.
18. Prendo un po' di/dello zucchero.
19. I miei amici vivono negli Stati Uniti.
20. Tu finisci alle sei?
21. Noi non capiamo il francese.
22. Quando mia sorella era giovane, suonava il pianoforte.
23. Da giovane, lei aveva i capelli biondi.
24. Ieri, mentre lui dormiva, io guardavo la TV.
25. Marco, mangiala!
26. Maria, non mangiarla!
27. Dammelo!
28. Signorina Dorelli, si alzi!
29. Che cosa è? È una nuova borsa.
30. Io te le ho date già.
31. Loro gliele hanno date.
32. Prima di mangiarle, voglio mangiare l'antipasto.
33. Maria starà in casa domani tutto il giorno.
34. Preferisco andare in macchina a lavorare.
35. Andremo con la macchina di mia sorella.

**C** 1. Io non conosco Roma affatto.
2. Loro conoscono un bel ristorante qui vicino.
3. Noi abbiamo avuto un incidente ieri.
4. Io la aiuto sempre, quando ha bisogno.
5. Lui non ha paura di niente. È molto coraggioso.
6. Lui è un bravo direttore d'orchestra.
7. Studiare è molto efficace.
8. Lei lavora in una fabbrica di motociclette.
9. Per quale ditta lavori?
10. Ieri non sono andato alla conferenza di italiano.
11. Quando hai letto quella rivista, fammela avere.
12. Quanti francobolli hai messo sulla busta?

# INDEX OF ITALIAN WORDS AND EXPRESSIONS

# SUBJECT INDEX